Bilingualism in the Spanish-Speaking World

Bilingualism has given rise to significant political, linguistic, and social changes in Spanish-speaking countries. In the United States, the increasing importance of Spanish has engendered an English-only Movement; in Peru, contact between Spanish and Quechua has brought about language change; and in Iberia, speakers of Basque, Galician, and Catalan have made their languages a compulsory part of school curricula and local government. This book provides an introduction to bilingualism in the Spanish-speaking world, looking at topics such as language contact, bilingual societies, bilingualism in schools, code-switching, language transfer, the emergence of new varieties of Spanish, and language choice – and how all of these phenomena affect the linguistic and cognitive development of the speaker. Using examples and case studies drawn primarily from Spanish–English bilinguals in the US, Spanish–Quechua bilinguals in Peru, and Spanish–Basque bilinguals in Spain, it provides diverse perspectives on the experience of being bilingual in distinct cultural, political, and socioeconomic contexts.

JENNIFER AUSTIN is an associate professor in the Department of Spanish and Portuguese Studies at Rutgers University, Newark.

MARÍA BLUME is an assistant professor in the Department of Linguistics and Literature at Pontificia Universidad Católica del Perú.

LILIANA SÁNCHEZ is a professor in the Department of Spanish and Portuguese at Rutgers University, New Brunswick.

Bilingualism in the Spanish-Speaking World
Linguistic and Cognitive Perspectives

JENNIFER AUSTIN

Rutgers University, Newark

MARÍA BLUME

Pontificia Universidad Católica del Perú

LILIANA SÁNCHEZ

Rutgers University, New Brunswick

CAMBRIDGE
UNIVERSITY PRESS

University Printing House, Cambridge CB2 8BS, United Kingdom

Cambridge University Press is part of the University of Cambridge.

It furthers the University's mission by disseminating knowledge in the pursuit of education, learning and research at the highest international levels of excellence.

www.cambridge.org
Information on this title: www.cambridge.org/9780521132978

First published 2015

Printed in the United States of America by Sheridan Books, Inc.

A catalogue record for this publication is available from the British Library

Library of Congress Cataloguing in Publication data
Austin, Jennifer, 1969–
Bilingualism in the Spanish-speaking world: linguistic and cognitive perspectives /
Jennifer Austin, Rutgers University at Newark; María Blume, Pontificia Universidad
Católica del Perú; Liliana Sánchez, Rutgers University at New Brunswick.
    pages   cm
Includes bibliographical references and index.
ISBN 978-0-521-11553-7 (hardback)
1. Bilingualism – Social aspects.   2. Spanish language – Social aspects.   3. Language
policies – Spanish-speaking countries.   4. Languages in contact – Spanish-speaking countries.
5. Spanish-speaking countries – Social aspects.   I. Blume, María, author.   II. Sánchez,
Liliana, author.   III. Title.
P115.45.A87   2015
306.44'6 – dc23   2015002315

ISBN 978-0-521-11553-7 Hardback
ISBN 978-0-521-13297-8 Paperback

Contents

Figures

Tables

---

[1] *BFLA* stands for *bilingual first language acquisition*.

Acknowledgments

We gratefully acknowledge the help of the children, schoolteachers, administrators, and students who helped us gather the data for our studies on bilingualism in Peru, Spain, and the United States. Thanks also to our editors at Cambridge University Press, Helen Barton and Helena Dowson, for their patience and their help in shepherding this project to completion. We would also like to thank our colleagues and students at UTEP and Rutgers University, the Aresty Research Program at Rutgers University, and the members of the VCLA for their assistance and advice. Finally, we are extremely grateful to our families on three continents, who have been instrumental in helping this endeavor come to fruition by providing intellectual companionship, childcare, logistical assistance, and unflagging support.

Suffix abbreviations

1	first person
2	second person
3	third person
ABS	absolutive
ACC	accusative
ACC-marker	accusative marker/ personal *a*.
ATT	attested
AUX	auxiliary
BEN	benefactive
CAUS	causative
CL	clitic
COMP	complementizer
DAT	dative
DER	derivative[1]
DES	desiderative
DET	determiner
DIM	diminutive[2]
DOM	differential object marker (= ACC-marker)
DUR	durative
ERG	ergative
EVID	evidential
F	feminine
FOC	focus
FUT	future
GEN	genitive
GER	gerund
IMP	imperative
IPFV	imperfective
IND	indicative
INF	infinitive
LOC	locative

[1] The derivative marker *-ri* in Quechua is used to mark courtesy.
[2] Diminutives in Quechua and Spanish may indicate small size but they are mostly used as markers of affection.

M	masculine
NOM	nominative
OBJ	object
PFV	perfective
PL	plural
POSS	possessive
PRS	present
PROG	progressive
PST	past tense
PTCP	participle
REFL	reflexive
REL	relative
REP	reportative
SBJ	subjunctive
SG	singular
TV	thematic vowel[3]

[3] Thematic vowels (TV) appear in Spanish verbs immediately after the root and indicate which conjugation the verb belongs to. TVs may be absent in some tenses, but they are for the most part very regular. Verbs of the first conjugation take the TV -a, verbs of the second conjugation take TV -e, and verbs of the third conjugation take TV -i. In some tenses, the TVs -e and -i are diphthongized into -ie. In the present subjunctive, verbs of the first conjugation take TV -e and verbs of the second and third conjugations take TV -a.

Introduction

In this book, we will examine the impact of bilingualism on the languages and minds of users of more than one language. In the past twenty years, there has been a dramatic increase in the number of studies published on bilingualism (Bialystok 2007), and this research has uncovered significant lifelong consequences for the linguistic and cognitive abilities of multilingual speakers. However, these studies have often been conducted on a particular subset of bilinguals, namely university-educated professionals (or their children) who are fluent speakers of the majority language. As a result, important questions regarding the cognitive effects of bilingualism are usually considered in isolation from how they are affected by the membership of the bilingual individual in communities with varying degrees of bilingualism. We examine how research on the effects of bilingualism on linguistic and cognitive development has been shaped by a wide range of (sometimes competing) theoretical assumptions, with examples and case studies drawn primarily from three bilingual communities: Spanish–English bilinguals in the USA, Spanish–Quechua bilinguals in Peru, and Spanish–Euskara (Basque)[1] bilinguals in Spain. We have chosen these groups because they provide diverse perspectives on the experience of being bilingual in distinct cultural, political, and socioeconomic contexts.

A further goal of this book is to shed light on the notion of degrees of communal bilingualism (referred to as bilingual continua). These continua of bilingualism are found in contexts involving language contact, the formation of *creole* varieties, and first language loss. By analyzing the results of previous work on the effects on bilingualism of different amounts of language input at home and in school and of different types of communicative interactions, we hope to provide a better understanding of some emerging conceptual views of bilingualism. One of them is the notion of the heritage speaker (Wiley and Valdés 2000), a widely used term that refers principally to bilingual speakers in the USA but covers a wide range of abilities from passive bilinguals (individuals who understand Spanish but are not able to engage in active conversation at an advanced level) to speakers who begin to acquire a formal register in college after a period of English-only education. Another theoretical construct that is examined closely is the notion of "incomplete acquisition," which contends that insufficient input in one of a

---

[1] Throughout this book we use the name *Euskara* to refer to the language otherwise known as Basque or Euskera since it is the term preferred by many speakers of the language.

bilingual's languages can impede linguistic development. By analyzing how these definitions have emerged in previous research we aim to clarify how the outcomes of bilingualism are shaped by variable access to input in the two languages.

In the remaining sections of this Introduction we present basic terminology used to describe bilingualism and language contact that the reader will need to understand in the rest of the book. We also present an overview of bilingualism in the world, as well as the factors that promote bilingualism and language shift. We then give a short historical overview of Spanish and describe its main grammatical characteristics. Finally, we introduce the typological characteristics of the other three main languages discussed in this book (English, Euskara, and Quechua), and present the circumstances of their contact with Spanish. The bibliography on Spanish language contact, bilingual education, and bilingualism, especially from a sociolinguistic perspective, is extensive and impressive. Rather than reviewing in detail that wealth of knowledge, we provide here the basic concepts and refer the reader to the relevant bibliography.

Chapter 1 addresses how to define bilingualism. In the past, bilingualism has largely been defined by three factors: (a) age of acquisition (successive/simultaneous), (b) cognitive development (additive/subtractive), and (c) competence (balanced/dominant in one language) (Grosjean 1982; De Houwer 1990; Romaine 1995). In this book, we analyze and compare the results of previous studies on bilingualism in the Spanish-speaking world that have privileged some of these perspectives in order to evaluate how these assumptions have shaped our understanding of bilingualism and of its linguistic and cognitive consequences. Our goal is to show that the same universal principles that guide language development in general can account for many patterns seen in bilingual acquisition, particularly the linguistic consequences of bilingualism.

Chapter 2 discusses recent findings regarding the cognitive and neurolinguistic effects of bilingualism, including language separation and cognitive control, concepts in the bilingual mind, the representation of more than one language in the brain, and the neuroanatomical consequences of bilingualism. In the cognitive domain, we show how these findings complement revised linguistic models of the interaction between the languages of a bilingual. We also show how contrasting approaches in studying bilingualism from a linguistic, cognitive, and neuroscientific viewpoint can reflect fundamental epistemological differences in these disciplines that for the time being have not been bridged.

In Chapter 3, we focus on the linguistic consequences of bilingualism such as cross-linguistic influence and convergence. We will explore the different ways that these phenomena are manifested in the language of child and adult bilinguals, as well as how they are affected by cross-linguistic differences in the typology of Spanish, English, Quechua, and Euskara. Comparing previously conducted case studies from the USA, Peru, and Spain will serve to illustrate the many universals in the ways that bilinguals use their languages. The chapter analyzes how research on the acquisition of bilingual lexicons parallels research on bilingual syntax and it draws attention to the need for studies that connect the different findings in these two subareas of bilingual studies.

I.1 Some basic terminology: bilingualism and second languages

Following common practice, we use the term *bilingualism* in this text as a general term for knowing two, three, or more languages; in using it, we are also referring to cases of *multilingualism*. In the same way, the term *second language* is used to refer to any language learned after the first language, be it the third, fourth, fifth, etc., unless we further specify the order of acquisition. In research on language acquisition, the abbreviations *L1*, *L2*, and *L3* are traditionally used for the first, second, and third language, respectively. Similarly, *L2 acquisition/learning* and *L2 speaker/learner* are used to refer to languages acquired after the first and to the individual's learning/acquiring those languages.

I.1.1 Language order

Linguists sometimes refer to bilinguals by mentioning the languages they speak, e.g., "English–Spanish speakers." The order in which the languages are listed is not arbitrary. In most cases a label such as "English–Spanish" bilingual means that English was the language that this person acquired first and Spanish was the language acquired later. In other instances, it can mean that English is this person's dominant language and Spanish is his/her non-dominant one, regardless of order of acquisition. In the primary literature the distinction between first and dominant languages is not always clearly drawn, and often it need not be, given that a person's first language is usually also his/her dominant language. However, in contexts of subtractive bilingualism or first language attrition – cases in which the acquisition of a second language goes hand-in-hand with the gradual loss of the first language – attention should be paid to this distinction, since a speaker's first language may have ceased to be his/her dominant language.

One of the recurrent themes of this book is the dynamic nature of bilingualism, not only at the societal level, but also at the individual level, and how these two levels are inextricably related. The characteristics of a person's bilingualism can change depending on his/her opportunities to use the language and the education available to him/her in the language. The fluctuations of language dominance at the individual level in turn drive the changes in bilingualism at the social level, sometimes leading to language shift and sometimes to language revitalization.

I.2 Language contact, transfer, interference, and convergence

Languages interact at the individual and societal levels, a topic we introduce here and which we will expand on throughout the book.

I.2.1   Language contact at the individual level

A common assumption in past research on bilingualism was that to be considered bilingual, one had to be a "perfect" speaker of two languages. The standard by which the level of proficiency of a bilingual was measured was, and still is to some degree – as we will see also in Chapter 1 – the monolingual speaker. Bilingual speakers were even rebuked for not behaving in each language like monolinguals, even though we now know that many of the phenomena under investigation are widespread even among highly proficient bilinguals. For instance, bilinguals have been criticized for not being able to keep their languages separated in production when code-switching, showing interference effects in comprehension and production even when told in experimental settings to use only one of their languages, and showing competence in each of their languages which was not equivalent to that of monolinguals.

In this book, we highlight new perspectives on bilingualism that have emerged from research in the last few decades into the cognitive and linguistic consequences of bilingualism. These studies have found that a bilingual person's languages interact at many levels, leading to mutual cross-linguistic influence. Therefore, by definition, their two or more languages are not the same as the one language in a monolingual brain. As a result, we should expect that the languages of a bilingual exhibit evidence of this sustained contact. In addition, other factors such as reduced input and an older age at the onset of acquisition may work in conjunction with cross-linguistic influence to create differences between bilingual and monolingual language outcomes. The linguistic abilities of monolingual speakers, therefore, should not be held up as a standard by which to measure bilinguals.

Having to accommodate two languages in one brain also creates language varieties that differ from those of monolinguals. In the same way that different social and regional varieties should not be stigmatized relative to standard varieties, we propose that variants that arise from language contact at the individual level should not be considered incomplete, but rather different from those of a monolingual speaker. From this perspective, the changes wrought by bilingualism are natural and inevitable responses of the language faculty to factors such as variable input and cross-linguistic contact, and as such should not be considered evidence of a deficit in linguistic competence or performance.

Furthermore, examples of multilingualism in the Spanish-speaking world underscore the fact that bilingualism is not unusual and rare, but rather, is the norm in most parts of the world. Far from a handicap, bilingualism is an advantage for many practical reasons (e.g., being able to communicate with more people, access to more job opportunities). Different languages come attached to different cultures, so being bilingual and bicultural brings enhanced awareness of different cultural practices across the world. Having to accommodate and control two languages also leads to important cognitive advantages, which we will review in Chapter 2.

The effects of language contact on the individual will depend on many factors, such as how similar the languages are, how frequently the speaker uses both of them, and his/her proficiency level in each language. Language contact is manifested in a number of ways that we explore in greater detail in later chapters. However, we will introduce some of the main concepts here.

Code-switching

A common outcome of bilingualism is code-switching, which is when a speaker uses two (or more) languages in his/her speech (or writing) at the same time. Code-switching is usually divided in two categories: inter-sentential code-switching when a speaker switches languages from one sentence to another (e.g., *I love bananas. Me las voy a comer todas* 'I love bananas. <u>I am going to eat them all</u>'), and intra-sentential code-switching when a speaker uses both languages inside the same sentence (e.g., *My mom <u>dice que</u> we have to clean our room* 'My mom <u>says that</u> we have to clean our room' or *Quiero ir al <u>football game</u> mañana* 'I want to go to the <u>football game</u> tomorrow'). While initially code-switching was seen as an indication of low competence in a language of bilingual speakers, research has shown that speakers code-switch for many discursive reasons, including emphasis, feeling that a word or expression in one of their languages expresses better what they want to convey, marking reported speech, and indicating intimacy (Zentella 1997). There is an extensive bibliography on Spanish–English code-switching because much of the research on code-switching was done on Spanish–English bilinguals in the USA. We will discuss this topic again in Chapters 2 and 3, but the reader is directed to Klee and Lynch (2009) for a good introduction to the topic and debates surrounding it.

Code-switching in young children who acquired both languages simultaneously is related to language dominance, i.e., whichever of the child's languages is strongest will have an effect on how he/she code-switches. Children tend to use more vocabulary from their dominant language, since code-switching may sometimes (but not always) be related to lexical gaps, and they tend to use the language already in use in the conversation – see Bedore, Peña, García, and Cortez (2005) and references within.

Language transfer

Another outcome of language contact is *language transfer*. The concept of transfer appeared first in studies of bilingualism and second language acquisition (see Jakobson 1938; Weinreich 1953; Gass 1979). Transfer occurs when a speaker assumes that the lexicon and structure of one of his/her languages is similar to that of his/her other language. Transfer is called *positive* when it facilitates language comprehension and production for bilinguals, for example when a Spanish–English bilingual guesses that *my elephant* means *mi elefante* in Spanish, realizing that *elephant* and *elefante* are cognates, or words that have similar forms (sounds) and meaning because they have a common origin. Transfer can also be *negative transfer* or *interference* (Gass and Selinker

1992) when it effectively disrupts language use, for example when one of the authors, with Spanish as her L1 and English as her L2, wrote *more subtle* instead of *subtler* in a draft of this chapter because in Spanish the equivalent form is *más sutil*. Transfer usually occurs from the speaker's first and/or dominant language to his/her second and or non-dominant language, but it can also occur in the other direction.

Convergence

Convergence is a type of transfer in which the speaker resolves a difference between his/her languages by adopting a characteristic of one of his/her languages for both languages, or by coming up with a novel form that does not correspond to either language (Muysken 2001). Rozencvejg (1976: 33) defined convergence as:

> The replacement in one and/or both languages of the characteristics and rules peculiar to it with corresponding (synonymous) characteristics and rules shared by both contact languages.

For example, when two languages have a similar sound, say Spanish has /e/ and /i/, and Quechua has only /i/, the language contact may create new possibilities for the bilingual speaker. When presented with these differences, the bilingual Quechua–Spanish speaker may produce an intermediate sound, for example [I], in both languages, saying [mɪsa] for both *mesa* 'table' and *misa* 'mass' in Spanish (Guion 2003). Transfer is an important area of research in language acquisition and language contact studies. For an introduction to the topic and the debates surrounding it with special reference to the Spanish-speaking world see Klee and Lynch (2009).

I.2.2   Language contact at the societal level

Languages also come in contact at the societal level when communities of speakers that use different languages interact with each other due to historical or economical factors. In turn, language contact leads to a multiplication of the linguistic options available to the bilingual speaker in a given situation, such as when will he/she use the different languages and why does he/she select one over the other and what consequences does language contact have for the speaker's languages? Appel and Muysken illustrate this point:

> many people find themselves at the frontier of two languages . . . there are many ways of coping with this situation. The structural characteristics of the languages involved impose an outer limit on the possible linguistic outcomes of language contact. Which strategy is chosen by any one speaker depends on many factors; the relation between the speaker and the languages, and the societal context in which the speaker finds himself. We continue to be amazed at the versatility and resourcefulness of speakers; multilingualism is

not just a problem; it can be a triumph of the human spirit.   (Appel and
Muysken 1987: 8–9)

One of the most common consequences of language contact is *borrowing*. Languages borrow elements from each other from different linguistic subsystems
(i.e., phonology, morphology, the lexicon, syntax) for various reasons (Appel and
Muysken 1987). Cross-linguistically, most borrowing occurs at the lexical level.
For example, Spanish has borrowed words such as *fax* and *club* from English,
English has borrowed words such as *taco* and *plaza* from Spanish, Spanish borrowed words such as *puma* 'mountain lion' and *cancha* 'field to play a game,
such as soccer' from Quechua, and it also borrowed *garúa* 'a fine rain' from
Euskara. Borrowed words (also called *loanwords*) are sometimes hard to tell
apart from instances of code-switching, and there is debate in the field as to how
they should be distinguished (see Myers-Scotton 2006 for an introduction to this
debate). The rule of thumb seems to be that if the word is known by the majority
of the population, even by the monolingual speakers, it is considered a borrowing (e.g., English speakers who use the word *taco* need not know any Spanish).
Sometimes the terms are borrowed with little adaptation (e.g., *fax*), and sometimes they are adapted to the phonetics of the recipient language (e.g., *escaner*
'scanner'). Sometimes, borrowed words change meaning slightly when they get
transferred from one language to the other (e.g., *plaza* in Spanish refers to an open
community space, usually with trees and benches and near a church; in English,
its most common meaning is that of a shopping plaza). Lexical borrowing is by
far the most common type of borrowing; but languages also borrow morphemes
from each other. For example, Andean Spanish[2] uses the Quechua suffix *-cha*
to indicate affection/diminutive, for example *Juanacha* for *Juanito* 'little Juan.'
Sounds may be borrowed as in the case of bilingual English–Spanish speakers
who reintroduced the phonemic contrast /b/ and /v/ in Spanish. Borrowings can
also be multiword structures, or *calques*; for instance, Andean Spanish speakers
sometimes place the verb at the end of the sentence as in Quechua *bien bonito*
es as opposed to Standard Spanish *es bien bonito* '(it) <u>is</u> very pretty' or use the
past perfect to express surprise *¡había sido grande el lago!* 'lit. (it) had been
large the lake!' as opposed to Standard Spanish *¡es grande el lago! / ¡estoy sor-*
prendida de que el lago sea grande! 'the lake is large! / (I) am surprised (by the
fact) that the lake is large!' As seen in most of these examples, less prestigious
languages tend to borrow from more prestigious ones, thus accounting for the
many borrowings from English into other languages. However, linguistic structures are also borrowed in the other direction (e.g., Quechua and Euskara words
borrowed into Spanish, Spanish words borrowed into English). What is more or
less prestigious depends on social, political, and historical factors in the particular
community. For example, Spanish is considered less prestigious than English by

---

[2] For an overview of this variety of Spanish, please see Section I.6.3.

some speakers in the USA, whereas in Spain it tends to be regarded as a more prestigious language than Euskara. In Latin America, Spanish is seen as more prestigious than Quechua by some Spanish speakers and even some Quechua speakers.

The extent of borrowing that occurs depends to a large degree on the extent of language contact between the languages. Thus, it is not surprising that there is more borrowing from English to Spanish in the region around the US–Mexico border than in other areas. Words such as *troca* 'truck' and *yarda* 'yard' are common in the Spanish of the speakers in this border region. In addition, the degree of typological proximity between languages influences borrowing, so that borrowing tends to occur more freely between similar languages than between more distant and different ones (Edwards 2006).

1.3   The extent of bilingualism

Globally, bilingual speakers are thought to outnumber monolingual ones. However, we have no precise numbers on how many people in the world are bilingual. What we do know is that there are about 7,000 languages (Lewis, Simons, and Fenning 2013)[3] spoken in about 200 nations,[4] so we can expect the majority of the speakers in the nations in the world to be bilingual. According to Crystal (1997),[5] 41 percent of English speakers (about 235 million people) are bilingual in English and some other language. Language distribution is not uniform across the world. Some languages are spoken by millions of speakers and others are spoken by only a few; in particular eleven languages are spoken by 70 percent of the population of the world. The five languages with the largest number of native speakers are Chinese, Spanish, English, Hindi, and Arabic.[6] Most countries in the world have more than one language. There are no truly monolingual nations. In some countries bilingualism is official throughout the country (e.g., Bolivia, Switzerland, and India), in some it is only in some territories (e.g., Canada, Spain), and in some cases the country has no official language (e.g., the USA).

In every nation with bilingual speakers several factors intervene to determine the makeup of bilingual and monolingual varieties in the region. For example, due to the influence of historical factors in Peru there was already a multi-ethnic and multilingual population when the Spaniards arrived bringing Spanish with them. Subsequently, the slave trade brought African natives to Peru, and the heavy immigration of Chinese, Japanese, and European natives has also contributed to the linguistic diversity of the country.

---

[3] www.ethnologue.com   [4] http://en.wikipedia.org/wiki/List_of_sovereign_states
[5] Cited in Bhatia (2006: 1).   [6] www.ethnologue.com/statistics/size

Table I.1 *Some estimates of numbers of L1 and L2 speakers of four languages*

	L1 speakers in millions	L2 speakers in millions
Chinese	1,200	15
English	427	950
Spanish	266	350
Hindi	182	350

I.3.1   Number of bilingual/L2 speakers

In some cases there are more speakers who speak the language as a second language than those who speak it as a first language, as seen in Table I.1 from Saville-Troike (2006: 9).

I.3.2   Minority and majority languages

In any multilingual society there is a majority language spoken by the majority of the population, whereas the other languages are minority languages (i.e., any language not spoken by the majority of speakers). In Spain, Spanish is the majority language and there are fourteen minority languages.[7] In Spanish-speaking countries in Latin America, Spanish is the majority language and there are many minority languages in each country (for example, Mexico has 281, Guatemala has 25, Honduras 9, Cuba 2, Colombia 83, Peru 93, Argentina 20, and Chile 9).[8] In the USA, English is the majority language and there are another 225 minority languages.[9]

In some communities the two or more languages are used equally for all activities and situations in the communities. In other societies, languages have restricted situations (called *domains*) in which they can be used, with one language usually ascribed to what are considered to be the most important activities, such as education and religion. This situation is called *diglossia* in linguistics, and the societies that engage in this practice are called *diglossic* societies (Ferguson 1959; Fishman 1967). Some level of diglossia exists between Spanish and the other languages it is in contact with, but there is no strict diglossia in the Spanish-speaking world.

I.3.3   Factors promoting bilingualism

When languages come into contact, the minority language may be affected by its status as a minority language. Sometimes bilingual speakers stop

---

[7] www.ethnologue.com/country/ES. We refer only to living languages for all the countries listed here.
[8] www.ethnologue.com/region/Americas   [9] www.ethnologue.com/country/US

using the minority language and start using (and teaching to their children) only the majority language. This is called *language shift* (Fishman 1967, 1991). In the most extreme cases, this leads to *language death* (Crystal 2000), that is, when speakers of a language stop teaching the language to their children and the language is kept alive by just the older speakers in the community. When these speakers die, the language dies with them. This has already happened or is happening now to most indigenous languages in the Americas.

However, that is not always the fate of minority languages, which may be preserved for a long time given adequate social support. This is the case with regard to Quechua in Latin America and Spanish in the USA. This outcome is called *language maintenance* (Fishman 1967, 1991; Baker 2011; Potowski 2013). We even see cases of language recovery, as with Euskara in Spain.

Factors that promote minority language maintenance include close proximity to a community of speakers of that language such as living in a border area, living in a multi-ethnic area, having an occupation that involves contact with members of other groups, being married or having a close relationship with speakers of another language, and, for heritage speakers, speaking the language with parents or grandparents. *Heritage speaker* is a term used for speakers who come from an immigrant family and therefore have learned the language the family spoke before migrating (and a minority language in the new country) by hearing it used by family members (Montrul 2004a, 2004b, 2008; Polinsky 2007; Valdés and Gioffrion-Vinci 2011). Many Spanish speakers in the USA and Quechua speakers in Peru are heritage speakers, whereas most speakers of Euskara have learned the language only at school. The availability and duration of bilingual education has a strong impact on minority language maintenance.

Another important factor that has a strong effect on language maintenance and use is the availability of bilingual education, the length of time it is available for, and the type of bilingual education provided.

I.3.4   Bilingual education

Bilingual education has existed for many centuries, but it has been traditionally available only for the elites in most areas of the world (e.g., upper/middle-class students learning a "prestigious" foreign language such as English or French throughout the world, Spanish education being offered only to the Inca elite in colonial times in Peru). For speakers of a minority language, the only available option has been usually to be educated exclusively in the majority language, sometimes with no support for learning it, and most commonly with no support for the maintenance of their first language.

In the Basque country, three out of four residents speak Spanish as their native language. Speakers who have Euskara as a first language constitute 20.56 percent of the population, and speakers who are bilingual from birth are 3.5 percent. Therefore, Euskara speakers comprise a total of 26.28 percent of the population, making Euskara a minority language in its own territory. Of these speakers, 13.88 percent use Euskara at home, 8.10 percent use both Euskara and Spanish, and 77.51 percent use only Spanish at home (Etxeberria 1997). In the USA it is estimated that 2,500,000 to 4,600,000 (7 to 10 percent) of the student population are language minority members (E. García 2008). These children arrive at the school with a wide range of English and American cultural knowledge. Some children are new arrivals into the USA, some were born in the USA but were primarily exposed to the minority language and culture, and some children are bilingual and bicultural to different degrees. Peruvian census data from 1993 (cited by Zúñiga, Sánchez, and Zacharías 2000: 20) provide the number of speakers between the ages of 5 and 14 who had one indigenous language as their first language in five *departamentos* 'states'[10] in southern Peru, the area with most indigenous language speakers. Of a total of 919,232 speakers of this age, 585,165 or 65 percent had an indigenous language as their L1. Percentages in the five *departamentos* went from 58.4 percent in Cusco to 72.4 percent in Apurímac. Zúñiga *et al.* in their study conducted in 1999 in the same five *departamentos* found 77.5 percent of children had an indigenous language as their native language.

Until the early twentieth century, most children across the USA and Latin America were educated only in the majority language. In the Basque Country, bilingual education existed since the early nineteenth century but was later forbidden by Franco's regime, as we will see below.

One of the principal problems in speaking about bilingual education is that the term *bilingual education* has been used to designate very different programs and practices, as Mackey (1970: 596–597) pointed out. These included schools in the UK where half of the subjects were taught in English, schools in Canada where only English was used to teach French-speaking children, schools in the Soviet Union where all topics were taught in English except Russian, or where some were taught in Georgian and some in Russian, and schools in the USA where English was taught as a second language, to name a few. This is one of the factors that have led to the replacement of the term by more precise terms from school programs' titles.

Mackey (1970) points out that there is no perfect model of bilingual education, a one-size-fits-all approach. Which model is best for a community will depend on the communities' characteristics, which are based on four intersecting factors (as cited by O. García 2008: 114–115):

1.   The relationship between the language(s) of the home and the school (or what Mackey called "the behavior of the bilingual at home," i.e., how many languages the speaker speaks at home and which of those languages, if any, is used in schooling);[11]

---

[10] Ayacucho, Apurímac, Cusco, Huancavelica, and Puno.
[11] The clarifications between parentheses are our additions to García's text.

2.   The curricular organization of the languages: the medium of edu-
        cation (i.e., are both languages used as a medium of instruction or
        not?), their pattern of development (i.e., does the school intend to
        maintain the minority language, develop it, or transition the child into
        the majority language?), the distribution of the languages in the cur-
        riculum (i.e., how much time is allotted for each one, are both used
        for all purposes or is there an intentional or unintended division of
        labor?[12]), their direction (i.e., is the intention to assimilate the chil-
        dren to the dominant culture, to resurrect dying cultural practices,
        or neither?), the transition from one language to the other (i.e., is it
        complete and abrupt or gradual? is language mixing in the classroom
        allowed?);
3.   The linguistic character of the community and the country (i.e., is
        the language used at home the one used in the immediate community
        and/or the nation?);
4.   The function, status, and differences, both regionally and internation-
        ally, of the various languages (i.e., which is the dominant language?
        how prestigious is the minority language? what are the domains of
        use of each language?).[13]

The principal models of bilingual education include:

- Submersion: children are placed in majority language classrooms for
  the entire school day. There is no formal program for developing
  second language skills.
- Sheltered (Pull-out): minority children are given separate classes in
  majority language development for part of the day. The amount of
  time varies greatly among schools. The usual amount is for one or
  two periods a day (or two to three periods a week). Instruction in all
  topics is in the majority language. Instructors do not have to speak
  the child's native language.
- Transitional bilingual education: use of two languages as medium of
  instruction only until the child has developed enough proficiency to be
  transitioned completely to dominant-language-only instruction. The
  native language is just a tool to help in second language learning. This
  type of program results in monolingualism in the dominant language
  and attrition of the minority language.
- Maintenance bilingual education (two-way/dual language): minority
  language and dominant language students are in the same classroom.
  Some programs seek only the maintenance of the first language and

---

[12] See Lee, Hill-Bonnet, and Gillispie (2008) for the finding that the division of languages in a
   dual language immersion school actually restricted children's possibilities to practice the second
   language in the school.
[13] For the definition of *domain* see Chapter 1.

development of the second. Others seek development of both languages. Dual language programs may start with a 50–50 percent distribution of the instructional time, or with 90 percent for the child's native language and 10 percent for English, gradually moving to the 50–50 percent model by fourth or fifth grade. These programs usually result in proficiency in both languages for minority language-speaking children and a good but less advanced command of the minority language by the majority language-speaking children. They also promote bicultural development.[14]

- Immersion: this model is used principally in Canada. Dominant-language students are educated in a minority language. Instruction is in the second language, but the teacher speaks the students' first language. The L2 is geared to the children's language proficiency at each stage so that it is comprehensible. The L1 is used only in the rare instances when the student cannot complete a task without it. The student thus learns the L2 and subject matter content simultaneously. This program is also used in communities who are attempting language revitalization.

- Content and Language Integrated Learning: this model is used in the European Union. All students from pre-school on receive education in their native language and in one additional language, which is commonly used to teach some content areas. Teachers need not have native proficiency, but they need to be highly fluent in the second language (O. García 2008).

- Multiple Multilingual Education: common in multilinguistic societies such as India, teaches students in at least three languages (O. García 2008).

The options adopted by language policy makers and the different school administrators depend in a large part on their view of bilingualism as a problem, as a resource, or as a right (Ruiz 1984).

The exact type of bilingual education model but, more importantly, the use of the child's two languages in the society have great effects on the language proficiency and dominance of speakers. Aldekoa and Garder (2002: 5–6) point out that even after the many efforts to bring back Euskara in the Basque Country through education, various factors seem to collude against equal proficiency in both languages for Basque students. The first factor is obviously the type of bilingual education the students are enrolled in. Classroom activities emphasize reading and writing over speaking, not giving the students enough experience to feel they can use the language outside the classroom. Not all the teachers are

---

[14] One problem with this type of program in the USA is that it is available only through elementary or at most middle school, with very few high schools continuing the minority language development; so even children who benefited from dual language education will end up having more developed abilities in terms of academic language in English (O. García 2008).

native speakers so some may not have enough competence in Euskara and even the native speakers do not have a good command of all the language registers in Euskara (Cenoz 2008).[15]

Other important factors that go beyond the school have to do with sociolinguistic characteristics of the community and with parental goals for their children: the frequency with which students hear Euskara at home, the fact that most students live in high-density areas dominated by Spanish, and the fact that parents are demanding more English in the school, which decreases the amount of time available for Spanish and Euskara. Similar factors are found to affect bilingualism across the world.

Several studies have shown that dual language programs are the most effective model for developing both of a child's languages, as well as for closing the achievement gap for language minority children (Collier and Thomas 2004). Studies in the USA have found that language minority children in these programs develop in English as well as children in monolingual English-only classrooms, but only 50 percent of the majority language children develop fluency in the minority language by the fourth or fifth grade, probably due to the strong dominance of English in the country (O. García 2008 and references therein).

Nevertheless, there is resistance to bilingual education in many communities – see Rossell and Baker (1996) and the critiques of this study by Krashen (1996a, 1996b) and Cummins (1999) – to the point that the term *bilingual* has been replaced by *English language acquisition,* even in programs which seek to maintain or develop the child's first language, now called *dual language education*, and legislation against bilingual education has been approved in California, Arizona, and Massachusetts (O. García 2008: 10).

In spite of these problems, dual immersion education helps students develop a better understanding of linguistic and cultural differences, foster appreciation for diversity, and provides most students with a good command of a second language (O. García 2008: 6). Bilingualism confers not only educational advantages but enhances cognitive abilities and auditory processing when high levels of proficiency are developed in both languages, as we will see in Chapter 2. Older adults exhibit problems in language such as difficulties in finding words, absence of more complex syntactic structures, and problems in comprehension of complex structures, probably due to generalized cognitive slowing, a shrinking working memory, increasing inability to inhibit distracting information, and loss of brain integrity. Balanced bilinguals who continue using their language into an advanced age experience these problems to a lesser degree (Schrauf 2008). Ramírez, Pérez, Valdez, and Hall (2009) – who studied the long-term effects a dual language program in California focused on maintenance and development of both English and Spanish and the development of a bicultural/multicultural identity and tolerance of diversity – concluded that their results confirmed previous findings that

[15] We find this same phenomenon for Spanish teachers in the USA.

such programs lead to long-term academic achievement, increased high school graduation rates, and enhanced academic performance in language arts.

I.4   Pidgins and creoles

Pidgins and creoles are the extreme instances of language contact which result in the creation of an entirely new language (Muysken 1981; Thomason and Kaufman 1988; Romaine 1992; Singler 1992; McWhorter 2001; Holm 2000). Pidgins are restructured linguistic systems that are used by speakers who do not share a language but need to communicate in situations where the exchange occurs infrequently (such as in trading situations). This system is used by adult speakers who have different native languages, none of which is the pidgin. Pidgins usually take their vocabulary from the most prestigious language. Creole languages emerge when the pidgins evolve, usually because they are taught as a native language to a new generation of speakers who develop the original pidgin into a fully fledged language. Sometimes creoles continue to be used as lingua francas but sometimes they develop further by adopting more characteristics of the dominant language (Appel and Muysken 1987). Despite the multilingual situation during the Spanish domination in the Americas, no Spanish-based creole language seems to have developed – see Klee and Lynch (2009) for a discussion of why this is so. For a fascinating set of studies relating language acquisition, creole languages, and language change, see DeGraff (1999).

I.5   Why study bilingualism/L2 acquisition?

Limiting research on language development to the study of monolinguals would exclude most of the world's population from our research, which would leave us with an impoverished understanding of how human beings acquire and use language. Understanding how we acquire more than one language and how our brain organizes and handles multiple languages in everyday use, and how they influence each other, is fundamental to understanding the human language capacity. Furthermore, bilingualism allows us to disentangle variables in the study of language acquisition which are confounded in monolingual speakers, such as the importance of age of acquisition and input in explaining certain developmental patterns. We will expand on these issues in Chapters 1 and 2.

I.6   Spanish language contact and bilingualism

In this section we provide a brief overview of the history of Spanish and its expansion and contact with other languages throughout the world. There

are many excellent books on these topics which provide a more in-depth coverage
and we refer the reader to them throughout this chapter.

I.6.1   Spanish across the world

Spanish is a Romance language that evolved from Latin, and which
began its expansion in Europe between 100 BC and AD 200. Modern Spanish
comes from the Castilian dialect, which originated around the ninth century near
Burgos and spread throughout the Iberian peninsula during the reconquest of the
peninsula from the Moors, who had dominated it from 711 to 1492. The larger
expansion of Spanish came through the conquest and colonization periods in
the fifteenth and sixteenth centuries, mainly to what is now Latin America and
parts of the Caribbean, the southern part of the USA, and also to Morocco and
Equatorial Guinea in Africa, and the Philippines.

According to Ethnologue (Lewis, Simons, and Fenning 2013), Spanish is spoken by about 405,638,110 speakers as a first language and by about 60,000,000
as a second language. The largest number of Spanish speakers is located in
Mexico, with 104,000,000 speakers according to 2011 data, followed by Colombia (42,300,000 speakers according to the 2011 census), Argentina (39,500,000
speakers according to 2011 census), the USA (34,200,000 speakers according to
the 2010 census), and Spain (29,900,000 speakers according to the 2010 census).
Spanish is used as a national language[16] in nine countries in South America,
where it is recognized as an official national language in the country's constitution, except in Argentina and Chile, six countries in Central America, as the
unofficial national language in Mexico, three countries in the Caribbean, and
Spain in Europe, plus Equatorial Guinea where regardless of its official status
it is the first language of few speakers. It is a provincial language in the USA,
a language for wider communication in Morocco in Africa, Andorra, France,
and Gibraltar in Europe, Belize in Central America, and Bonaire, Sint Eustatius,
and Saba (ex Netherlands Antilles) in the Caribbean, an educational language in
Trinidad and Tobago, and a dispersed language in Curaçao in the Caribbean.[17]

[16] This and the rest of the classification terms used in this paragraph come from Lewis *et al.* 2013
(www.ethnologue.com/about/language-status). The terms used here are defined as follows:
1. National: the language is used in education, work, mass media, and government at the national
level.
2. Provincial: the language is used in education, work, mass media, and government within
major administrative subdivisions of a nation.
3. Wider Communication: the language is used in work and mass media without official status
to transcend language differences across a region.
4. Educational: the language is in vigorous use, with standardization and literature being sustained through a widespread system of institutionally supported education.
5. Dispersed: the language is fully developed in its home country, so that the community of
language users in a different country has access to a standardized form and literature, but
these are not promoted in the country in focus via institutionally supported education.
[17] We include this long list – and other similar ones in this chapter – to underscore the enormity of
the Spanish-speaking world, as well as the diverse range of languages that Spanish is in contact
with. Being aware of the many places where languages are spoken should highlight how much

I.6.2   An overview of our four main languages

In this section we provide a brief overview of the four languages selected to exemplify different types of language contact and bilingualism: three European languages, Spanish, English, and Euskara, and one American language, Quechua.[18] The description of the languages here is of their basic attributes. Other characteristics will be reviewed in more detail in the subsequent chapters. Suggested readings in this section point to canonical and fairly introductory texts on these languages where readers can find references to other works.

Grammatical overview of Spanish

Spanish is a SVO language that also allows VOS and VSO orders (Zagona 2002). It is a head-initial language where nouns precede their complements,[19] determiners[20] precede nouns, and verbs precede all complements. As in other Indo-European languages, movement is overt, with, for example, *wh*-words (*qué, quién, cuándo,* etc.) being moved to the beginning of sentences for question formation. Spanish also shares with many Indo-European languages a rich morphology, with verbal inflectional morphology being richer than nominal inflectional morphology (Zagona 2002). As is the case with many Romance languages, Spanish is a *pro-drop* language (i.e., it allows null subjects Ø *Lo miro* '(I) see it,' *llueve* '(it) rains'), it has clitics (*Yo lo miro* 'I see **it**,' *la niña se baña* 'the girl bathes **herself**'), and it allows negative concord (e.g., ***Nadie** me habló* / ***No** me habló **nadie*** 'No one spoke to me / lit. Not to-me spoke no one'). Spanish-specific characteristics include *personal a*, a Case marker that looks like the preposition *a* and precedes animate direct objects (e.g., *Vi **a** un león* '(I) saw a lion'), and the existence of clitic doubling, which can be more or less extended depending on the dialect, i.e., the coexistence of a direct or indirect object with a clitic (e.g., ***Lo**vi **a Juan*** '(I) saw Juan,' ***Le** di un regalo **a mi hijo*** '(I) gave my son a present'). Hualde, Olarrea, Escobar, and Travis (2010) present a thorough basic introduction to Spanish history and characteristics. We refer readers to Zagona (2002) and Bosque and Gutiérrez-Rexach (2009) for more detailed information on Spanish syntax.

Grammatical overview of Euskara

Euskara is the only living language isolate in Europe, meaning that it is not related to any other known language in the world. Not being an Indo-European language, it is not related to Spanish at all, unlike the other languages spoken in Spain. Euskara seems to have been a native language of the Iberian

---

work there is to do in bilingualism studies to obtain a more accurate picture of bilingualism across the world.

[18] Here we are referring to the origin of the languages, obviously, since Spanish and English are used outside their European context.

[19] Adjectival phrases, prepositional phrases, genitives, relative clauses.

[20] Articles, numerals, demonstratives, and possessives.

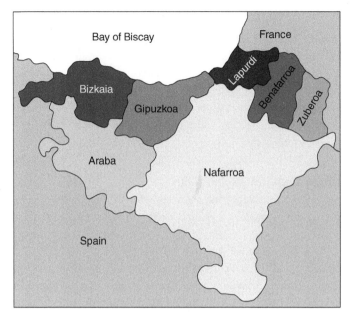

Figure I.1 *Map of the Basque Country. Adapted from http://lokarri.org/index .php/en/documentation/parties*

peninsula, and therefore it predated the arrival of Latin. Euskara is spoken by about 580,000 people in Spain and roughly 80,000 in France (Trask 1997) in a small area of the Pyrenees shown in Figure I.1.

Throughout its history Euskara was mostly a rural, spoken language, which favored the creation of different dialects. Luis Luciano Bonaparte, a nephew of Napoleon Bonaparte, was the first to study Euskara scientifically and to try to establish its dialects in the nineteenth century (Etxeberria 1997). Much of the Euskara used today is actually a standardized variety established in 1982, based on the Navarran and Guipuzcoan dialects and called *Euskara Batua*. Euskara is the minority language in the Basque Country and most speakers are bilingual with Spanish or French, which are the main languages in the cities. Euskara is only used more frequently than Spanish or French in everyday communication in some limited areas of the Basque Country (Cenoz 2008).

Euskara is an SOV, head-final language, which also shows overt movement. It is morphologically agglutinative, meaning that it has several inflectional and derivational morphemes that attach to a root. Each morpheme has one specific meaning – as opposed to fusional languages, such as Spanish where morphemes may fuse more than one meaning; see example (9) for Quechua. The grammars of Euskara and Spanish are different in two main regards: case and agreement patterns, and branching direction.

Euskara is an ergative language in which subjects of transitive verbs receive a special nominal case called *ergative*, and subjects of intransitive verbs and direct objects receive a different case called *absolute*. Trask (1997: xiv) calls its morphology an "extraordinarily rich and elaborate verbal system . . . [including] the most thoroughgoing morphological ergativity on the planet." To clarify the Euskara case system, we need to make an excursion into one of the areas of linguistics with most confusing nomenclature.

The term *ergativity* is used to refer to two things: (a) a type of argument structure in verbs of any language and (b) the type of case marking system found in Basque, as well as other languages such as Inuit and Walpiri.

In the first sense (describing argument structure), an *ergative* verb can be either transitive or intransitive. When it is intransitive its subject corresponds to its direct object when transitive (e.g., transitive: *He broke the window* vs. intransitive: *The window broke*). Intransitive verbs can be *ergative* (e.g., *The window broke* where the subject has a theme/patient theta role), *unaccusative,* i.e., an intransitive verb whose subject has a theme/patient role[21] but does not have an ergative version where such a subject could be an object,[22] or *unergative* (i.e., what we most commonly think of as a typical intransitive verb, one with only a subject with an agent theme, *I ran*).

In the second sense of the word, ergative languages require a separate case marker (or verbal inflection) used with transitive verbs. Euskara uses this ergative marker for transitive verbs as well as unergative verbs, as seen in (1) and (2). In (1), *irakurri* 'to read' is a transitive verb whose subject is marked with the ergative morpheme -*k*, and its direct object is zero-marked (Ø), corresponding to the absolutive case. In (2), *eseri* 'to sit' is an unaccusative verb whose subject has the same absolutive case marker (Ø), the same case used for direct objects of transitive verbs:

Transitive verb
(1)   *Nik liburua- Ø irakurri dut.*
           Ni-k liburu-a- Ø   irakurri dut
           I-ERG book-DET-ABS read   AUX.3SG.ABS.1SG.ERG
           'I have read the books.'

Unaccusative verb
(2)   *Ni eseri naiz.*
           Ni-Ø   eseri naiz
           I-ABS sit   AUX-1 SG.ABS
           'I have sat.'   (Examples from Austin 2001)

---

[21] Hence the name *unaccusative* since direct objects typically take the accusative case (e.g., *they fell*).

[22] Intransitive ergative verbs are therefore a subtype of unaccusative verbs. In Spanish, subjects of unaccusative verbs can appear in postverbal position (e.g., *Llegaron los estudiantes* 'The students arrived'). While other Romance languages have a clear grammatical marking of unaccusative verbs which take a copula as their auxiliary (*être* in French and *essere* in Italian) and unergative verbs which take the auxiliary to *have* (*avoir* in French and *avere* in Italian), Spanish marks both types of verbs with *haber*.

The subjects of unergative verbs take the ergative case, as shown in example (3).

Unergative verb

(3)   *Nik korritu dut.*

Ni-<u>k</u>   korritu   dut

I-ERG   run   AUX-3SG.ABS.1 SG.ERG

'I have run.'   (Examples from Austin 2001)

In contrast, in Spanish all subjects take the nominative case and all direct objects take the accusative, as shown in (4)–(6):

Unaccusative verb

(4)   *Ellos han llegado tarde.*

Ell-o-s.∅   h-a-n   lleg-a-do   tarde

They-M-PLNOM   have-TV-PST.3 PL   arrive-TV-PSTPTCP late

'They have arrived late.'

Unergative verb

(5)   *Ellos han dormido*

Ell-o-s.∅   h-a-n   dorm-i-do

They-M-PLNOM   have-TV-PST.3 PL   sleep-TV-PST.PTCP

'They have slept.'

Transitive verb

(6)   *Ellos han leído los libros*

Ell-o-s.∅   h-a-n   le-í-do   l-o-s   libr-o-s

They-M-PLNOM   have-TV-PST.3 PL   read-TV-PST.PTCP the-M-PL book-M-PL

'They have read the books.'

A second syntactic feature which distinguishes Euskara from Spanish is the order of the constituents in a sentence, because Euskara is a head-final language. For example, in Euskara, the verb precedes the auxiliary, whereas in Spanish, the auxiliary precedes the verb, as shown in (7). Similarly, in Euskara relative clauses are placed before the noun they modify while in Spanish they are after, as shown in (8):

Euskara (examples from Austin 2001)

(7) a.   *Guk liburu asko irakurri dugu.*

Guk   liburu asko <u>irakurri</u> <u>dugu.</u>

We.ERG   book a lot read   AUX.ABS.3SG.ERG.1 SG

'We have read a lot of books.'

   b.   *Ikusi duen gizona.*

<u>Ikusi</u> duen   gizon-a

seen   man-DET AUX.ABS.3SG.ERG.3SG.REL

'The man that she saw.'

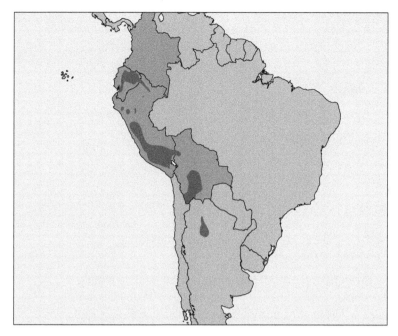

Figure I.2 *The distribution of Quechua in South America. http://en.wikipedia*
.org/wiki/File:Quechuan_langs_map.svg

Spanish (examples from Austin 2001)
(8) a.   *Nosotros hemos leído muchos libros.*
           Nosotros he-mos   le-í-do   much-o-s   libr-o-s
           We.NOM   have-PST.1 PL.NOM read-TV-PST.PTCP many-M-PL book-M-PL
           'We have read many books.'
    b.   *El hombre que he visto.*
           El   hombre que he   visto
           DET man   REL AUX.PST.1 SG.NOM see.PST.PTCP
           'The man that I saw.'

Other grammatical aspects of Euskara will be presented in the book to explain
the examples of language contact and bilingualism in Chapters 2 and 3. See Trask
(1997) for further information on Basque history and grammatical structure.

Grammatical overview of Quechua

Quechua, or Runa Simi, is spoken in Bolivia, Colombia, Ecuador,
Peru, and in the north of Chile and Argentina. It is the most widely spoken
indigenous language in America. There are 8 to 12 million speakers[23] (mainly in
Ecuador, Peru, and Bolivia).

---

[23] Quechua is considered a family of related languages, so it is difficult to estimate number of
   speakers.

Quechua is an SOV language, although SVO, VSO, VOS, OVS, and OSV orders are also possible. It is a head-initial language and it is an agglutinative language, as shown in (9)[24] in comparison to Spanish which is fusional (10).

Quechua

(9)   *Yachachishawarankupis.*
       Yacha -chi -sha   -wa -ra -n -ku -pis
       learn -CAUS-PROG -1SG PST -3 PL too
       '(They) were teaching it to me too.'

Spanish

(10)   *(Ellos) me lo estaban enseñando a mí también.*
       (Ellos) me =   l   -o =   est -a
       (They) CL.1 SG.DAT = CL.3.SG.ACC -M =   be -TV
       -ba   -n   enseñ -a   -ndo   a   mí   también
       PST.IPFV -3.PL   teach -TV -PROG to   me.1 SG.DAT too.
       '(They) were teaching it to me too.'

Other grammatical aspects of Quechua will be presented in the book to explain the examples of language contact and bilingualism in Chapters 2 and 3. Cerrón-Palomino (1987) provides a fascinating introduction to Quechua history and grammar.

Grammatical overview of English

English is spoken in countries throughout the world. It is a national language in Antigua and Barbuda, Bahamas, Dominica, Grenada, Jamaica, Saint Kitts and Nevis, Saint Lucia, Saint Vincent and the Grenadines, and Trinidad and Tobago in the Caribbean; Belize in Central America; the USA[25] and Canada in North America; Guyana in South America; Botswana, Cameroon, Gambia, Ghana, Kenya, Lesotho, Liberia, Malawi, Mauritius, Namibia, Nigeria, Rwanda, Seychelles, Sierra Leone, Somalia, South Africa, South Sudan, Sudan, Swaziland, Uganda, Zambia, and Zimbabwe in Africa; Brunei, India, Malaysia, Pakistan, Philippines, and Singapore in Asia;[26] Australia,[27] Fiji, Kiribati, Marshall Islands, Micronesia, New Zealand,[28] Nauru, Papua New Guinea, Palau, Tonga, Samoa, Solomon Islands, Tuvalu, and Vanuatu in Oceania; and the United Kingdom,[29] Ireland, and Malta in Europe.[30] It is spoken

---

[24] We thank Ellen Courtney for the Quechua example.
[25] And its multiple territories: American Samoa, Guam, and Northern Mariana Islands in Oceania, and Puerto Rico and US Virgin Islands in the Caribbean.
[26] Along with Hong Kong.   [27] And Norfolk Island, its territory.
[28] And its territories: Cook Islands, Niue, and Tokelau.
[29] And its multiple territories: Anguilla, Bermuda, the British Virgin Islands, the Cayman Islands, Monserrat, and Turks and Caicos in the Caribbean; the British Indian Ocean Territory in Asia; Pitcairn in Oceania; and Gibraltar in Europe.
[30] Other English-speaking European territories include Bonaire, Sint Eustatius, and Saba located in the Caribbean, which is part of the Netherlands, Sint Maarten also in the Caribbean, which belongs partially to France and partially to the Netherlands.

by around 334,800,758 according to Lewis, Simons, and Fenning (2013). It is also a second language for about 150,000,000 people.

English is an SVO, head-initial language, with the exception of adjectives and possessives which appear before the noun, a feature of its Germanic ancestry. It also shows overt movement. English has very limited inflectional morphology.

Other grammatical aspects of English will be explained as needed in the rest of the chapters. Radford (2004) is a good resource for English syntax.

I.6.3   Spanish in contact with other languages

Spanish has been in contact with Catalan, Galician, and Euskara inside its territory, and also, as we mentioned before, with Arabic during the Muslim occupation between the eighth and the fifteenth centuries. Starting in the fifteenth century, Spanish also expanded to territories in America, Africa, and Asia.

Bilingualism in Spain: the case of Euskara

Bilingualism in the Basque Country has a long history, stretching back many centuries. Euskara and Spanish have been in contact since Spanish evolved from Latin, leaving many traces of mutual influence. Euskara was originally spoken in a much wider area, from southwestern France to what is now Catalonia. In the Middle Ages, Euskara began to lose ground to Spanish and French, and survived primarily in rural areas. For centuries, there was a form of diglossia without widespread bilingualism, with Euskara spoken by the rural population and Spanish as the language of commerce and the Euskara upper classes.

In the Basque Country at the end of the nineteenth century, some schools were bilingual or even trilingual (in Euskara, Spanish, and French). Unfortunately, these schools disappeared during the Franco dictatorship from 1936 till 1975 in which there was an attempt to assimilate Basques – and all the non-Spanish-speaking population in Spain – linguistically and culturally to Spanish. The use of Euskara was banned in schools from 1939 till 1975. At the same time, immigrants began moving into the Basque Country seeking jobs in its industries, and also as part of a government strategy to make the region Spanish-speaking. The immigrants nearly quadrupled the population of the Basque Country. Since most immigrants and their children did not learn Euskara, the percentage of the population that spoke Euskara declined considerably, causing it to become a minority language. In the early twentieth century, some private schools called *ikastolas* opened which taught content in Euskara. They operated in secret throughout many of the Franco years, and were not officially recognized as part of the school system until the death of Franco (Arzamendi and Genesee, 1997). The law of *Normalization of the Basque Language* in 1982 made Euskara an official language in the Basque country and bilingual education options were expanded (Cenoz 2008).

Since the death of Franco, Euskara has made a significant recovery in the Basque Autonomous Community, thanks largely to language-planning policies and widespread, compulsory bilingual education. The Basque Country became officially bilingual in 1978. Additionally, in 1982 a law mandated that all government services be provided in Euskara, as well as access to bilingual education for all public school students. These measures represent significant progress towards the survival of Euskara because they have introduced the language into prestigious spheres of use which had previously been restricted to Spanish (Haddican 2005). Another important step in the preservation of Euskara has been its standardization through the creation of Euskara Batua (Unified Euskara) (Amorrortu 2003; Haddican 2005).

The Basque Country's school system provides the students with three different models of bilingual education. Model A consists in mostly teaching in Spanish with Euskara as a subject area, which seeks to give students a good comprehension of Euskara, allow them to talk in Euskara about everyday events, and create a positive attitude towards Euskara. This model treats Euskara as a second language rather than as a language of instruction. Model B consists in teaching academic content in both languages with both languages also as subject areas (similar to dual-language programs in the USA). There is no model C. Finally, model D consists in teaching most of the curriculum in Euskara with Spanish as a subject, so it acts as a language maintenance program with some Spanish for Euskara-speaking pupils and as an immersion program for Spanish-speaking pupils. Therefore, only students in system D receive enough Euskara input to counteract its status as a minority language.

Model D (Euskara) is the most popular with 60.47 percent of the primary level and 52.64 percent of the secondary level students; followed by model B (Spanish and Euskara) with 29.96 percent and 27.54 percent of students, respectively. Spanish-only education attracts just 8.80 percent of primary level students and 19.08 percent of secondary level students (Cenoz 2008).[31]

Language contact between Spanish and Euskara has produced the following specific linguistic forms:[32]

Iterative compounds for emphasis
(11)   Solamente los *pobres pobres*
        Only   the poor   poor
        'Only the very poor ones'   (Klee and Lynch 2009: 40)

More frequent occurrence of non-SVO structures than in Standard Spanish
(12)   Tres   sobresalientes tiene Juan.   (OVS)
        Three outstandings   has Juan
        'Juan has three outstanding (grades).'   (Klee and Lynch 2009: 41)

---

[31] For interested readers, both Cenoz (2008) and Zalbide and Cenoz (2008) provide detailed overviews of the achievements and challenges of bilingual education in the Basque Country. These findings refer to the Basque Autonomous Community only; for Navarre, see Oroz Bretón and Sotés Ruiz (2006).
[32] In examples (11) and (12) we have not indicated the morphological structure since it is not necessary in order to understand the examples.

Use of clitic le *to refer to feminine direct objects*

(13)   *¿La hija le va a dejar a la madre?*

       ¿La hija   <u>le</u>   va   a dejar a la madre?

       The daughter CL.3 SG.DAT = go.PRES.3 SG to leave to the mother?

       'Is the daughter going to leave the mother?' (Klee and Lynch 2009: 48)

Omission of third-person accusative clitics

(14)   *Yo ya he leído.*

       Yo ya   Ø he   leído.

       I   already Ø have.PRS.1 SG read.TV.PST.PTCP

       'I have already read (it).' (Klee and Lynch 2009: 52)

There are many other characteristics that Klee and Lynch present as possible effects of Euskara–Spanish contact but for which confirmation is needed with more research; see Klee and Lynch (2009: 39–56).

Bilingualism in the Americas

There are many native language families in the Americas. Since they are so numerous, we list here the ones with over 50,000 speakers. Since indigenous languages do not respect country or continental division, we have included in Table I.2 the language families with number of speakers and geographical area organized by number of speakers.

The native speakers of languages of the Americas were decimated by war, disease, and forced labor in the first centuries of contact with the Europeans. As Mackey (2006: 608) summarizes bilingual speakers that speak a native American language in North America are found "from southern California northward up through the Canadian west coast and Alaska, eastward along the Arctic shorelands and across the sparsely populated Canadian north all the way down the coast of Labrador." Escobar (2011) points out that bilingualism between Spanish and Quechua is the third most important one in the Americas in terms of number of speakers after Spanish–English bilingualism in the USA and English–French bilingualism in Canada.

Bilingualism in Latin America: the case of Quechua

At the time of conquest there were about 2,000 languages in America.[33] Peru and Mexico were the main viceroyalties of Spain. Several languages disappeared during the first period of the colonization (e.g., Taino[34] spoken

---

[33] It is not absolutely clear how many languages there were in each country due to the fact that it is sometimes difficult to determine when two speech varieties are different languages or dialects of the same language, and to the fact that the same languages sometimes were referred to by more than one name (e.g., Matlatzinca, Ocuilteco, and Tlahuara in Mexico, and Cashobo, Managua, and Hagueti in Peru).

[34] Even though it disappeared early, Taino lent many words to Spanish, for example *canoa* 'canoe,' *cacique* 'tribal chief,' *maíz* 'corn,' and *tabaco* 'tobacco.'

Table I.2 *Main indigenous language families in the Americas*

Quechuan	9,096,020	Argentina, Bolivia, Chile, Colombia, Ecuador, and Peru
Mayan	6,523,182	Belize, Guatemala, and Mexico
Tupian	5,028,652	Bolivia, Brazil, French Guiana, Paraguay, and Peru
Aymaran	2,808,740	Bolivia and Peru
Uto-Aztecan	1,910,412	El Salvador, Mexico, and the USA
Otomanguean	1,686,494	Mexico and Nicaragua
Maipurean	705,169	Bolivia, Brazil, Colombia, Guyana, Honduras, Peru, Puerto Rico, Suriname, and Venezuela
Chibchan	306,667	Colombia, Costa Rica, Honduras, Nicaragua, and Panama
Totonacan	282,250	Mexico
Mapundungu	260,620	Chile
Tarascan	235,000	Mexico
Eyak-Athabaskan	207,614	Canada and the USA
Misumalpan	192,450	Nicaragua
Mixe-Zoquean	153,650	Mexico
Algic	138,184	Canada and the USA
Chocoan	113,300	Colombia and Panama
Eskimo-Aleut	110,310	Canada, Greenland, Russian Federation, and the USA
Jivaroan	89,630	Ecuador and Peru
Cariban	67,396	Brazil, Colombia, Guyana, Suriname, and Venezuela
Paezan	61,000	Colombia
Matacoan	60,280	Argentina, Bolivia, and Paraguay
Guaykuruan	50,100	Argentina and Brazil

in the Caribbean and Venezuela and Chibcha spoken in Panama and Colombia). Now, there are eighteen primarily Spanish-speaking countries plus Puerto Rico in Latin America.

In the Caribbean, Spanish also came into contact with African languages through the presence of slaves. Non-Caribbean countries also had contact with these languages through slavery but the greatest influence seems to have occurred in the Caribbean. The first contact of the Spaniards with the native American cultures outside the Caribbean was with the Aztecs in Tenochtitlan, Mexico. The viceroyalty of New Spain was created and in the first period of the colonization it became the most important territory of the Spanish colonies. After 1540 the viceroyalty of Peru became more important.

During Inca times, Quechua was in constant contact with two other indigenous languages in the Andean region, Aymara and Puquina (Cerrón-Palomino 1987). Aymara is still spoken in the southern Andes Altiplano area in Peru, around lake

Titicaca and in Bolivia, while Puquina has now disappeared. Puquina was the language reserved for the Inca elite. Language contact between Andean languages and Spanish was nevertheless limited to specific sectors of the population during the colonial era. Even though the Incas dominated territories inhabited by speakers of other languages, they did not begin to impose the use of Quechua till the fifteenth century. It was the Spaniards, in their need for a common language for evangelization and administration, who expanded Quechua beyond its original frontiers, as they became frustrated after a failed first attempt to learn many of the multiple languages well enough. Quechua, Nahuatl, Mapudungu, and Guaraní were adopted as lingua francas for administrative and religious purposes (Escobar 2011). The Jesuits established bilingual schools with the intent to evangelize the indigenous people and teach them Spanish; but they were available for the native elite only. Philip IV decided later on to go back to the original idea of teaching Spanish to the natives in 1634. In 1770, Charles III ordered a stronger imposition of Spanish and the eradication of the native languages and expelled the Jesuits from the Spanish territories. From then on, schooling was available in Spanish only. However, in the rural areas the *encomenderos*, members of the high class who had been given Indian workers, did not want them to learn Spanish for fear of losing their position of power; this resulted in Quechua being maintained in rural areas while Spanish became dominant in urban areas (Klee and Lynch 2009). The other lingua francas followed similar paths with the exception of Guaraní. In Paraguay, Spaniards and Guaraní speakers joined forces early on to defeat other indigenous peoples and many mixed families were formed. The Jesuits in Paraguay formed *misiones*, protected areas where Guaraní speakers were more isolated from the Spaniards and where their language and culture was respected with the effect that, as opposed to what happened in other areas, Guaraní speakers were not made to believe their language was inferior and widespread bilingualism exists to this day in Paraguay.

The language contact between Quechua and Spanish in Peru has produced two different results, Andean Spanish and what Alberto Escobar (1978) called *interlect*, and Anna María Escobar (1994) calls *Bilingual Spanish*. Bilingual Spanish is spoken by native speakers of Quechua or Aymara who are in the process of acquiring Spanish as a second language. Andean Spanish is a dialect of Spanish spoken by native speakers (and sometimes monolingual speakers of Spanish) in the Andean region, which has characteristics borrowed into Spanish from the Andean languages due to intense contact. Both forms of Spanish have different characteristics, and therefore it is important to distinguish when speaking about bilingual speakers and contact varieties, which one of these varieties of Spanish one is speaking about. All constructions that differ from the Spanish Standard variety that are found in Andean Spanish are also found in Bilingual Spanish but not vice-versa, according to Escobar (1994). The characteristics that differentiate the two varieties include the different constructions exemplified below, which come from Escobar (2011):

Replacement of Spanish mid vowels by high vowels
(15)   *Pelota* [pilúta]
          'Ball'   (Escobar 2011: 328)

Omission of articles and prepositions
(16) a.   *Escribe carta.*
            Ø *escribe*   Ø   *carta*
            write.PRS.3 SG   Ø   letter
            '(He/she) writes (a) letter.'   (Escobar 2011: 328)
     b.   *La casa ingeniero*
            L-a   cas-a   Ø   ingenier-o.
            The-F   house-F   Ø   engineer-M
            'The house (of the) engineer'   (Escobar 2011: 328)

Lack of number and gender agreement
(17) a.   *La escuela nocturno.*
            L-a   escuel-a   nocturn-o
            The-F   school-F   nocturnal-M
            'The night school'   (Escobar 2011: 329)
     b.   *Niños sucio.*
            Niñ-o-s   suci-o
            Child-M-PL   dirty.M.SG
            'Dirty children'   (Escobar 2011: 329)
     c.   *Es necesario que ellos habla su quechua pues.*
            Es necesario que ellos   habla[35]   su   quechua pues.
            Is   necessary that they.3.PL   speak.PRS.IND.3 SG   their Quechua then.
            '(It) is necessary that they speak their Quechua then.'   (Escobar 2011: 329)

Morphological regularization
(18) a.   *Ponieron* (for *pusieron*).
            '(They) put.'   (Escobar 2011: 329)
     b.   *Hacerán* (for *harán*)
            '(They) will do.'   (Escobar 2011: 329)

Features of Andean Spanish, the Spanish spoken by even monolingual speakers in the Andes, include:

Loan blending
(19)   *Cachi-caldo*
          Salt (Q)-broth (S)
          'Broth with salt'   (Escobar 2011: 329)

Borrowing of Quechua plural marker -kuna, *topic/focus markers* -ga/-ka/-qa, *derivative marker used for courtesy* -ri, *and the negative emphatic* -tan
(20) a.   *Oveja-kuna*
            Sheep (S)-PL (Q)
            'Sheep (PL)'   (Escobar 2011: 330)

---

[35] In addition, this form would be subjunctive in Standard Spanish.

b.   *Ahí-ka   barrio   chiquito.*
        There-FOC   neighborhood   small
        'There small neighborhood'   (Escobar 2011: 330)

c.   *Espera   -ri-me.*
        Wait.2.IMP.2 SG   -DER = CL.1 SG.ACC
        'Wait for me, please.'   (Escobar 2011: 330)

d.   *Nada   más   -tan.*
        Nothing   more   NEG
        'No more!'   (Escobar 2011: 330)

The omission of third-person object clitics in answering questions or when the direct object is dislocated to the left

(21)   *¿Sabes que el señor Quispe se murió?*
        'Do you know that Mr. Quispe died?'
        Ø No   Ø he   sabido.
        Ø Not   Ø have.PRS.1 SG   known
        '(I) have not know (it)/ (I) did not know (it).'   (Escobar 2011: 331)

The frequent use of the Quechua diminutive -cha, and the Spanish diminutive -it, even in gerunds

(22) a.   *Mama-cha*
        Mother (S)-DIM (Q)
        'Miss'   (Escobar 2011: 330)

b.   *Corr-ie -nd   -it   -o*
        Run-TV   -PROG   -DIM   -M
        'Running'   (Escobar 2011: 332)

Other characteristics of Andean Spanish and Bilingual Spanish will be reviewed in Chapter 3.

According to Escobar lexical borrowing from Quechua into Spanish occurred primarily in the early colonial period (sixteenth and early seventeenth centuries). However, she claims that other types of contact phenomenon (phonological, morphological, and syntactic–structural interference) require "widespread bilingualism, a high degree of interaction between the bilingual and the monolingual speech communities, and active bilingual use of the second language for ordinary communicative purposes" (Escobar 2001: 80). She proposed that although these language contact phenomena did occur at the individual level, Andean Spanish, as an established variety of Spanish could not have appeared till the twentieth century, when social mobility and a massive immigration from the rural to urban areas created a large bilingual community (but see Cerrón-Palomino 2003 for arguments in favor of a much earlier creation of this variety).

Although acceptance of Andean Spanish has slowly been growing in Peru due to the enormous migration from rural areas to the cities in the twentieth century due to poverty and terrorism and has helped spread features of this dialect to the varieties of the coast and even to the standard variety in Lima, a study by Vigil (2003) found that in educational texts on Spanish provided to the schools by the Ministry of Education for free, some structures provided to the students as examples of incorrect Spanish were examples of grammatical constructions in Andean Spanish.

After their wars of independence, the new Latin American nations did little to improve the availability of bilingual education for the indigenous population. Things started to change when, in 1953, a UNESCO resolution said it was necessary to teach children how to read and write in their native language. In Mexico, the support and interest in the indigenous languages started earlier, in the 1920s (Hidalgo 1996), but nevertheless indigenous people have continued shifting in their majority to Spanish. The population who spoke a native language went from 14 percent in 1930s to 6.2 percent in 2002 (Klee and Lynch 2009). In Peru, even though interest in the indigenous languages became strong in the 1920s and 1930s with the *Indigenista Movement* and though the law has supported bilingual/bicultural education since the 1960s, its implementation has been very slow, based mostly on pilot projects that never became common practice. In general, Latin America has been slow in recognizing the language and educational rights of their indigenous peoples. In 1911, the Mexican Constitution forbade the use of indigenous languages in education, a situation which continued until 1936 when a new law promoted bilingual education, which supported mainly a transitional model[36] (López 1997). In the 1950s the Summer Institute of Linguistics started working in Latin America and created the first materials and programs to prepare bilingual teachers. In 1972, a law on bilingual education started some programs to try to incorporate bilingualism and biculturalism into the curriculum in Peru. In 1975, in Velasco's government, Quechua, but not the other indigenous languages, was declared an official language of Peru. In 1977, the teaching of Quechua at all educational levels became mandatory and several grammars and dictionaries of the different varieties of Quechua were created, while some experimental projects on bilingual education were started, but their efforts were not successful due to lack of funding and teacher preparation and because bilingual education was seen by most people in power as unnecessary and even dangerous to national unity. When Velasco's government ended, also in 1975, though, the mandate for bilingual education was abandoned (Zavala 2002).[37] In the 1930s, 39 percent of the population spoke an indigenous language; this number had been reduced to 19 percent in 2005 (Klee and Lynch 2009). Changes in Bolivia started in 1983 with a national literacy and education plan for the indigenous peoples. In Colombia, the linguistic and educational rights of indigenous peoples were recognized in the 1991 Constitution. In 1993 Mexico recognized the rights of indigenous peoples in their Constitution, but no mention is made of their linguistic and educational rights. In 1990 Guatemala created the Academy of Mayan Languages (Zimmermann 1997). Ecuador and Guatemala created Bilingual Intercultural Education Programs in 1983 and 1995, respectively, through collaborations between their

[36] Models of bilingual education are explained below in this section.
[37] Pozzi-Escot (1988) provides a detailed history of Peruvian bilingual education till the 1980s.

Ministries of Education and the German Gesellschaft für Technische Zusammenarbeit (GTZ).[38] In Peru, after Velasco's government, there were isolated projects on bilingual education, most of them funded by international organizations and private foundations – see Zavala (2002) and references therein. In 1997 the Ministry of Education created the Unidad de Educación Bilingüe e Intercultural 'Bilingual and Intercultural Education Unit,'[39] and since then bilingual education in Quechua, Aymara, and some Amazon languages has reached sixteen *departamentos* in the nation. Information provided by the Ministry in 2000 and cited in Zavala (2002: 65) indicated that at that time there were 4,280 bilingual schools and almost 100,000 children receiving bilingual education.

In general, in the Andean region there is a positive attitude towards bilingualism from native indigenous speakers, but there is also an almost complete lack of support for majority language speakers to learn the minority languages.[40] In Zúñiga *et al.*'s (2000) study it was found that regardless of the fact that the communities and teachers were bilingual with dominance in the indigenous language, Spanish was the only language used for literacy instruction, even when the children's proficiency in Spanish was limited. Even though the teachers favored bilingual education, this study concluded they were ill prepared to implement it, or to teach Spanish as a second language.

Several challenges have hindered the development of bilingual education in Latin America. The first one is the large amount of language and dialect diversification in the area and the lack of precise information on the number of speakers.[41] This is compounded by the need to train well-prepared bilingual teachers in large numbers and the lack of consistent funding and support by the governments.

Bilingualism in the USA: the case of Spanish

There were about 500 to 1,000 native languages in the USA before the European settlers arrived. The main colonial languages were English on the east coast, Spanish in the south (Florida to California), French in Louisiana and northern Maine, German in Pennsylvania, Dutch in New Amsterdam (now New York), Swedish in Delaware, and Russian in Alaska.

The predominance of English was reinforced by new immigration in the seventeenth and eighteenth centuries. By 1776 the USA was mostly English-speaking, with 60 percent of the population of English descent, 18 percent of Scottish and

---

[38] The German Society for Technical Cooperation.

[39] Now renamed as the Dirección General de Educación Intercultural, Bilingüe y Rural 'the General Directorate for Intercultural, Bilingual, and Rural Education.'

[40] At the moment of writing a well-intentioned bill has been presented to the Peruvian congress proposing that all university students show proficiency in Quechua in order to obtain a Bachelor's degree. However, the law does not take into account the problems in acquiring a language that is very different from Spanish in adulthood, nor does it mention where the resources would come from to train the number of teachers such endeavor would require.

[41] In the Second National Congress of the Brazilian Association of Linguistics in 1999, a systematic study of the indigenous languages of Latin America was proposed to promote comparative studies (http://www.unicamp.br).

Irish descent, and 9 percent of German descent. However, in the US Constitution, English was never declared as the official language of the USA, and to this day there is no official language. Until the mid nineteenth century, however, bilingualism was well tolerated. For example, Pennsylvania was German-dominant, with newspapers written in German and German used as the language of instruction in schools. Cashman (2006: 43–45) provides a historical overview of the pervasive shift to monolingualism in the USA. Slaves on plantations were isolated linguistically from each other by being placed with speakers who did not share a common language. Native Americans were forced to assimilate in the late nineteenth century; their children were forcibly taken away from their parents and placed in boarding schools where they were punished for speaking their languages. During the two World Wars German, Japanese, and Chinese nationals as well as German-, Japanese-, and Chinese-Americans suffered virulent discrimination and even imprisonment in internment camps, and many states passed laws making English the sole language of instruction in schools. In the early to mid twentieth century an Americanization campaign attempted to assimilate recent immigrants linguistically and culturally. All of these factors served to promote monolingualism and reduce linguistic diversity in the United States.

Spanish arrived in what is now the USA with the *conquistadores* between 1513 and 1543. The territories that belonged to the Spanish crown included Florida, Louisiana, Texas, New México, Arizona, California, Nevada, Utah, and parts of Colorado, Wyoming, Kansas, and Oklahoma. The territories in the southwest were incorporated later, in 1598. When Mexico became independent most of these territories became Mexican. Texas became an independent republic in 1836 and was annexed to the USA in 1845. Later, Mexico lost many of these territories after the USA–Mexico war of 1846, which culminated in Mexico handing over half of its territory to the USA when it signed the Guadalupe–Hidalgo Treatise in 1848. This treatise guaranteed the rights of the ex-Mexican citizens in these areas but did not guarantee their right to continue using Spanish. English soon became dominant in these areas, although some remnants of the Spanish spoken at the time still exist in New Mexico (Bills 2005). In 1898, the USA entered into the war of independence between Cuba and Spain, and gained control over Cuba, Puerto Rico, and Guam. Cuba became independent in 1902. Many Cubans later migrated in Florida in 1959, fleeing from Castro's government in Cuba after the fall of the Batista regime that had been supported by the USA.

Cubans, Puerto Ricans, and Mexicans are still the largest Hispanic groups in the USA. Many Puerto Ricans, as American citizens, travel back and forth between Puerto Rico (which remains predominantly Spanish-speaking) and the USA, which has helped this community maintain their Spanish. Cubans settled mainly in Miami, becoming the majority of the population of the city by the 1970s, and immigration by Cubans and other Latin Americans (Nicaraguan, Colombian, Argentinian, and Venezuelan) has continued for three decades into Miami and surrounding areas, with 60 percent of the population being Hispanic and with Spanish being spoken in 62 percent of the homes. Mexicans are by far

Table I.3 *Languages spoken at home in the USA according to the 2010 census*

Language	Number of speakers
English	225.5 million
Spanish	34.5 million
Chinese	2.5 million
Other languages with at least 1 million speakers	
Tagalog	1.5 million
French	1.4 million
Vietnamese	1.2 million
German	1.1 million
Korean	1.1 million

the largest group of Hispanics in the USA and today reside mainly in the areas that belonged to the Spanish crown but have also become established throughout the country. This great variety of origins has created different varieties of Spanish in the USA and also different contact varieties of English (Lipski 2008).

During the nineteenth century and the beginning of the twentieth century Spanish speakers in the USA comprised only 2 percent of the population of the country, with a majority of other non-English speakers coming from Europe. From the mid twentieth century this changed to a majority of immigrants coming from Latin America, due to economic and sociopolitical turmoil in the Latin American countries. With the Mexican revolution of 1910 there was an increase in immigration to the USA. There was a second large wave of immigration during the American depression in the 1930s, when the USA government created the *bracero* program to bring agricultural workers into the country. In 1965 immigration law was reformed to allow the provision of a green card to any immigrant from a western country, but in the 1970s this program became unavailable for Mexican citizens.

These days, the United States is a multilingual country that is home to many bilinguals. According to the 2010 census,[42] the USA has 281 million inhabitants of which 55.4 million (or 20 percent) report that they speak a language other than English at home.[43] Table I.3 shows the distribution of languages spoken at home in the USA.

An estimated 225 languages are spoken besides English in the United States. Millions of speaker of other languages come into the USA or are born in it. Although it is a country with great linguistic diversity, there are no federal

---

[42] See www.census.gov/newsroom/releases/archives/american_community_survey_acs/cb10-cn58. html for a summary and www.census.gov/hhes/socdemo/language/ for more detailed data.

[43] The US census has information only on citizens and legal residents. For information on undocumented Hispanics consult the Pew Hispanic Center website (www.pewhispanic.org) which estimates that 11.7 million undocumented Hispanics lived in the USA in 2012.

policies to protect the rights of minority language speakers. As a consequence, bilingualism at the individual level is not very strong. The descendants of speakers of this wide variety of languages tend to lose the non-English language by the third or fourth generation. As Hakuta (1986: 166) noted, "in its short history, the United States has probably been host to more bilingual people than any other country in the world. One of the most fascinating aspects of bilingualism in the United States is its extreme instability, for it is a transitional stage towards monolingualism in English." Several researchers (Ruiz 1984; Crawford 1992) have pointed out the paradox that even though learning an L2 is well regarded in the USA for employment or educational reasons, bilingualism and the maintenance of heritage languages is not, and as a consequence little support is provided for dual language programs. Cashman (2006: 42) summarized these paradoxical attitudes toward bilingualism in her excellent article about researcher responsibilities towards the populations they study in an anti-bilingual society:

> Languages may alternatively be seen as a problem, a right or a resource (Ruíz, 1984). The choice of which metaphor to apply is related to the value placed on its speakers by the hegemonic group. In the case of language minorities in the USA, language diversity is most often seen by those in power as a problem to be solved rather than as a right to be protected or as a resource to be conserved. Differential bilingualism (Aparicio, 1998) describes the unequal value accorded by the English monolingual majority to the bilingual skills of Anglo members of the language majority, which tend to be seen as a resource and an achievement, and those of Latinos and other language minority or immigrant groups, which tend to be seen as a problem and a deficiency.

Even though the USA has no federally recognized official language, twenty-eight states have adopted English as their official language and Hawaii has both English and Hawaiian as official languages.

Notice that the census question asked whether people speak a language other than English at home but not whether that is the only language they speak at home. The census does not give us information on how many of these 55.4 million people are bilingual at home. The majority of these speakers reported that they spoke English very well. The percentage of speakers in all groups who report speaking another language at home that say that they also speak English very well goes from 50 percent for speakers of Asian or Pacific languages to 70 percent for speakers of other languages.

Most Spanish-speaking bilinguals live on the east and west coasts of the United States, as seen in the map in Figure I.3.

States in which Spanish is spoken include Texas, New Mexico, Arizona, California, and Puerto Rico with more than 30 percent of Spanish speakers, and Florida, Colorado, and Nevada with between 20 percent and 29.9 percent. Of the 34.5 million speakers of Spanish in the USA, 52.6 percent said they spoke English

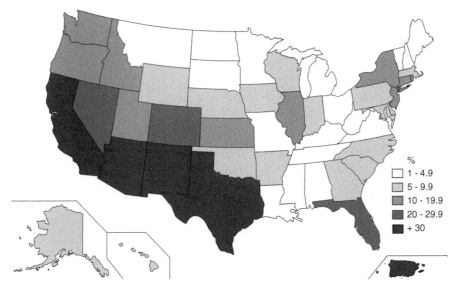

Figure I.3 *Spanish speakers in the United States (US Census Bureau, 2010 Census, Summary File 1). Taken from http://upload.wikimedia.org/wikipedia/ commons/e/e9/2010_US_Census_Hispanic_map.svg since the USA Census website was unavailable at the time of writing due to the Government Shutdown*

very well, 18.3 percent said they spoke it *well*, 18.4 percent said they spoke it *not well*, and 10.7 percent said they did not speak English at all. Because census figures rely on self-reported data, the accuracy of the responses is impossible to gauge (e.g., we do not know how the respondents understood the difference between speaking English *well* and speaking English *very well*, or whether they even had the same notion of what *well* meant). The data indicate that the majority of Spanish speakers (almost 71 percent) also know English at least well, and that only a minority has not learned English. One interesting characteristic of the Spanish-speaking population is that while the majority of speakers of languages other than English and Spanish in the USA are foreign born, almost half of the Spanish speakers in the USA are native born (17 million) while foreign-born speakers constitute 17.5 million speakers. This points to the fact that Spanish-speaking families in this country tend to use Spanish with their children and that these children have a better chance of maintaining their language than children of other populations in the USA.

This achievement is particularly impressive given the prevalent view of bilingualism as a problem and even as a threat to national unity in the USA. In Texas 43 percent of the schoolchildren speak a language other than English at home, and of those 90 percent speak Spanish. At the national level, three out of four of the English language learners are Spanish speakers. According to data from the 2000 US Census cited in O. García (2008: 178), the overwhelming majority of the school-aged children who spoke a language other than English at home (from

84.8 percent to 92.02 percent) were considered bilingual (and not only emergent bilinguals).

Title VII of the Civil Rights Act in 1964 finally created language policy for the protection of non-English speakers in the workplace. In 1980 the Equal Employment Opportunity Commission protected the linguistic characteristics of workers (as well as cultural and physical characteristics). Language minority children were immersed in English-only programs with little help to develop their English skills or maintain their native languages. This caused elevated dropout rates, lower academic achievement, and low access to college level-education. The Bilingual Education Act (Title VII of the Elementary and Secondary Education Act) gave funding for schools to implement programs that used the children's native language as a medium of instruction in 1968, mainly due to pressure from parents. However, school participation was voluntary until 1974, when the US Supreme Court decided that minority children provided only with English-language materials were receiving unequal treatment. Unfortunately, the type of bilingual educations programs to be implemented was not specified, with the result that most programs became transitional programs rather than dual language ones. Lately educational and civil right matters have been decided using public referenda or ballot propositions instead of being discussed by the legislators. Voters poorly informed on matters of bilingual education and language policy have further reduced the support for minority-language speakers' rights.

Despite the success of dual immersion programs in developing children's proficiency in English while simultaneously promoting their overall academic achievement (Collier and Thomas 2004), in 2008 only twelve states mandated bilingual education, twelve states permitted it, one forbade it, and twenty-six states had no legislation about it (E. García 2008). In 1998, California passed Proposition 227, which mandated English-language instruction for all children. Children who speak a minority language are assigned to English as a second language programs and transitional programs only, although parents can request a waiver. In 2000 Arizona also eliminated bilingual public education. Half of the children who attended bilingual education programs in California and Arizona were reassigned to English-only programs. Massachusetts passed a similar law in 2002 (Montrul 2013). The Bilingual Education Act was terminated in 2001 with the passing of *No Child Left Behind* by the US Congress, which emphasized accountability in English only, and mandates that all students be tested yearly in English, with the result that much more time is now devoted in schools for learners to develop English skills than to create for them a successful learning environment.

Although Spanish speakers tend to conserve their language to a greater degree as a group, language maintenance is not guaranteed at the individual level. Third- and fourth-generation immigrants do maintain some competence in Spanish, but they are dominant in English. Heritage speakers usually have a system that differs from native varieties of Spanish (see Chapter 1, Section 1.9.2). Even though individuals lose their Spanish, the continual influx of new Hispanic immigrants, and the fact that at least some of the Mexican and Puerto Rican speakers and their descendants frequently travel back and forth between their countries of origin and the USA, has helped maintain Spanish at a societal level.

The Spanish varieties in the USA have several characteristics that were brought by first-generation speakers from their regional varieties in Latin America – for a brief overview see Escobar (2010), for a detailed explanation see Lipski (2008). Here, we will only discuss those features that are characteristic of the Spanish spoken in the USA – see Escobar (2010) and references therein.

Use of English discourse markers
(23)   *So a los trece años me gradué de sexto, entonces a los católicos vine a séptimo, so este estaba atrasada y'know.*
         'So at age thirteen (I) graduated from sixth (grade), then to the Catholic (school I) came in seventh (grade) so ehh (I) was delayed y'know.'
                                                              (Escobar 2010: 477)

Omission of que *'that'*
(24)   *Yo creo Ø inventaron el pronombre.*
         'I think (that they) made up the pronoun.'   (Escobar 2010: 478)

Redundant use of subject pronouns
(25)   *Mañana nosotros vamos a visitarte.*
         'Tomorrow we (will) go to visit you.'   (Escobar 2010: 478)

Redundant possessive pronouns
(26)   *Nos   lav-a-mos   nuestras mano-s antes de com-e-r.*
         REFL = wash-TV-PST.1 PL   our   hand-PL before of eat-TV-INF
         '(We) wash our hands before eating'   (Escobar 2010: 478)

Use of nominalized gerunds or as adjectives
(27) a. *Lo que hace es comparando precios.*
         'What (he/she) does is comparing prices.' (vs. Standard Spanish *Lo que hace es comparar precios* with an infinitive instead of the gerund, Escobar 2010: 478)
    b.   *Las compañeras enseñando español.*
         'The colleagues teaching Spanish.' (vs. Standard Spanish *Las compañeras que enseñan español* with a relative clause instead of the gerund, Escobar 2010: 478)

Extended use of passive construction
(28)   *Mis padres fueron muy queridos.*
         'My parents were very loved.'   (Escobar 2010: 478)

Use of para + *subject pronoun* + *infinitive*
(29)   *No hay tiempo para yo poder comprar algo.*
         'There is no time for me to be able to buy something.'   (Escobar 2010: 478)

Reduction in the use of the subjunctive
(30)   *Me habló como si no pasó nada.*
         '(He/she) spoke to me as if nothing had happened.' (vs. Standard Spanish
         Me habló como si ni hubiera pasado nada with a pluperfect subjunctive
         form of *pasar* instead of the past perfective [pretérito] one, Escobar 2010:
         478)

I.7   Conclusions

In this chapter we have introduced many of the key terms and concepts which will be discussed at greater length in the rest of the book. We have
also presented a basic overview of the languages we will discuss, as well as a
brief introduction to their complex histories of language contact. We have also
discussed bilingual education in Peru, Spain, and the USA, and how educational
support for minority languages affects bilingualism at the individual and societal
levels. Comparing contact varieties of Spanish in the three countries also illustrates the importance of a language's status as a majority or minority language in
determining the outcomes of language contact.

The history of bilingual education in the three regions is quite different. In Peru,
as in most of Latin America, bilingual education is just beginning to be taken
seriously, and will require decades of work to improve educational outcomes
for the indigenous populations. In the USA, the need for bilingual education is
also evident. Despite research showing the efficacy of dual immersion education,
bilingual education generates little political or popular support in the USA, and
many regions have been cautious about expanding bilingual programs for more
students. In contrast, linguistic policies regarding bilingualism in the Basque
Country are more established than in the USA or Peru and far more ambitious in
reach, and have achieved some success in introducing Euskara into more spheres
of use. The continued survival of Euskara, a minority language with a small
number of speakers, will depend upon sustained efforts to preserve the language
through universal bilingual education programs.

1   What does it mean to be bilingual?

> The bilingual is not two monolinguals in one person.
>
> (Grosjean 1989: 1)

1.1   Who is bilingual?

The hypothetical case histories – adapted from Hoffmann (1991) to the Spanish-speaking world – in Table 1.1 illustrate how different the bilingual experience can be.

For bilingual speakers, many of these stories will sound familiar, but for a monolingual speaker, the examples in Table 1.1 illustrate the heterogeneity of the experience of being bilingual. Case histories such as these can be categorized in four groups according to the speakers' reasons for becoming bilingual:

- Group A: children who are bilingual from birth or simultaneous bilinguals, either having two languages at home or one at home and one outside the home (playgroup, daycare, other family members).
- Group B: early bilinguals who start learning a second language sometime after birth,[1] normally having one language at home and one outside home.
- Group C: people who learned a second language in adulthood[2] who use it for work-related activities, in academia, as translators/interpreters, for reading specialized literature, or because they have jobs that require contact with several international colleagues.
- Group D: immigrants who must learn a second language to survive in the new country or speakers of a minority language in their own country who must learn the dominant language.

This grouping is just a simplification of all the possible variations of bilingualism in the world. Most of the cases we talk about in this book fall under type D, adults and children who are in a minority language situation either in their own country or because they immigrated. In two of our case studies, the Basque Country and

---

[1] We will see later in Section 1.5.4 what "sometime after birth" means.
[2] Obviously, some of the children in groups A and B may later become part of groups C or D.

Table 1.1 *Cases of bilingualism (adapted from Hoffmann 1991)*

The 2-year-old who is beginning to talk, speaking English to one parent and Spanish to another.

The 4-year-old whose home language is Euskara and who has been attending a Spanish playgroup for some time.

The schoolchild from a Peruvian immigrant family living in the United States who increasingly uses English both at home and outside but whose older relatives address him in Spanish only.

The American child from New York who comes from an English-speaking background and attends an immersion program consisting of half a day of schooling taught in Spanish.

The young graduate at a Mexican university who has studied English for eleven years.

The 60-year-old scholar who has spent a considerable part of her life working with manuscripts and documents written in Mayan.

The technical translator.

The personal interpreter of an important public figure.

The Spanish chemist who can read specialist literature in his subject written in English.

The Argentinian airline pilot who uses English for most of his professional communication.

The Quechua-speaking immigrant worker in Lima, Peru, who speaks Quechua at home and with his friend and work colleagues, but who can communicate in Spanish, in both the written and the oral forms, with his superiors and the authorities.

The wife of the latter, who is able to get by in spoken Spanish but cannot read or write it.

The Chilean immigrant in Mexico who has had no contact with Mapudungu for the last forty years.

The Paraguayan government employee who lives in bilingual Asunción, whose friends and relatives are mainly Guaraní speakers but who works in an entirely Spanish-speaking environment and whose colleagues in the office (whether they are Guaraní speakers or not) use Spanish as well.

The fervent Catalanist who at home and at work uses Catalan only, but who is exposed to Castilian Spanish from the media and in the street and has no linguistic difficulty in the latter language.

Peru, Spanish is the majority language. In contrast, in the USA, Spanish is the minority language. In the Spanish-speaking world cases of bilinguals of types A through C can also be found.

Opinions as to who is a bilingual differ between monolingual people who have little contact with bilingualism and bilinguals themselves (and linguists). Grosjean (1982) asked monolingual and bilingual college students to answer: "If someone told you that X was bilingual in English and French, what would you understand by that?" His results are presented in Table 1.2.

Table 1.2 *Different opinions about bilingualism from monolinguals and bilinguals according to Grosjean (1982: 231)*

	Monolinguals	Bilinguals
X speaks both languages fluently	36%	31%
X speaks English and French	21%	46%
X speaks and understands English and French	18%	–

As can be seen, the majority of monolinguals considered fluency a necessary criterion for bilingualism, but bilinguals themselves did not consider fluency as important as monolinguals did. This is not surprising since bilinguals may be more aware of the difficulties involved in achieving fluency in both languages and of the different levels of proficiency a bilingual can have. For a definition of proficiency and fluency see Section 1.3; for the different situations that may affect a bilingual's performance see Section 1.3.3.

1.2   Bilingualism vs. bilinguality

There is a lack of consensus even among experts on bilingualism as to who should be considered bilingual. See the following well-known examples:

> The practice of alternately using two languages will be called BILINGUALISM, and the persons involved, BILINGUAL.   (Weinrich 1953: 1)

> In . . . cases . . . where perfect foreign-language learning is not accompanied by loss of the native language, it results in bilingualism, native-like control of two languages.   (Bloomfield 1933: 55–56)

> Bilingualism is the condition in which two living languages exist side by side in a country, each spoken by one national group, representing a fairly large proportion of the people.
> (Aucamp 1926, in Beziers and Van Overbeke 1968: 113)

These three definitions are very different. Weinrich's definition focuses on the individual speaker and does not say anything about the amount of use of each language by the speaker or of his/her proficiency in them.[3] Bloomfield's definition implies a very negative view of foreign-language learning since he assumes that it is most likely accompanied by language loss. He focuses on the individual speaker and mentions only the learning of a foreign language, without taking into consideration the case of learning another language in someone's own country. He furthermore defines bilingualism as native-like control of two languages. Finally, Aucamp defines bilingualism at the societal and not at the individual

---

[3] We will use the term proficient here just to indicate a general level of language knowledge. We will define the term more precisely in Section 1.3.

level. Unfortunately, there is no universally accepted definition of what it means to be bilingual. Most authors use the term *bilingualism* to refer both to the bilingual individual and the bilingual society. Nevertheless, Hamers and Blanc (2000) distinguish between *bilingualism* and *bilinguality*.

> The concept of bilingualism refers to the state of a linguistic community in which two languages are in contact with the result that two codes can be used in the same interaction and that a number of individuals are bilingual (societal bilingualism); but it also includes the concept of bilinguality (or individual bilingualism). Bilinguality is the psychological state of an individual who has access to more than one linguistic code as a means of social communication; the degree of access will vary along a number of dimensions which are psychological, social, sociological, sociolinguistic, sociocultural and linguistic (Hamers 1981).   (Hamers and Blanc 2000: 6)

In this book, we use the term *bilingualism* to refer to both societal and individual bilingualism. Although in this book our three case studies are cases of bilingualism at the societal level, we will be mainly interested in the effects of bilingualism on the individual, and therefore on *bilinguality*.

Note that in addition to the distinction between society and individual, the previous definitions differed in terms of the speaker's language ability, usually referred to as *proficiency* in our field.

There are different views on who we consider to be bilingual, ranging from Haugen (1953),[4] who said we should consider bilingual someone who can produce meaningful sentences in non-native languages, to Halliday, McKintosh, and Strevens (1970) who proposed that a "true bilingual" was a person who is capable of functioning equally well in either of his languages in all domains of activity and without any traces of the one language in his use of the other.[5] Haugen's point of view represents what we call the *minimalist* view of bilingualism, while Halliday *et al.*'s is the *maximalist* view.

Even within these two different points of view, there are differences. For the maximalist view, it is not clear whether the speaker needs to be native-like in the four basic skills (speaking, writing, reading, listening) to be considered bilingual. Different interlocutors and domains of use affect bilinguals' performance (as we will see in Section 1.3.3), so this "perfect bilingual," if he/she exists, is not the most common type of bilingual across the world. On the other hand, for the minimalist view, how much is enough? Is someone bilingual if he/she can sign a song or say *goodnight* in a different language? There are no clear-cut answers to these questions. Since bilingualism is a continuum from the minimalist to the maximalist view, where one draws the line depends on the person's theory, training, and personal views. What is important, therefore, is that one always defines clearly in research and academic writing what kind of bilinguals one has selected as participants or is writing about.

---

[4] Also see Macnamara (1967).   [5] Also see Bloomfield (1933).

1.3   The challenges of defining proficiency

Bilinguals are usually classified in terms of language knowledge, amount of use of both languages, domains of use of both languages, and their skills (speaking, understanding, reading, and writing). It is important to remember that someone's level of command may fluctuate in all these areas throughout his/her lifetime; so bilinguals need to be assessed at different points in their development. Grosjean (2008: 26) says that "the age at which a language was acquired, how it was acquired, and the amount of use it has been given over the years has an impact on how well a language is known, how it is processed, and even the way the brain stores and deals with it."

1.3.1   Proficiency vs. competence

There are different terms used to describe a speaker's knowledge and ability. One frequently used term in the literature on bilingualism is that of *proficiency*. Unfortunately, it is difficult to find definitions of this term. The term *proficiency* can have different meanings. In general, it is used to refer to:[6]

- Formal competence: knowledge of abstract rules of grammar.
- Communicative competence (Hymes 1967, 1972): the knowledge and ability to use language in socially acceptable ways; including grammatical, sociolinguistic, strategic, and discourse competence (Canale and Swain 1980; Canale 1983).

As Butler and Hakuta (2006: 124) put it:

> there is no simple answer to how to conceptualize language proficiency and how to measure it. Does proficiency refer to the mastery of one's knowledge of language or does it include the ability to use such knowledge? Is knowledge of language limited to knowledge of grammar, or does it include other psycholinguistic and socio-cultural aspects of language? Which components of communicative competence should be considered as the subjects of proficiency? To what extent should non-linguistic cognitive factors and non-cognitive factors (e.g. "motivation" and other affective factors) be included in measuring proficiency? How are all these different aspects of language related? How do different domains and contexts relate to proficiency?

Hernández-Chávez, Burt, and Dulay (1978) proposed that proficiency was made up of three major components; each of these components and its subareas is partially autonomous and therefore the speaker may have different abilities in each of them:[7]

---

[6] For an in depth discussion of the different uses of the term, see Butler and Hakuta (2006).
[7] Another well-known model is Bachman's (1990) model. We will refer to that model through footnotes to avoid complicating the text too much.

1.   The linguistic components[8]
       a. Phonology
       b. Syntax
       c. Semantics
       d. Lexicon
2.   Modality[9]
       a. Oral mode: oral production (speech) and comprehension
       b. Written mode: writing and reading
3.   Sociolinguistic performance
       a. Usage: the relationship between style and function:
          i. Style: alternate levels of formality expressed by linguistic words
             or structures which are distinct in form but equivalent in func-
             tion: for example: *buy* vs. *purchase*; *isn't* vs. *is not*; *May I help
             you?* vs. *What do you want?* (Hernández-Chávez *et al.* 1978:
             42).
       b. Use: sociolinguistic factors defined by the interplay between vari-
          ety and domain:
          i. Variety: a form of speech normally used by a given speech com-
             munity for a particular set of purposes. Each variety is employed
             by the speech community within a set of domains, i.e., situations
             defined by who the speakers are, the purposes of their interac-
             tion, and the content of their discourse (Hermández-Chávez *et al.*
             1978: 42).[10]

Hernández-Chávez *et al.* propose that these factors interact and therefore there
could potentially be sixty-four intersections of proficiency that we could need to
test to have a complete picture of someone's proficiency.

Differences in *usage* and *use* will determine if one is looking at *conversational
competence* (Cummins 2000) – also called *surface fluency* by Skutnabb-Kangas
and Toukomaa (1976) – or *academically related aspects of language competence*.

In this book, we will use the term *competence* to refer to *formal competence*
and *proficiency* to refer to *communicative competence*.

1.3.2   Fluency

Fluency is sometimes used as an equivalent of *competence*, but in a
narrower sense it refers to the capacity of speaking without major problems or
hesitations during a conversation as a native-speaker would. Although the term
fluency is being replaced in definitions of bilingualism by information on amount
of language use and quality of language competence, in many research studies

---

[8] The *grammatical* part of Bachman's (1990) *organizational competence*.
[9] This includes Bachman's *textual competence*, which deals with written and oral cohesion, another
   subcomponent of *organizational competence*.
[10] Hernández-Chávez *et al.*'s *usage* and *use* are fairly similar to Bachman's *Illocutionary Competence* and *Sociolinguistic Competence*, both part of *Pragmatic Competence*.

subjects are selected in terms of their language dominance, which is frequently measured by language fluency tests (see Grosjean 2006: 36). Therefore, even if *fluency* is not mentioned so frequently nowadays, it is still used in the context of selecting research participants, either by classifying speakers as being native or native-like because they are fluent speakers or by classifying them as non-native due to their lack of fluency in speech, as in the case of heritage speakers or receptive bilinguals. See Sherkina-Lieber, Pérez-Leroux, and Johns (2011) for an interesting study on grammatical competence of non-fluent speakers, which highlights the fact that fluency may not be a clear indicator of grammatical competence.

1.3.3   Who is bilingual? Who is an L2 speaker/learner?

Some researchers consider speakers bilingual when they have native-like control of two languages. So what does *native-like* mean? Are there any good measures of *nativeness*? Do all monolingual native speakers have identical abilities in all the areas of their competence? Not all native speakers are alike. Some know more vocabulary than others. Some have better reading or writing skills than others. At least at the performance level, one can observe variations among native speakers in any given language. There are even differences among native speakers with high levels of education (Valdés and Figueroa 1994).

The definition of the term *native speaker* is more complicated than it seems at first glance (Gass and Glew 2008). Part of the problem is that it can mean two different things. A native speaker can be defined as someone who either (i) learned a language as an L1 or (ii) has the same competence/proficiency that a native speaker has.

Considering the first definition, some questions arise: what about a sequential bilingual who started learning a second language a few months after the other? Is he/she *native* or *near-native*? What about someone who learned a language as an L1 but who has basically stopped using it? Is that person still a native speaker?

In the second sense, a speaker is considered native if he/she has the same competence/proficiency that a native speaker should have. But how do we define what that competence or proficiency is? Note that by selecting *competence* over *proficiency* or vice-versa, we are asking for very different sets of skills from the speaker.[11] Moreover, we know language proficiency is a very complicated construct and native speakers may vary in their command of the different areas (see Section 1.3.1). What are the implications for bilinguals? Even simultaneous bilinguals may not be equally proficient in all areas due to input and domains of learning and use, as we will see in Section 1.4. So in this case, a simultaneous bilingual, therefore a *native* speaker in the first sense, may turn out not to have *native-like* proficiency after all.

---

[11] See also Birdsong's (2005) interesting discussion of nativeness in second language acquisition in relationship to the critical period hypothesis.

Another, frequently used term is *near-native*, which is based on the second definition of *native*, and which carries all the same problems that this definition has. As Gass and Glew (2008: 268) put it:

> In general, we have two different ways of thinking of the concepts of native and near-native – the practical and the technical. In practical terms, native speakers are those who, in everyday conversation, are indistinguishable from other native speakers,[12] and near-native speakers are highly proficient speakers who are distinguishable from native speakers, but in only small ways. The technical definition refers to a native speaker as someone who is indistinguishable in a scientific sense (through comparative performance on tests designed specifically to measure the outer reaches of proficiency) from other native speakers – a near-native speaker is an individual who in casual conversation may be indistinguishable from native speakers but who may differ in subtle ways from native speakers...   (Gass and Glew 2008: 268)

Note than even the technical sense of Gass and Glew does not indicate what the "subtle ways" in which native and near-native speakers differ are. Since it is the technical sense which is important in research, investigators need to agree on standard ways of determining *nativeness* and *near-nativeness*, and other commonly used terms defined in relation to *nativeness* such as *advanced language learner* (defined in twelve sometimes contradictory terms in forty-six studies according to Bardovi-Harlig 2004), *intermediate learner, beginner learner, heritage speaker,* and *second language speaker/learner* (see Gass and Glew 2008). The definition also depends on the field of the researcher.

It is interesting to note, as Cook (1995) does, that L1 acquisition is usually described in terms of the development, capacities, and achievements of the child, while adult L2 acquisition is usually portrayed in a negative light, by focusing on the failure of most adult L2 speakers to become native-like speakers, by always comparing the L2 speaker to the monolingual native model. Instead of focusing on the adult L2 learner capacities – L2 learners are native speakers of one language and in addition they know at least something of a second language – research tends to focus on the many ways in which they are not native-like.

What is native-like? How much should we expect a second language learner to resemble a native speaker so that we call him/her near-native? That is what Birdsong asks:

> How are results of L2 A upper limits research to be used and interpreted?... I ask whether all aspects of L2 learners' linguistic behaviors should be fair game for comparison with those of natives, and suggest that the standards of nativelikeness and non-nativelikeness should not be applied to the CPH/L2 A[13] debate in an unconstrained fashion. I also consider the nature of

---

[12] Therefore, they are referring to the second definition of *native*.
[13] *CPH* stands for *Critical Period Hypothesis*, which we discuss in Section 1.8. *L2 A* stands for *second language acquisition*.

bilingualism. In bilingualism, there are inevitable interactions, with functional repercussions, of the L1 on the L2, and of the L2 on the L1. Neither of the two languages of a bilingual can be expected to resemble that of a native monolingual. Accordingly, non-nativelike performance is not necessarily indicative of compromised language learning abilities, as assumed under the CPH/L2 A.   (Birdsong 2005: 320)

Birdsong asks, for example, if an English speaker who passed for a native French speaker in everyday interactions should be denied being native-like because he shouts *Ouch!* when he burns himself with coffee instead of the French *Aïe!*. Obviously, this is an extreme case, but it is unclear where to set the limit. Are we talking about *competence* or *proficiency?* Birdsong suggests we need an inventory of native controls' performance in multiple tasks to provide a benchmark for comparing L2 learners. He believes that nativelikeness may be achieved in the areas of grammar, lexicon, and phonology, but may not be attainable in language processing tasks. However, as he points out, more new research, replication studies, and studies of late learners whose L2 is the dominant language are needed in order to set a group of elements we can use to judge L2 learners' nativelikeness.

A common view among second language acquisition researchers is that *bilingual* refers to an endpoint, to the ultimate attainment by the L2 learner. An alternative view held in some other fields is that *bilingual* can refer to a person with the ability to use more than one language that is still in the process of acquiring the L2 (Gass and Glew 2008).

Grosjean (2006) analyzed the ways in which several studies described their bilingual subjects and found that subjects were chosen very differently; some in terms of fluency (using various tests and scales to measure it); language stability; contexts of learning; and actual screening tests and biographical data. Later he points out that since determining bilingualism in terms of language fluency is complicated, many researchers and bilingual speakers are now referring to language use as the defining criterion (Grosjean 2008: 22).

For decades, Grosjean has been a pioneer in changing the common perception of bilingualism as a deficit. Because bilinguals do not have the same proficiency in both their languages, with whom and when they use a given language will determine to a large degree the lexicon and perhaps even the syntactic structures under a bilingual's command. Therefore it is important to distinguish *knowledge* from *use*. Table 1.3 shows the different types of conversational partners (targets) and domains of speech that can affect a speaker's proficiency, according to Baker. These factors will affect the speaker's ability to use the language in these particular contexts (proficiency), but would not necessarily affect their competence (knowledge). In our understanding, these targets and domains would allow the speaker to show more or less proficiency, thus affecting their communicative competence but not their formal competence.

For example, Cooper (1971) found that Spanish–English bilinguals had different scores on word naming tasks depending on domain: family, neighborhood,

Table 1.3 *Language targets and domains that may affect proficiency (Baker 2011: 5)*

Language targets
 1. Nuclear family
 2. Extended family
 3. Work colleagues
 4. Friends
 5. Neighbors
 6. Religious leaders
 7. Teachers
 8. Presidents, principals, other leaders
 9. Bureaucrats
10. Local community

Language contexts (domains)
 1. Shopping
 2. Visual and auditory media (e.g., TV, radio, records, cassettes, CDs, video)
 3. Printed media (e.g., newspapers, books)
 4. Cinema/discos/theater/concerts
 5. Work
 6. Correspondence/telephone/official communication
 7. Clubs, societies, organizations, sporting activities
 8. Leisure and hobbies
 9. Religious meetings
10. Information technology (e.g., computers)

school, or religion. Most tests don't take into account the different domains in which a language is used.[14] Butler and Hakuta (2006) believe that the domain also determines the extent to which bilinguals can code-switch and/or keep their languages separate. So, we again see that the bilingual experience is fundamentally different from that of monolinguals, since targets and domains may affect a monolingual person's style but usually not their proficiency, or not to the same degree as they affect it in bilinguals.

> One cannot determine bilinguals' proficiencies in relation to monolingual native speakers' proficiencies if linguistic abilities between these two groups are qualitatively different . . . it does not make sense to use the monolingual norm as the guideline for bilingual proficiency.
>
> (Butler and Hakuta 2006: 125)

As we mentioned above, an important task for the field is to create new and better instruments specifically designed to test bilinguals.

It is also very important to take into account the differences between oral and written mode. Oral skills include speech and comprehension of aural language.

---

[14] Grosjean (1982) warns us that assessment methods and measures used by educators and clinicians are largely monolingual and monocultural when most children are bilingual.

The written mode includes reading and writing. Many fluent and balanced bilinguals may be able to speak and understand but not write one or both languages. Many bilinguals who acquired a language late in life may also differ from native speakers in one or more subareas of linguistic competence (phonology, morphology, extent of vocabulary, correctness of grammar, etc.).

Mackey (1968) says that to determine a speaker's degree of bilingualism it is necessary to:

- Test for comprehension and production both orally and in writing.
- Look at the domain of use of each language: home, school, church, work, etc.
- Look at the language's internal use for counting, praying, cursing, dreaming, etc.
- Determine the person's aptitude for learning and using a language that may be determined by sex, age, intelligence, memory, language attitude, and motivation.
- Study their ability to alternate languages, how much, in what conditions?

Grosjean (2008) suggests that we also should gather information on the person's language history to classify bilinguals, since bilinguals usually do not have the same amount and type of input in each language.

Cummins (1987) incorporates the effect of contextual support available to help the speaker express or understand meaning as well as degree of cognitive demands of the language task to give a more accurate description of a speaker's variable proficiency. Contextual support can vary in a continuum between *context-embedded* (more typical of every day life where speakers can request feedback and rely on many contextual cues) and *context-reduced* communication (more typical of many classroom activities where the information is presented with no or very little context). The degree of cognitive involvement is also a continuum between *cognitively demanding* (e.g., persuading someone, writing an essay) and *cognitively undemanding* (or automatized) tasks (e.g., answering when welcomed), which is determined by the amount of information that must be processed simultaneously or in close succession by the speaker. With development, some tasks that were initially cognitively demanding may become more automatized. The more context embedded the task is, the easier it will be carrying it out.

1.4   Why do we need to define who is bilingual?

The number and types of bilinguals in a particular region needs to be measured for governmental, educational, and research purposes. Governments measure numbers of speakers of different languages and their distribution through censuses. Censuses usually gather very basic language information, such as the languages used other than the dominant language of the country and level of

proficiency in the dominant language (see Baker 2011: 35–39 for details and limitations on censuses). We mentioned some of these limitations in the Introduction
when discussing the US census. Most other classifications are for educational
or research purposes. Schools and researchers are interested in the selection of
participants, to group them for research or for placement in different educational
levels or programs. Schools are also interested in summative assessments which
give an overall view of the proficiency that a student has reached at a certain
point (e.g., at the end of the school year) and formative assessments, to provide
feedback during the learning process and help shape future teaching practices
(Baker 2011).

In research involving bilinguals it is extremely important to include a well-
defined and homogeneous group of bilingual speakers so that our data are repli-
cable and comparable to that of other studies (Grosjean 2006). If a homogeneous
group of bilingual participants is not selected for a certain study, the study results
may be unreliable and even controversial since the same theoretical assumptions
or models cannot be applied to all groups of speakers (Wei 2007). However,
selecting a homogeneous group is a challenging task since bilingual speakers
vary according to their language proficiency, age of acquisition of the second
language, patterns of exposure to their languages, language use, and language
attitudes.

Lack of methodological standards in selecting participants provoked until
the early 1990s confusing results in bilingualism/second language acquisition
studies, as Grosjean (2006) noted when he did an overview of the description of
subjects in several studies and concluded that insufficient factors were considered
when bilingual speakers were selected for a study (e.g., speakers were classified
according to age of acquisition, but patterns of use were not considered). Different researchers relied on different criteria when selecting the participants for
their studies and used various assessment tools to collect information about the
speaker's language proficiency and language history. In many cases, speakers
were asked to self-rate their proficiency. Baker (2011: 26–27) mentions several
problems with self-rating. One is that questionnaires used for self-rating usually
ask very broad questions such as "how well can you write in English?" with a
five-point scale to choose from, without any further explanation of what is meant
by the term "write": write simple sentences? write longer texts? write different
types of texts? (e.g., an e-mail, an essay), how many grammatical or spelling
errors fit into each of the points of the scale, etc.? They usually have no indication
of context or domains of use (e.g., speaking at an appropriate level for shopping
or for teaching a class). People may not rate themselves accurately because for
societal reasons they may want to appear as more (or less) proficient in a language
than they actually are; or just because they are not consciously aware of their
capacities, an issue that is specially relevant with children. This causes different groups of bilinguals to be analyzed in different studies and does not allow
researchers to reliably compare the results of such studies. There are no clear
standards for classifying bilingual/L2 speakers across studies, and therefore it is

impossible to tell if the results of a given study will generalize to other groups of bilingual/L2 speakers.

The fields of bilingualism and second language acquisition have standardized their methodology to a certain point in the last twenty years, but it is always necessary to judge carefully the participant selection of different studies to see whether their participant pool is really comparable.

1.4.1   Possible solutions

Researchers should provide as much information as possible about the participants, the criteria used to classify them in different groups, and the language assessment tools used in their study.

Grosjean (2008)) suggested several factors that should be considered when collecting information about bilingual speakers and describing them in a study report:

- *Language history and language relationship:* which languages were acquired (when and how)? What skills were acquired and when? What was the pattern of language use? Were the languages learned in a formal or natural setting, or both?
- *Language stability:* are one or several languages still being acquired? Has a certain language stability been reached? Are some of the languages being influenced by a more dominant language?
- *Function of languages:* which languages are used for what purposes, in what context and to what extent?
- *Language proficiency:* what is the bilingual's proficiency in the four skills in each language?
- *Language modes:* Grosjean (1999: 136) defines *language mode* as "a state of activation of the bilingual's language and language processing mechanism." A speaker is in a bilingual mode when engaging in activities that require use of his/her two languages (e.g., interacting with other bilinguals, translating) or a speaker is in a monolingual mode when he/she is trying to use only one of his/her languages (e.g., interacting with monolinguals, reading a text in one language, etc.). Therefore the availability of these modes is influenced by contextual factors which determine how often and for how long a bilingual is in monolingual and bilingual mode, and when in a bilingual mode, how much code-switching and borrowing takes place.
- *Biographical data:* what is the bilingual's sex, age, socioeconomic status, etc.?

Devising tools to gather these pieces of data is not without complication. Take, for example, a questionnaire about language use that asks for which purposes and with which interlocutors a person uses a particular language, which fails to ask about frequency of use. As Baker and Hinde (cited by Baker 2011) illustrate:

> A person who says she speaks Welsh to her father (mostly away at sea), her grandparents (seen once a year), her friends (but tends to be an isolate), reads Welsh books and newspapers (only occasionally), attends Welsh Chapel (marriages and funerals only) but spends most of her time with an English speaking mother and in an English speaking school might gain a fairly high 'Welsh' score.   (Baker and Hinde 1984: 46)

De Groot (2011: 16) reminds us that many studies on bilingualism are carried out in bilingual communities where language-pure exposure does not occur. Therefore, *monolingual* refers to subjects whose exposure to each language is extremely unbalanced (e.g., 95 percent vs. 5 percent). *Bilingual* means that the subject has a more balanced language exposure (e.g., at least 40 percent for each language).

1.4.2   Methods for determining levels/types of bilingualism

We review in this section some of the common methods used to determine a speaker's level and type of bilingualism.

Determining language proficiency

Recall Hernández-Chávez *et al.*'s sixty-four elements comprising proficiency. Given that it would be almost impossible to test the proficiency of each speaker in these sixty-four combinations and given that testing the dominance of a bilingual speaker would mean testing him/her in 128 areas (without taking into account the complications involved in finding comparable items and structures to test in two different languages),[15] the authors attempt to select the most central aspects which will substantially represent the other complexes or skills or permit inferences about them. They, therefore, provide the following suggestions for the direct measurement of language proficiency:

- Eliminate style and function given that their content is still relatively unspecified and we do not know enough of these areas to be able to test them.
- Eliminate variety and domain since we do not have any good methods to test them besides naturalistic observation in a variety of social contexts.
- Avoid the use of the written modality in proficiency testing in minority language situations.

Paradoxically, and as the authors note, after considering the sixty-four possibly relevant dimensions, this leaves us with the four traditional linguistic components to test (what we have called here *competence*); however, they recommend testing

---

[15] Hernández-Chávez *et al.* mention, among others, the sociopolitical contexts of learning and of use. For example, foreign language learning in the USA focuses on literacy and metalinguistic knowledge; but in minority language contexts the oral mode may be more developed than the written mode.

them using both a natural communication task and a linguistic manipulation task to have a better picture of the speaker's proficiency.

Different tasks and methods are used to classify speakers and to measure their proficiencies. For an overview see Hamers and Blanc (2000), Baker (2011), and De Groot (2011). Language assessment for educational purposes is achieved through two types of tests: *norm reference* tests and *criterion reference* test. *Norm reference* tests compare one speaker with another (e.g., by comparing the student's score to an average for his/her age). *Criterion referenced* tests look at particular language skill[16] and see how developed this skill is in a particular speaker. Baker (2011) points out that while norm reference tests tend to highlight what the speaker cannot do, criterion reference tests focus on communicative skills and therefore on what learners can do. The most commonly used method in the USA is the *ACTFL Proficiency Guidelines*, which classify speakers in the four traditional language areas, speaking, writing, listening, and reading. In each area speakers are classified as *distinguished*, *superior*, *advanced*, *intermediate*, and *novice*. The three lower levels have subclassifications in *high*, *mid*, and *low*. The ratings are based on types of tasks the speaker should be able to handle at each level. Each task is associated with particular contents, contexts, accuracy levels, and discourse types. The guidelines also present the limits that speakers should encounter when attempting to function at the next higher major level. For example, speakers at the *distinguished level*:

> are able to use language skillfully, and with accuracy, efficiency, and effectiveness. They are educated and articulate users of the language. They can reflect on a wide range of global issues and highly abstract concepts in a culturally appropriate manner. Distinguished-level speakers can use persuasive and hypothetical discourse for representational purposes, allowing them to advocate a point of view that is not necessarily their own. They can tailor language to a variety of audiences by adapting their speech and register in ways that are culturally authentic.
>
> Speakers at the Distinguished level produce highly sophisticated and tightly organized extended discourse. At the same time, they can speak succinctly, often using cultural and historical references to allow them to say less and mean more. At this level, oral discourse typically resembles written discourse.
>
> A non-native accent, a lack of a native-like economy of expression, a limited control of deeply embedded cultural references, and/or an occasional isolated language error may still be present at this level.
>
> (*ACTFL Proficiency Guidelines* 2012: 4)

While *advanced speakers*:

> engage in conversation in a clearly participatory manner in order to communicate information on autobiographical topics, as well as topics of community, national, or international interest. The topics are handled concretely by means

---

[16] According to Baker (2011: 24), language skills tend to refer to highly specific, observable, measurable, clearly definable components such as handwriting.

> of narration and description in the major time frames of past, present, and future. These speakers can also deal with a social situation with an unexpected complication. The language of Advanced-level speakers is abundant, the oral paragraph being the measure of Advanced-level length and discourse. Advanced-level speakers have sufficient control of basic structures and generic vocabulary to be understood by native speakers of the language, including those unaccustomed to non-native speech.
>
> (*ACTFL Proficiency Guidelines* 2012: 5)

And *novice speakers*:

> can communicate short messages on highly predictable, everyday topics that affect them directly. They do so primarily through the use of isolated words and phrases that have been encountered, memorized, and recalled. Novice-level speakers may be difficult to understand even by the most sympathetic interlocutors accustomed to non-native speech.
>
> (*ACTFL Proficiency Guidelines* 2012: 9)

Similar descriptions are provided for each level in every skill. Speaking ratings are based on 20–30-minute face-to-face or telephone interviews with a human interviewer or delivered online with a computer avatar as interlocutor. The listening test and the reading tests are also online with listening passages or reading passages and multiple-choice questions. The writing test is a proctored standardized test.

In Europe there is the *Council of Europe's Common European Framework of Reference for Language Assessment*, which also defines levels of proficiency. For English the *International English Language Testing System* is also used. In this test speakers are placed in one of the nine levels, which go from *Expert User* to *Non User* by means of an interview.

The guidelines, as can be seen, are very general. A critique by Douglas (1988) of the early ACTFL guidelines points out that they were devoid of any reference to specific domains of language use, which have been shown to greatly affect performance. The current guidelines do not seem to have incorporated this concept yet. However, according to Baker (2011), in the USA assessment in schools is usually supplemented by other sources of information such as inspection of students' work in school and at home as well as by teachers' observations.

Determining language dominance

We can use various psychometric tests to determine whether one of the speaker's languages is more accessible than the other (i.e., their dominant language and less dominant language). This list is taken from Baker (2011: 35) where the reader can find a detailed description of each.

- Speed of reaction in a word association task.
- Quantity of reactions to a word association task.

- Detection of real words of both languages in a nonsense word[17] that contains sounds and syllables that are possible in both languages.
- Time taken to read sets of words in both languages.
- Amount of mixing (switching and borrowing) from each language to the other.

However, these tests are coarse instruments, which only tap into limited types of linguistic performance. Assessing a bilingual speaker's phonological and grammatical competence in each language is much more problematic, given that such knowledge is not static but may change with exposure to input, especially at younger ages. In addition, divergence from monolingual norms may reflect cross-linguistic influence, rather than lower proficiency per se.

Bedore *et al.* (2005) propose that young bilingual children's vocabulary needs to be assessed differently from that of monolinguals for correctly identifying children who may need language intervention. They point out that a bilingual child's (or a bilingual adult's) vocabulary is distributed across their languages. Translation equivalents (words referring to the same object in two languages, such as *juguete* and *toy*) comprise about 30 percent of children's vocabulary before age 2;00 (Pearson, Fernández, and Oller 1995), which means the majority of their lexical items are known in one language only. Therefore they propose one should use *conceptual* scoring instead of *monolingual* scoring. In monolingual scoring, children are tested as if they were two monolinguals in one, and therefore expected to know word equivalents in both languages. However, we know that in children at early stages of acquisition, and sometimes also in adult speakers, the number of vocabulary items may be different in each language due to differences in language input and use. Therefore, if we test bilingual children using monolingual scoring they get lower scores than monolingual children in each language and are therefore wrongly assessed as at-risk children. *Conceptual* scoring respects the fact that a bilingual's vocabulary may be spread across the languages he/she speaks, therefore a child gets credit for knowing a word irrespective of which language the word is in. When using conceptual scoring, bilingual children's scores were in the average range of the monolingual children. Therefore, it is important to recognize that bilingual children are not two monolinguals in one and that they are not delayed because they may know less vocabulary than a monolingual child in each of their languages. The field is actively working on creating instruments that measure the specific bilingual language experience in a more accurate and fair way.

Language dominance is also determined by giving participants questionnaires that ask about their language use, language proficiency, and language history. These instruments give us important information but should not be the only instrument used to assess a bilingual's dominance and proficiency. Lust, Flynn,

---

[17] A nonsense word is a word made up by the researchers which does not really exist in the speaker's language(s) but which resembles real words of the language(s) in terms of sound and morphological structure.

Blume, Park, Cang, and Yang (2014) compared two 4-year-old Korean–English sequential bilingual children whose parental reports gathered through a multilingualism questionnaire predicted their development should be fairly similar, with the exception that one of the children received more English input than the other in terms of amount of hours of exposure. Therefore, a difference in their English proficiencies was expected. However, the children's proficiency in English and Korean was also tested through elicited imitation. These tests revealed unexpected differences in the children's Korean development. Pease-Álvarez, Hakuta, and Bayley (1996) in a similar study also found that answers by the participants and their parents in interviews predicted less Spanish proficiency for their 8- to 10-year-old Spanish–English bilingual participants than direct testing showed.

1.5   Classifying bilinguals

There are numerous classifications of bilingual speakers. We have here taken most classes and definitions from Wei (2007: 6–7); we have added a few terms, and organized them depending on what aspect of the bilingual experience they focus on: competence (with its multiple subtypes), use, input and learning environment, or age. Deviations from Wei's definitions are noted in the footnotes.

1.5.1   According to competence

This first group deals with bilingual competence; usually depending on how close the bilingual resembles a monolingual native speaker of the language. Terms are organized here from more native-like to less native-like.

- *Maximal bilingual/ Proficient bilingual/ Near-native:* someone with near native control of two or more languages.
- *Functional bilingual:* someone who can operate in two languages with or without full fluency for the task in hand.
- *Non-proficient bilingual*: someone whose control of the language is more than minimal but not near-native.[18]
- *Incipient bilingual:* someone at the early stages of bilingualism where one language is not fully developed.
- *Minimal bilingual:* someone with only a few words and phrases in a second language.

Notice that depending on the researcher's view of bilingualism, the group of people who we call bilingual will vary. If one holds a maximalist view of bilingualism, only maximal bilinguals will be included. If one holds a minimalist view, even minimal bilinguals will be included. Researchers vary on whether they include second language learners under the term *bilingual* or not. Some

---

[18] This class does not appear in Wei.

researchers include even beginner learners in the group. Other researchers will only consider advanced language learners in the bilingual group.

Thiery (1978: 146) claimed that "A true bilingual is someone who is taken to be one of themselves by the members of two different linguistic communities, at roughly the same social and cultural level," and decided to study what was necessary for this achievement. According to him, bilinguals who were as balanced as he proposed had learned the two languages before age 14, had spoken both languages at home, had moved from one language community to another during their school years, and had been taught in both languages.

In recent years very interesting research has emerged on heritage speakers and receptive bilinguals which questions the somewhat simplified classification of speakers in terms of language competence presented in this classical division. We analyze the case of heritage speakers in detail in Section 1.9 in this chapter and again in Chapter 3. The particular case of heritage receptive bilinguals is, however, worth mentioning here. Sherkina-Lieber *et al.* (2011) conducted a study with Labrador Inuttitut heritage receptive bilinguals showing that even those speakers that could be considered "minimal" or "incipient" bilinguals in terms of their productive competence (classified by the authors as low-proficiency receptive bilinguals and high-proficiency receptive bilinguals), had "a clear knowledge of the basic properties of word structure," thus showing greater competence than their production or proficiency would predict.

According to language abilities or skills

This classification deals with the bilingual's command of the four basic language skills: production and comprehension of spoken language, reading, and writing. In terms of language abilities, bilinguals can be classified in broad terms as:

- *Receptive bilingual / asymmetrical bilingual / passive bilingual / semibilingual:* someone who understands a second language, in either its spoken or its written form, or both, but does not speak or write it.
- *Productive bilingual:* someone who not only understands but also speaks and possibly writes in two or more languages.

According to language dominance

In terms of which language they know better, a language that sometimes – but not always – coincides with the language they use more, bilinguals can be classified as:

- *Balanced bilingual / ambilingual / equilingual / symmetrical bilingual:* a bilingual who has equal command in both languages.[19]
- *Dominant bilingual / unbalanced bilingual:* a bilingual who is more proficient in one of his/her languages than in the other.[20]

---

[19] This definition is different from Wei's; the language was simplified but the definition is very similar.

[20] See previous note.

- *Semilingual:* someone with insufficient knowledge of any language. This term was used at early stages of the studies on bilingualism but it has come into disuse due to the fact that it stemmed from a misunderstanding of bilingual speech. It is now believed that such bilinguals do not really exist.[21]

Notice that this classification is based on comparing the bilingual's relative command of both languages, but it says nothing about how much competence they should have in each. In practical terms, though, we expect a balanced bilingual to be someone who should be at least native-like in both languages since we assume semilinguals do not exist. A dominant bilingual, however, could go from minimal to functional bilingual in his/her non-dominant language. A dominant bilingual could also be only a receptive bilingual in one of the languages. It will depend on the different authors whether such a person is called *a bilingual* or a *second language learner.* Whatever we choose to call them, we must recognize that bilingualism is a large proficiency continuum and it can be divided at different points, therefore it is very important in research to give as much information about the subjects as possible.

Grosjean (1982) surveyed thirty bilinguals from eight different countries and found only seven who felt perfectly balanced in the four major linguistic skills (understanding, speaking, reading, and writing). Baker reminds us that "Someone may listen with understanding in one context (e.g. shops) but not in another context (e.g. an academic lecture). These examples show that the four basic abilities can be further refined into sub-scales and dimensions" (Baker 2011: 5).

According to the effect of the L2 on L1
- *Additive bilingual:* someone whose languages combine in a complementary and enriching fashion.[22]
- *Subtractive bilingual:* someone whose second language is acquired at the expense of the aptitudes already acquired in the first language (i.e., someone whose development in a first language stops or whose first language abilities actually diminish when that person starts developing a second language. Language loss is called *attrition.* We discuss attrition further in Section 1.9.1.)

According to interference of L1 in L2
- *Subordinate bilingual:* someone who exhibits interference in his or her language usage by changing the patterns of the second language to those of the first.[23]

---

[21] We have changed "either language" in Wei's definition to "any language" to include cases of multilingualism. The explanation of the use of the term is ours.

[22] Wei said "two languages" but we deleted "two" to include cases of multilingualism.

[23] We used the term "changing" instead of Wei's "reducing."

As we have seen in the Introduction, some level of interference usually exists in a bilingual speaker's two languages and though interference from the first language to the second is most common, interference from the second language to the first is also possible.

According to development in L2

- *Ascendant bilingual:* someone whose ability to function in a second language is developing due to increased use or learning.[24]
- *Recessive bilingual:* someone who begins to feel some difficulty in either understanding or expressing him or herself with ease, due to lack of use.

A recessive bilingual would be someone undergoing language attrition in a second language.

According to bilingual memory organization

These terms were first proposed by Weinreich (1953). In these definitions we differ from Wei's definitions since he defined the terms in relation to language-learning contexts.

- *Compound bilingual*: a bilingual whose two forms of a cognate or translation equivalent are linked to just one concept or meaning representation.
- *Coordinate bilingual*: a bilingual whose two forms of a cognate or translation equivalent are linked to two independent concepts or meaning representations, one in each language.
- *Subordinate bilingual*: a bilingual who accesses a concept by linking the form from the weaker language to the form in the dominant language that is in turn linked to the meaning. Therefore he/she does not have a meaning linked directly to the weaker language's form.

We review these concepts in more detail in Chapter 2.

1.5.2   According to type of input/learning environment

- *Natural bilingual/ primary bilingual:* someone who has not undergone any specific training but has learned the language by exposure to it (e.g., by living in an L2 environment, someone who learned the language "in the street").[25]
- *Secondary bilingual:* someone whose second language has been added to a first language via instruction.

---

[24] Wei's definition does not include "or learning."
[25] Here we eliminated the translation capabilities mentioned by Wei and have added the explanation on language exposure.

Two frequently used terms in second language research are related to this classification. When second language acquisition occurs in a natural setting, it is referred to as *second language acquisition*; when it takes place in a formal setting without a group of speakers of the language in the community (e.g., learning Quechua in the USA) it is referred to as *foreign language learning*.

1.5.3   According to language use

*   *Dormant bilingual*: someone who has only minimal opportunity to use one of his/her languages.[26]

Dormant bilingualism will sometimes lead to language attrition, which we will discuss in Section 1.9.1.

1.5.4   According to age of acquisition

Age of acquisition seems to be one of the most important factors in determining second language competence and proficiency. We will explore this topic further in Section 1.8 and in Chapter 2.

Are the two languages acquired at the same time?[27]

*   *Simultaneous bilingual:* a bilingual whose languages were acquired from birth.
*   *Successive/sequential/consecutive bilingual:* a bilingual whose L2 was acquired after birth. All speakers who have acquired their second language as adults (L2 speakers) fall in this category.

In the case of simultaneous bilingualism, authors currently speak about *bilingual first language acquisition*,[28] to highlight the fact that in simultaneous acquisition there is no real L2. Both languages are considered first languages, native languages. Notice that in this sense *native* takes into account the time of acquisition of the languages, and not the child's level of proficiency in both, since both languages can develop at the same time but not necessarily to the same level.

When are the two languages acquired?

*   *Early bilingual / ascribed bilingual*: a bilingual who has acquired both languages before puberty.[29]
*   *Late bilingual / achieved bilingual*: a bilingual who has acquired his/her second language after puberty.

---

[26] This definition differs from Wei's since we do not restrict it to cases of immigration.
[27] Our definitions here differ from Wei's since he speaks about onset of speech and we believe bilingualism from birth is possible. Our different definition of *simultaneous bilingual* also caused us to diverge from Wei's definition of *successive bilingualism*.
[28] Meisel (1989, 2001) uses the term *2L1*.
[29] We have changed Wei's broader "early in childhood" to "before puberty."

The definitions of early vs. late bilinguals have changed throughout the years and mostly in relation to our definition of *critical period*, see Section 1.8.

1.6 How do children become bilingual?

Bhatia and Ritchie (1999) said that in the late 1990s there were relatively few studies on child bilingualism, in part because bilingual acquisition was considered more complex than monolingual acquisition and many researchers believed that we had to wait for better knowledge on monolingual acquisition before embarking on bilingual acquisition research.

However, in the last decade, interest in child bilingualism has increased because of the recognition that bilingualism is not really the exception across the world, but the norm; that we would therefore have an incomplete version of normal language acquisition if we did not study bilingual acquisition. The bilingual child offers a unique opportunity to resolve issues in language acquisition since the bilingual child constitutes the perfect matched pair for comparing acquisition of different languages in research, since we can assume that in a bilingual speaker factors that usually affect language development and that researchers control for by looking for participants with similar characteristics (such as age and gender) remain constant (De Houwer 1990: 1).

Most of the early research on child bilingualism looked at western middle- to upper-class families where children were simultaneous bilinguals and who for the most part adhered to the *one parent, one language* rule where each parent speaks to the child in one language. Research has been also, for the most part, restricted to first-born children. Therefore, what we say below about bilingual acquisition is only an indication; it is what we know so far. Research on other types of bilingual acquisition is fundamental to being able to generalize to other cases.[30]

In general, the development during bilingual first language acquisition is very similar to that of monolingual acquisition in the relevant languages. In certain areas, bilingual children may develop more slowly or faster than monolingual children, but the differences last usually only a few months.

Bilingual children sometimes produce one language more than the other due to domain and input factors. There may also be differences in comprehension in both languages; however, there is very little research on language comprehension, except for differences in the lexicon.

Bilingual children are able to select from an early age the appropriate language for a given situation, in the case of some children as early as 2 years of age (Sinka and Schelleter 1998). They are also able to switch quickly from one language to

---

[30] We do know, however, that children in other cultures may acquire comprehension of spoken language by overhearing adults speak in a language in which they are never addressed; but they do not develop production skills in that language (Kulick 1992).

the other or to code-switch depending on the domain (De Houwer 1990; Genesee, Boivin, and Nicoladis 1996; Deuchar and Quay 2000).

Considering simultaneous vs. sequential bilingualism, there are very specific language development outcomes that can be linked to this difference. In sequential bilingualism, when the bilingual-to-be child – to use De Groot's (2011: 6) accurate term – is exposed to the second language, he/she already has some knowledge of his/her L1 and is more biologically and cognitively mature. In this situation, transfer may occur between the child's languages, usually from the L1 to the L2. In simultaneous bilingualism, it is now agreed in the field that the two languages develop independently from each other (e.g., Genesee, Nicoladis, and Paradis 1995; Meisel 2001; De Houwer 2005). Chapter 3 reviews previous proposals of mixed development and the studies that changed the view in the field towards that of independent development of the child's languages. An interesting recent proposal by Amaral and Roeper (2014a) indeed suggests that all speakers – monolingual, second language learners, and bilinguals – may actually develop different simultaneous grammars and therefore the differences among these speakers' grammars is just one of degree (see also Amaral and Roeper 2014b's clarifications to the points and concerns raised by the other contributors to the same volume).

1.6.1   Different exposure patterns

In the case of child bilingualism, the relationship of the child's languages to the languages of the community is very important in establishing early bilingualism (Lanza 2004).

There are three important factors in the input (Romaine 1995):

- The language(s) the parents use to interact with the child
- The parents' native language(s)
- The extent to which the parents' languages(s) reflect the language(s) of the community.

Vihman and McLaughlin (1982) distinguish between three patterns of language use:

- Each parent using one language (*one person, one language*)
- Mixed use by each parent
- An environment-bound language, e.g., one language is used at home and the other is the language of the community

Children, and adults, usually have a dominant language due to exposure and use. Children also move from a monolingual mode to a bilingual mode (Grosjean 2006), and may regress and progress in the two languages depending on the situation. Some bilingual children travel frequently to visit family; in which case input in one of their languages may be stopped while they may get more input than usual in the other language.

Table 1.4 *Parental home language input patterns and child bilingual use (De Houwer 2009: 10)*

	In how many families do the children speak both the majority and a minority language?
Two-parent families	
1. Both parents speak just a minority language or at most one parent also speaks the majority language.	In 96% of the 665 families.
2. Parents both speak both languages or one parent speaks a minority language.	In 79% of the 562 families.
3. Parents both speak the majority language and one parent speaks a minority language.	In 36% of the 353 families.
Families headed by a single parent	
4. The single parent speaks just a minority language.	In 42 of the 46 families [91.3%]
5. The single parent speaks both a minority language and the majority language	In 50 of the 75 families [66.7%]

A study in Flanders by De Houwer (2007) found that even when children were exposed to two languages from birth, they might not in fact speak both languages. In only 71 percent of the 1,356 two-parent families she studied did the children speak the minority language[31] as well as the majority language, Dutch. De Houwer found that the patterns of language use in the home had a clear effect on the child's knowledge and production of both languages, as we will see in the next section.

Bilingualism at home

The findings of De Houwer's (2007) study and further analyses of the same data are summarized in Table 1.4.

There was an even greater possibility of success if the language that the parents spoke at home was the minority language and not the dominant language, and this seems to be the most decisive factor for the child's successful productive bilingualism. As shown in cases 3 and 5 in Table 1.4, when the minority language is supported by just one parent, the rate drops dramatically.

Interestingly, though there have been many studies on the *one parent, one language* situation, and even when many manuals for parents of bilingual-to-be children recommend this strategy, De Houwer (2007) reports in her survey that the *both parents, both languages* strategy seemed to be more successful in having the children produce both languages (four out of five, or 80 percent) than the *one*

[31] De Houwer found seventy-three different minority languages in her sample.

Table 1.5 *Three main patterns of parental language presentation in BFLA (De Houwer 2009: 110)*

One parent, one language[a]	Both parents speak both languages[a]	One parent uses one language and the other uses both	Totals	Source
16.75%	42.35%	40.91%	1457[b]	De Houwer 2007
23.00%	27.00%	44.00%	188[c]	Yamamoto 2001

Note: BFLA stands for *bilingual first language acquisition.*
[a] Includes single and dual-parent families.
[b] Number of families in which a particular pattern was used in Flanders (regardless of number of children).
[c] Number of children in dual-parent families in Japan.

parent, one language one (74 percent). De Houwer reports that Yamamoto (2001) found similar results and that there may be an effect of input frequency. Again, comparing her own study to Yamamoto's, De Houwer (2009) provides a table of the most frequent parent-language patterns in both studies (see Table 1.5).

In both studies the *one parent, one language* pattern turned out to be the least frequent one, which indicates that the majority of the studies on bilingual acquisition may not be representative of the experience of the majority of bilingual children. This is even more salient if most bilingual children turn out to be sequential and not simultaneous bilinguals.

Other relevant factors are whether the parents are native speakers of the languages, and if not, what their degree of proficiency is; and whether they mix languages and code-switch or not. We do not have studies looking at what effect this may have, given that in the majority of these cases children are also exposed to the relevant language by native speakers; in which case their competence and proficiency seems to be similar to that of children who only received native input.

Most studies look at parental input only, when studying young children, but the sources of input for a child may vary greatly with the country and culture. As Bhatia and Ritchie (1999) remind us, it is important not to underestimate the language of other family members. An example from Nair (1984) is relevant. Nair's study focused on a child raised in New Delhi. The child lived with parents, grandparents, an uncle and an aunt, and family employees. The father spoke Bengali, the mother spoke Malayalam, and they spoke Hindi and British English to each other; they code-switched. However, following Indian tradition, immediately after birth the paternal grandmother took care of the baby for the first forty days (if the parents work this practice continues for longer). Therefore the child typically had more exposure to the language of grandparents and household employees than to the parents' language. This particular child was exposed at home to Hindi, Harayanavi (a dialect of Hindi), Indian English, Punjabi, and Oriya.

It is important to take into account also that when one of the child's languages is spoken at home only, if the child attends daycare, he/she may get much more exposure to one language than the other. Even in the *one parent, one language* situation, one parent may spend much more time with the child than the other. Another very important factor to take into consideration is whether the child is the first-born or not. For first-born children, exposure to the dominant language usually increases after toddlerhood, when they start attending daycare; but second-born and later children will usually be exposed to the dominant language at home by their older siblings.

It is frequently claimed that even children who are exposed to both languages from birth receive less exposure to each language than a monolingual child and the input of each language is intermittent with that from the other. However, De Houwer (2009: 119–120) points out that there is a large variability in the amount of input monolingual children get depending on how much parents talk and their speaking rate; therefore, it is not necessarily true that bilingual children will receive less input in each language than monolingual children.

There is also a difference between children who are raised in a bilingual society where most people are actually monolingual or where language mixing is considered incorrect and children raised in a bilingual community where most people speak both languages and language mixing is common.[32] Two studies indicate than in these cases, the child's language mixing is very similar to that of the parents (Huerta-Macías 1981; Quay 2008).

Bilingualism at school

We have already discussed bilingual education in the Introduction, focusing mainly on its effects on minority language children, acquiring a majority language. In many cases, the majority language will also be a second language for these children. However, even for children who are bilingual from birth, schooling may have an important effect on their language development. For simultaneous bilingual children, starting school or daycare constitutes a major change in their language input, since most bilingual children do not attend schools that support both their languages. They will therefore receive not only more input in one of their languages, but also a different quality of input since academic language will start to be introduced.

---

[32] De Houwer proposes that in those cases children may not actually be receiving bilingual input, in the sense of being exposed to two different languages, but utterances combining words in two languages. According to De Houwer, "they are not hearing two different ways of speaking that they need to differentiate between in order to learn to speak themselves. Rather, they are hearing one particular contact variety which happens to include elements that are relatable to two separate languages" (De Houwer 2009: 105). However, studies of code-switching have shown that to be able to code-switch one needs to be able to obey the rules of the two independent languages, so children do need to differentiate both in order to speak in their community's particular variety. Nevertheless, we agree with De Houwer's point that these children's experience is very different from others' and requires careful study.

Most children are not bilingual from birth. For sequential bilinguals either their first contact or the major contact with a second language starts at school. What type of experience they have and their success in both languages will greatly depend on the type of language education they get, monolingual or bilingual, and also on the different kinds of bilingual education. In many cases it will unfortunately mean the beginning of the loss of their minority language.

1.6.2   Problems in defining bilingual children

Sequential bilingualism can be clearly distinguished from simultaneous bilingualism when the second language was acquired after childhood. However, a clear criterion has not been defined for the classification of child bilinguals.

De Houwer (1990) proposed that for a child to be truly considered a simultaneous bilingual, he/she had to be exposed to the second language not more than a week after birth (and exposure to the first language). She also required regular exposure to both languages, meaning that the child should be addressed in both languages almost every day. McLaughlin (1978) proposed that children should be considered sequential bilinguals if their second language was acquired after the age of 3;00.[33] Even though this criterion is highly arbitrary since language development differs in each child at this early age, the assumption is that by the age of 3;00 children have acquired the basic structure of their language. Genesee (1989) proposed to avoid the age limit by stating that acquisition will be considered simultaneous if both languages are acquired during the "period of primary language development." On the other hand, sequential acquisition occurs when the second language was acquired after the "period of primary language development." Now the problem is defining what that period is.

Another important factor is that children at the age of 3;00 still have to acquire some structures of their L1 such as passives, constraints on the interpretation of pronouns, subjunctive/indicative moods, copular distinctions (in Spanish). Therefore, as Lakshmanan (2009) points out, some areas of language may be acquired sequentially by the child but these later developments may occur simultaneously. Thus, L2 acquisition does not necessarily mean sequential acquisition of all aspects of language.

Another issue is when do we call a child *bilingual* vs. a *second language learner*. The definition of these terms clearly depends on the researcher. For example, if a child learned an L2 at the age of 2;00, he/she is usually considered an early bilingual. Is this child also considered an L2 learner? Will his/her competence be considered native or only near-native? Based on McLaughlin's criteria we could say that a child is a sequential bilingual if he/she acquired the

---

[33] In language acquisition studies, ages are indicated in the format shown here, indicating years and months; therefore this number should be understood as 3 years and 0 months. When more precision is needed, usually for younger children, days may also be included, for example 1;02;07 indicates one year, two months and seven days.

L2 after the L1 but before the age of 3;00, and a second language learner if he/she acquired the L2 after 3;00; but not every researcher will agree with this classification.

De Houwer (2005: 5) proposes that early second language acquisition starts between 1;06 and 4;00, and that many bilinguals are more formally exposed to second language acquisition between 5;00 and 6;00 when exposure to formal instruction starts in schools. We have no good terminology to refer to cases when children start out monolingual but are exposed to an L2 during the first year of life. There is also need for research to find out if there are differences between BFLA, early second language acquisition, and these cases.

1.7   Are L1 and L2 acquisition the same?

Why is distinguishing between bilingual first language acquisition and early sequential bilingualism so important? Partially because there are indications that first language acquisition and sequential bilingualism have different characteristics and outcomes. We need to understand all types of language acquisition to have a solid linguistic theory if we believe that language is one of the innate capacities of human beings.

Most studies on second language acquisition have looked at second language acquisition in adulthood, so we will start by comparing L1 acquisition with adult L2 acquisition.

1.7.1   L1 acquisition and adult L2 acquisition

The speech of both adult L2 speakers and children in the early stages of acquisition is different from that of native-speaker adults. They both produce grammatical errors, misuse vocabulary, and have pronunciation errors. In L2 acquisition studies, the speech produced by L2 language learners is called *interlanguage*.

An interesting fact is that not all the errors produced by L2 speakers can be explained as interference from L1. For example, adult L2 learners typically produce a sentence such as (1) when learning negation, where they put the negative element before the subject:

(1)   No you are playing here. (Ellis 1994: 100)

This cannot be a transfer error because it is commonly produced by speakers from varied native language backgrounds, and even by speakers whose languages place negation after the subject as in English.

Another similarity is that even though both groups produce grammatical errors, those errors are not random but rule-governed. Both groups also show variability in their production, meaning they may get a grammatical feature right in a sentence and immediately produce another sentence lacking the correct feature – for example, the person may say sentences (2a) and (2b), one immediately after

Table 1.6 *Stages in the acquisition of negation (Ellis 1994: 100)*

Stage	Description	Example
1	External negation (i.e. 'no' or 'not' is placed at the beginning of the utterance).	No you are playing here.
2	Internal negation (i.e. the negator 'no', 'not' or 'don't' is placed between the subject and the main verb.)	Mariana not coming today.
3	Negative attachment to modal verbs.	I can't play that one.
4	Negative attachment to auxiliary verb as in target language rule	She didn't believe me.
		He didn't said it.

the other – which makes it difficult to judge whether he/she has acquired certain grammatical features or not. The usual measure used in research for monolingual adults is 90 percent production in obligatory contexts (for example, how many times did the L2 speaker provide definite articles in places where they are obligatory in adult monolingual speech?).

(2) a.   My father likes bananas
    b.   He like-Ø them with honey.

Both adult L2 learners and child L1 learners go through staged development. For example, Ellis studied the acquisition of negation and found that adults, as had been reported for children (Bellugi 1967; Bloom 1970; Wode 1977), went through stages in the acquisition of negation, and that these stages corresponded very closely to the ones reported for children (see Table 1.6).

Brown (1973) reported that certain grammatical morphemes are acquired in a predictable order by children learning English as an L1, no matter how frequently they may occur in the input. Dulay and Burt (1974) investigated how accurately children learning English as an L2 would produce the same grammatical morphemes. They tested sixty Spanish-speaking children and fifty-five Chinese children. The order of accuracy was quite similar for the two groups, and the researchers claimed that order of accuracy reflected order of acquisition. Bailey, Madden, and Krashen (1974) found a similar order of accuracy for adults from varied native language backgrounds. However, the orders for the L1 English speakers and the L2 English speakers were not the same, even though both groups appear to acquire /-ing/ relatively early and third-person singular /-s/ relatively late.

On the other hand, L1 acquisition and adult L2 acquisition are not exactly alike. Table 1.7 shows the differences that are most frequently found in the literature.

The main differences are in rate and effort in acquisition, ultimate attainment and the factors affecting it (affective factors, formal instruction), and the effects of the L1 when it exists. We will come back to these issues when we discuss the *Critical Period Hypothesis* in Section 1.8.

Table 1.7 *Differences between L1 and adult L2 acquisition*

L1	Adult L2
Fast	Slow
Apparently "easy"	Laborious
Achieves perfect proficiency	Does not achieve native proficiency (Fossilization)
L1 learner doesn't know another language.	L2 learner already knows another language (Transfer)
Children develop clear intuitions about correctness	L2 learners often do not have clear grammatical judgments
Instruction is not needed	Instruction is helpful or necessary
Affective factors usually do not play a role.	Affective factors usually play a major role in determining success.

1.7.2   Child L2 acquisition

A recent area of study that could help us shed light over several of the unknowns in L2 acquisition is the area of child L2 acquisition. As Lakshmanan (2009) reminds us, the study of child language acquisition should cover all children: monolingual, simultaneous bilinguals, and L2 learners.[34] Moreover, we need to have a clear image of L2 acquisition to distinguish L2 learners from children with language disabilities. Another reason why child L2 acquisition is interesting is because in the case of bilinguals and L2 learners there may be more "poverty of stimulus" than for a monolingual child.[35]

Where is the division between child L2 acquisition and adult L2 acquisition? The most frequently used definition is that child L2 acquisition is concerned with children who are sequential bilinguals who start learning their second language after the age of 3;00 but before puberty. Schwartz (2003) proposes that the limit for child L2 acquisition should be age 7;00 based on the findings by Johnson and Newport (1989) that only L2 learners who had learned English before the age of 7;00 performed like native speakers in a grammaticality judgment test. Foster-Cohen (2001) recommends that we set different boundaries for the different areas of language acquisition.

1.7.3   Adult and child L2 acquisition

There are some similarities among all L2 learners, adult or child:

• Both adult and child L2 learners have already acquired an L1 (albeit the child's may not be fully developed, it is assumed that after age 3;00 children have already acquired the fundamental aspects of an L1).

---

[34] There are interesting differences between L1 acquisition and child L2 acquisition which go beyond the scope of this book. See Lakshmanan (2009) and Montrul (2004a).

[35] But see De Houwer 2009 for a different opinion.

- Contrary to popular belief, not all child L2 learners acquire a perfect phonology of their L2 (MacKay, Flege, and Imai 2006); and not all adult L2 learners fail to achieve it. (Flynn and Manuel 1991; Bongaerts, Planken, and Schils 1995), although the general trend is that child L2 learners do better in ultimate achievement than adults.

There are also differences between adult and child L2 learners, as seen in Table 1.8.

- Child L2 learners are usually successful in acquiring a second language; adults may not be.
- Although inflectional morphology is absent at the first stages of child L2 acquisition, child L2 learners have been reported to become near native around the tenth month of exposure (Lakshmanan 1994; Kakazu and Lakshmanan 2000); some adults never achieve this.
- Child L2 acquisition is usually naturalistic through immersion in the L2,[36] adults usually have some formal training.
- Children learning an L2 may go through a silent period lasting from one to six months; this has not been reported for adults.

Several topics of research will help us further understand the differences between L1 and L2 acquisition and their causes. Some of these are listed by Lakshmanan (2009: 379–382):

- How much does the developmental sequence of child L2 mirror that of L1 acquisition? For example, even if one assumes that Universal Grammar (UG) constrains child L2 acquisition, is L2 acquisition different due to the fact that child L2 learners are more cognitively mature than L1 learners?
- How many of the L2 phenomena are due to an influence from L1?
- A comparison of the pattern of development in child L2 acquisition with the pattern of development of simultaneous bilingual acquisition, keeping the two languages constant across the comparisons, can shed light on the role played by language dominance in the directionality of transfer effects.
- A comparison of child L2 acquisition and adult L2 acquisition allows us to study the availability of UG in adult L2 acquisition; assuming that children before the age of 7;00 who are sequential bilinguals still have access to UG.
- Are some aspects of UG not available at the initial stages of language acquisition since they mature later? The study of L2 acquisition can help us determine if this is true, since those aspects of UG should be already available for a child who is acquiring an L2 after age 3;00.

---

[36] Although this will obviously vary when the child enters school, depending on the type of bilingual education he/she receives, if he/she receives any at all.

Table 1.8 *Differences between child and adult L2 acquisition*

Child L2	Adult L2
May go through an initial "silent period."	Adults do not go through silent period.
Typically successful in acquiring L2.	May not succeed in acquiring L2.
Typically in naturalistic/ immersion settings.	Typically in formal instructed setting.
Child L2 learners seem to acquire phonology better than adults; but it is not true that all child L2 learners have no foreign accent.	Adult learners typically do not achieve native-like pronunciation.
Children's ultimate attainment is better (Krashen, Long and Scarcella 1979; Genesee 1988; Snow 1983, 1987; Ellis 1985; Flege 1987)	Adults seem to progress faster.

1.8   The critical period hypothesis

The classification between early and late bilinguals was originally closely related to the notion of a critical period in first language acquisition. A critical period is a period of time with a distinct onset and offset during which experience can lead to learning by an organism. This period is assumed to be innately programmed and irreversible. An example of critical periods proposed for other species are the development of visual cognition in primates and imprinting in geese.

In the case of bilinguals, it is proposed that early bilinguals achieve native or near-native proficiency in both their languages, while late bilinguals fail to achieve native proficiency in some aspects of their second languages (e.g., they have a foreign accent), although several exceptions of "good language learners" can be found.

One explanation proposed for this difference is that of a critical period for language acquisition.

The critical period hypothesis for language was introduced by Penfield (1963/1981) and Penfield and Roberts (1959). Penfield proposed that children were better at language acquisition than adults due to the fact that their brain had more plasticity than the adult brain, which became increasingly rigid with age. This advantage was thought by Penfield to last till age 9, when the rigidization began, probably due to increases in myelination. Lenneberg (1967) proposed that there was a period in the maturation of the human organism, from approximately 2 years of age to puberty, during which effortless and complete language acquisition is possible, and after which it is not possible. Both Penfield and Lenneberg based their proposals on the observation of children's recovery of language after brain damage and its comparison to adult recovery.

> Between the ages of two and three years language emerges by an interaction of maturation and self-programmed learning. Between the ages of three and the early teens the possibility for primary language acquisition continues to be good; the individual appears to be most sensitive to stimuli at this time and to preserve some innate flexibility for the organization of brain functions to carry out the complex integration of sub-processes necessary for the smooth elaboration of speech and language. After puberty, the ability for self-organization and adjustment to the physiological demands of verbal behavior quickly declines. The brain behaves as if it had become set in its ways and primary, basic skills not acquired by that time usually remain deficient for life.   (Lenneberg 1967: 158)

Lenneberg studied human and animal behavior and came up with a list of characteristics of an innate behavior that according to him applied to language:

    i.   The behavior emerges before it is necessary.
    ii.   Its appearance is not the result of a conscious decision.
    iii.   Its emergence is not triggered by external events.
    iv.   Direct teaching and intensive practice have relatively little effect.
    v.   There is a regular sequence of "milestones" as the behavior develops, and these can be correlated with age and other aspects of development.

Notice that Lenneberg was talking about acquiring a first language. About second languages, he says:

> Most individuals of average intelligence are able to learn a second language after the beginning of their second decade... A person *can* learn to communicate in a foreign language at the age of forty. This does not trouble our basic hypothesis on age limitations because we may assume that the cerebral organization for language learning as such has taken place during childhood, and since natural languages tend to resemble one another in many fundamental aspects..., the matrix for language skills is present.   (1967: 176)

So he does not extend the notion of critical period for second language acquisition.

Lenneberg linked the critical period to cerebral lateralization, which he believed occurred between the ages of 2 and 13. Research has shown that the relationship between the critical period and lateralization doesn't seem to hold. Lateralization is present at birth and complete by age 5 (Kinsbourne 1975; Kinsbourne and Hiscock 1977; Krashen 1973).

Another problem is that there have been multiple formulations of the critical period, as Singleton (2005) points out. There are variations in the onset (6 months of fetal life or age 2;00) and offset ages (age 1;00, 2;00, 4;00, 6;00–8;00, 7;00; 9;00, 12;00, 15;00, 15;00/16;00 or puberty) for the period. In terms of the capacities it affects, it has been proposed to affect many different areas of our competence (only phonetics/phonology; non-innate elements of grammar, innate elements of grammar, particular subparts of innate elements; implicitly acquired elements, or general capacity). There is also disagreement about its underlying causes (neurobiological, cognitive-developmental, or affective-motivational, with several variations under each). Singleton attempts to give a summary of all the positions to find a common definition of the critical period. However, as can be seen, the resulting definition seems meaningless:

> For some reason, the language acquiring capacity, or some aspect or aspects thereof, is operative only for a maturational period which ends some time between perinatality and puberty.   (Singleton 2005: 280)

It is clear, therefore, that a better definition and much more research to reach a consensual definition are needed.

1.8.1   Is there a critical period for L1 acquisition?

There is some evidence in favor of a critical period for first language acquisition. The evidence comes from two types of cases: deprived children and deaf signers exposed to sign language after birth.

Deprived children

Deprived children are children who were lost or abandoned in areas away from civilization – for whom we have very little information of previous history or conditions during deprivation – and children who were raised in exceptional circumstances of low stimulation due mainly to parental mental problems. There are three famous cases of deprived children: Victor, Kamala and Amala, and Genie.

Victor (Itard 1962) was found at age 11 or 12 in 1799 in Aveyron, France. He was subsequently educated and studied by Dr. Itard, who eventually gave up on his language development. At the end of four years of training, he was reported to be able to produce only two expressions *lait* 'milk' and *Oh, Dieu!* 'Oh, God!', the second of which was a common expression used by his governess. He also produced the nonsense syllables *la* and *li/gli*. Itard speculates that this second expression may have been used to refer to Julie, the governess's daughter. Even though his case is well documented by Dr. Itard himself, we do not know enough about his condition before and during his isolation to be able to draw any conclusions about the case. There are also some researchers (Firth 2003) who have suggested that he may have suffered from autism, which may have led to his abandonment in the first place.

Kamala and Amala were found by Reverend J. A. L Singh in 1920 in a forest in Midnapore, India (Singh and Zingg 1942/1966). Kamala was about 6 or 8 years old and Amala was about 4 to 6. Amala died the following year of a kidney infection. Kamala learned around forty words in five years. She died in 1929, at age 16. However, there are indications that the whole case may have been exaggerated or fabricated.

Genie was found in California at age 13;07. She is the only one of the famous cases for which we have good documentation. She was immediately put under the care of a team of specialists at the Children's Hospital in Los Angeles. In particular, her linguistic development was studied by Susan Curtiss (Fromkin, Curtiss, Krashen, Rigler, and Rigler 1974; Curtiss, 1977; Curtiss, Fromkin, and Krashen 1978; Rymer 1993; Jones 1995). Genie's general cognitive development after treatment reached a level of 6 to 8 years of age by the next year. We will describe Genie's linguistic development in more detail below.

Skuse (1993) studied several cases of children who had suffered extreme deprivation during early childhood and focused on their later outcome. These children were raised in extreme isolation, not only deprived of language but sometimes also deprived of perceptual and social stimulation, in some cases lacking any meaningful and normal human contact. One of the cases studied by Skuse was Genie's. The ten children that Skuse studied had these common characteristics: they initially lacked basic speech and social skills, and after removal from impoverished conditions, they usually made a fast and remarkable recovery, but not in all areas.

All the children, except Genie, were found before the alleged offset age of the critical period of 7 years of age. Genie, on the other hand, was either beyond the critical period or just on the verge of it if one believes in the puberty offset. Skuse was looking at how resilient language was, so we need to see how many of these children achieved proper language development. Of the nine children besides Genie, we cannot tell what would have happened with Anna since she died early. Of the eight remaining children, seven "reached virtually age appropriate levels within a few years" (Skuse 1993: 42). The only exception was a child named Mary who Skuse reports to have had autistic behavior. Therefore, it seems that even in the most dire circumstances, language is achievable after deprivation if consistent language input starts before the age of 7. Even Anna was showing signs of progress before her death.

Most of the children had some form of minimal communication. Another child, Isabelle, had been locked away with her deaf–mute mother and had shared some signs with her, and some others were twins, so they had each other for company, e.g., the Koluchova, Douglas, and Sutton twins. In another case, the children were siblings; Louise had a sibling called Mary, even if the latter didn't speak. It might be argued that some form of minimal communication is needed. The only other completely isolated case besides Genie, Adam, was rescued at an earlier age (1;06) than the other children, who were rescued between the ages of 3;06 and 6;11, when children raised in normal circumstances have already developed the core elements of language.

So what about Genie, the only child who seems to have been found after the critical period? Her language behavior is reported by Curtiss:

> In contrast [to her lexical acquisition], her utterances remained largely agrammatic and hierarchically flat. Her ability to produce sentences developed only in so far as she was able to produce increasingly longer strings and strings

that increased in propositional complexity. Her speech, even after 8 years [of
language training and testing], remained essentially devoid of closed class
morphology and of most syntactic devices and operations.

(Curtiss 1989: 118)

We will come back to her case after we review the evidence on other speakers
who acquired language past the critical period.

Deaf children

Newport (1990) studied the signing abilities of congenitally deaf
children of hearing parents who were exposed to American Sign Language (ASL)
at three different ages: at birth, before age 6, and after age 12. She found that after
thirty years of using ASL, native signers were better than early signers who were
better than late signers. However, these late signers had some knowledge of ASL
morphology and syntax. Boudreault and Mayberry (2006) obtained similar results
with a grammaticality judgment task. Late learners had the most trouble with
questions and relative clauses. However, these adults were not isolated like the
children we saw above. They must have developed some form of communication
with their families, or what we call *homesigns*. These forms have been studied
by Susan Goldin-Meadow and her colleagues (Goldin-Meadow and Feldman
1977; Goldin-Meadow and Mylander 1984; Goldin-Meadow 2003) and have
been found to share several characteristics with natural languages. Therefore,
these adults must have had a foundation for language similar to that which
Isabelle had.

In this respect, two cases studies are interesting: Chelsea (Curtiss 1989) and
E.M. (Grimshaw, Adelstein, Bryden, and MacKinnon 1998).

Chelsea was misdiagnosed as mentally retarded and, even though the mother
suspected she was deaf, because they lived in a remote, rural community without
access to the help she needed, she received no medical help or instruction in sign
language. However, unlike Genie, she seems to have had a normal childhood
with a loving family. At age 32 she was finally fitted with hearing aids with
which her hearing improved within the normal range, and cognitive evaluation
and language instruction begun. A full-fledged report on Chelsea has not been
published to the best of our knowledge. Since information on Chelsea is hard to
find,[37] we reproduce here Curtiss' description of her language and her examples.
It is unclear how long Chelsea had been receiving language instruction at the
point of this description:

Chelsea's linguistic performance exhibits marked discrepancies between
her lexical abilities and her ability to combine vocabulary into appropriate, semantically well-formed, and grammatical utterances. Her lexicon has
steadily increased and appears to be organized along normal semantic lines,
as evidenced by her above-12th-grade-level performance . . . In contrast, her

---

[37] There are only short descriptions in Curtiss (1988, 1989, and 1994), and an unpublished
manuscript by Curtiss (1996). Dronkers and Glusker both presented independent papers on
the case in 1987 but have never published them either.

multiword utterances are, almost without exception, unacceptable grammatically, and often propositionally unclear or illformed as well. Her lexical knowledge seems limited to (denotative) definitional cores and does not appear to encompass either subcategorization information or logical structure constraints (in contrast to Genie and probably Kaspar Hauser as well). Likewise, her expressive language appears at its best, limited to the production of combinations of semantically relevant substantives, unelaborated morphologically, and ungoverned by constraints on word order, as illustrated in the following examples:

Examples of Chelsea's Utterances

a.	*The small a the hat*
b.	*Richard eat peppers hot.*
c.	*Orange Tim car in.*
d.	*Banana the eat.*
e.	*I Wanda be drive come.*
f.	*The boat sits water on.*
g.	*Breakfast eating girl.*
h.	*Combing hair the boy.*
i.	*The woman is bus the going.*
j.	*The girl is cone the ice cream shopping buying the man.*

(Curtiss 1989: 119–120)

E.M. is a similar case. He was profoundly deaf since birth and grew up in a rural area in Mexico where he used homesigns with his family. Preliminary analyses of his homesigning indicate that it was much more elaborate than that described in younger children. At age 9 he spent one year in the regular school system where they tried to teach him to read, and at age 12 he spent several months in a day school for the deaf where he had oral training. At age 15;09, he was fitted with hearing aids that corrected his hearing loss to 35 db. Then he began to learn verbal Spanish just by exposure to the language, with no additional instruction. He then spent six months a year with his family in Mexico, where he continued to use his homesigns and Spanish, and six months with relatives in Canada, where he was exposed to Spanish only since his family decided not to have him learn sign language because he would have no support for it in his rural community. However, he still used signs and oral language at the same time. Grimshaw *et al.* (1998) report on his development after four years since his acquisition of hearing aids. The researchers used translations of the tasks that Curtiss used with Genie to test him.[38] E.M. began to learn vocabulary within days of exposure. In terms of grammar, after eight months, he demonstrated knowledge of singular/plural.

---

[38] Although one of the authors is said to be a native Spanish speaker, we have noted with surprise some spelling errors in several of the test instructions provided in the article, and more importantly, at least one ungrammatical sentence (before/after word order task, p. 249), which raises concerns about the authors' ability to test and judge Spanish knowledge. We hope these are only typos at the time of writing the report which do not reflect errors on the test items.

After thirty-four months, he still did not understand verb tense, *before/after* constructions, negation, pronouns, and prepositions. In terms of syntax, also after eight months he had comprehension of comparatives and superlatives.

In production, his mean length of utterance (MLU) was of less than 2. He never babbled, he never imitated or asked questions.

Comparing Genie, Chelsea, and E.M.

Genie started using single words after five months, and her vocabulary grew quickly. Her words were cognitively complex; she had terms for color, number, and superlatives. However, her syntax was not normal. For example, she attempted to do recursion (embedding one sentence into another) and although it is possible to understand what she meant, her sentences lacked necessary grammatical elements.

(3) a.   Ask go shopping.
              '(Someone/I) ask (to) go shopping.'[39]
    b.   Father hit Genie cried long time ago.
              'Father hit Genie (and she) cried (a) long time ago.'

She has been reported to have several grammatical deficits on word order, absence of auxiliaries and contractions, difficulty with pronouns and an irregular use of inflection.[40]

So what do these three cases tell us about language acquisition after puberty? The children do not seem to have had any problems in acquiring semantics and lexicon. They all seem to have problems mainly with syntax and morphology, although their profiles are different in terms of what areas they succeeded in and in which ones they didn't. While Genie had trouble with discourse markers and social expressions such as *hello*, Chelsea seems to have used them without any problems. There is no information on E.M.'s abilities in this respect, so we cannot judge whether Genie's problems were due to her earlier isolation. Genie and E.M. exhibited great variability in performance, between sessions and across items. We do not have enough information on Chelsea to see if that was also the case for her.

One salient difference is that the report on E.M.'s attainment was done after only four years of exposure to language, so we cannot be certain how much he was able to develop later. However, in two years of testing he did not show improvement in any of the subtests. Also, he had a functional homesign that may

---

[39] Some inflection may be missing on the verb also depending on the sentence's subject and intended tense.

[40] Jones (1995), however, has noted that there are some discrepancies in the way Genie's data have been portrayed by Curtiss, which suggest that at some point around 1977, Curtiss started having a much more negative view of Genie's linguistic development than she did in her earlier writings. For example, in later writings she noted that Genie was unable to acquire the morphology of English, while in Fromkin *et al.* (1974) the authors noted that Genie had begun to use the progressive marker *-ing* and to mark plurals and possessives. To the best of our knowledge Curtiss has never answered Jones' questions.

have been a deterrent for him to put much effort into oral language acquisition, even though he did not have a community with whom he could use his homesigns during six months of the year.[41]

It does seem to be true from the three cases studied, and from the reports of late signers, that syntax and grammar are the areas more impacted by late acquisition. However, the early report on E.M., the discrepancies in Genie's report, and the scarcity of the data on Chelsea's language make it impossible for the moment to judge whether there is any clear critical period effect.

1.8.2   Is there a critical period for L2 acquisition?

So, there does seem to be some support, albeit not conclusive, for a critical period for first language acquisition. Is there a critical period for L2 learning?

The general belief is that adult L2 speakers learn language less efficiently than children and have an accent while children do not. The simple view of second language acquisition is that of "the younger the better." Even though there is some evidence that, at the first stages of naturalistic exposure, older children and adults progress faster than younger children (Krashen, Long, and Scarcella 1979; Harley 1986; Long 1990; Cook 1991; Ellis 1994) the consensus is that in terms of long-term outcomes younger learners in general attain better proficiency than older learners. Support for this comes from Snow and Hoefnagel-Höhle (1978a, 1978b) who conducted a longitudinal study of sixty-nine English L1 speakers learning Dutch as an L2, and from Patkowski (1980) who studied the syntactic proficiency of sixty-seven highly educated immigrants to the USA who had lived in the US for at least five years. The studies done on formal L2 instruction point to the same initial advantage for older learners (Singleton 1989), but no study has looked at longer-term outcomes. This fact does not, however, presume that all child L2 learners achieve native-like proficiency, nor that no adult is able to achieve it, as we will see below.

The main support for a critical period comes from the two studies by Johnson and Newport (1989, 1991). They did a grammaticality judgment task and studied the English abilities of native speakers of Korean or Chinese who had begun exposure to English between the ages of 5 and 39 years of age and who had been exposed to English for at least three years. Their results show that subjects who had acquired English before puberty showed a strong correlation between proficiency and age of acquisition. Only speakers who had learned the L2 before age 7;00 performed like native speakers. However these studies have been criticized because the authors did not control for other factors, such as L1 maintenance and development, language dominance, and amount of each language use. Patkowski (1980) found a strong negative correlation between age of arrival and syntactic

---

[41] It is unclear from the report where E.M. was tested. If he was tested in Canada, the researchers themselves may have been a community with whom he may have been able to use his homesigns.

competence. The thirty subjects who had arrived before age 15 had high scores while the rest of the speakers showed a normal curve of competence decline.

Many authors, however, do not believe there is a critical period for adult language acquisition. Long (1990) and Flynn and Manuel (1991) argue that if we can find even one adult who is native-like, that would prove a critical period for L2 does not exist. Neufeld (1977) and Flynn and Manuel (1991) claim that some adults can acquire accent-free speech[42] while some child learners (preadolescents) do show evidence of non-native accents (Flynn and Manuel 1991). Patkowski (1980), for syntax, also found that five of the subjects who had arrived in the US after age 15, nevertheless scored in the same range as the early learners. Ioup (1995) studied two L1 speakers of English who had learned Egyptian Arabic as an L2, one with formal instruction and the second one by immersion, although she did take notes on her errors and corrections. Ioup found that they had comparable grammatical competence in Egyptian Arabic and that both were native-like.

If there is no critical period, we need to find explanations for the differences between child and adult language acquisition where they do occur (Flynn and Manuel 1991; Martohardjono and Flynn 1995). Martohardjono and Flynn (1995) suggest that if we were to find a critical period for L2, it would apply to the core elements of grammar and not to language-specific characteristics. They argue against a critical period by looking at the participant's capacity to apply principles that are not applicable in their native language, to reset parameters and phonology. For phonology, they cite several studies[43] showing that adults are able to acquire phonemes, perceive phonemic contrasts, and produce sounds which did not exist in their L1, and others showing they are able to reset VOTs to resemble those of the L2, even though their VOTs are not identical to those of native speakers. For syntax, they first look at Chinese and Indonesian L2 learners of English and their ability to recognize subjacency violations that would not occur in their native languages where *wh*-words stay *in situ* (Martohardjono 1993). Results show that both groups of L2 learners showed solid knowledge of the subjacency principle, against what the existence of a critical period would predict. Next they looked at parameter resetting by Japanese speakers (who have a left-branching language) learning English (a right-branching one). Papers in Lust (1987) had found that speakers of right-branching languages expected a pronoun to follow its antecedent and in left-branching languages, speakers expected the pronoun to precede its antecedent. Flynn (1983, 1987) presented the Japanese speakers with possible English left-branching constructions where the antecedent preceded the pronoun (as in Japanese) and found that contrary to predictions, Japanese speakers found them extremely difficult, as L1 English-speaking children do, showing that they had been able to reset the parameter for English.

---

[42] See also Bongaerts, Planken and Schils (1995).
[43] See references in Martohardjono and Flynn (1995).

Flege and his colleagues (Flege, Yeni-Komshian and Liu 1999 and Flege and Liu 2001) have shown that when one controls for the educational background of the subjects, the age effects disappear.

Note that the existence of a critical period for second language acquisition has some important practical implications for the grade levels at which second language teaching is recommended for schools and on the expectations for proficiency we can set for adult language learners.

1.9   Outcomes of bilingualism

There are several possible outcomes when people come into contact with a second language. Some may remain, to a certain level, mostly monolingual in their first language. Others may become bilingual and remain bilingual. Others may become bilingual and later switch into using the second language only or predominantly. In this case, attrition of the first language may occur.

1.9.1   Language attrition and loss

The term *attrition* refers to a decrease in competence or proficiency in a speaker that no longer uses one language or has less contact with it than before. *Language loss* is the complete disappearance of linguistic abilities in a given language. Language attrition is discussed at greater length in Section 2.4.5 of Chapter 2.

Many bilinguals who have receptive abilities in only one language or who have suffered from language attrition engage in what Saville-Troike (1987) calls *dilingual conversation*, in which their parents speak to them in the minority language and they answer in the majority language.

1.9.2   Heritage language speakers and the question of ultimate attainment

"Heritage speaker" (Wiley and Valdés 2000) is a widely used term that refers principally to bilingual speakers in the USA who learned a language other than English at home, but have been immersed in English since childhood and often exclusively schooled in it. This category covers a wide range of abilities from passive bilinguals (individuals who understand their home language but are not able to engage in active conversation at an advanced level) to speakers who begin to acquire a formal register in college after a period of English-only education.

Several researchers have discovered that heritage speakers of Spanish do not perform identically to Spanish-speaking monolinguals on various tests of syntactic competence, suggesting that heritage bilinguals have either experienced language attrition in their L1 or that they never acquired certain syntactic distinctions (e.g., Silva-Corvalán 1994; Montrul 2002, 2004; Montrul and Potowski 2007; Silva-Corvalán 2008). These studies have pointed to age of acquisition as a critical factor in determining whether a heritage speaker's grammar will diverge from monolingual norms, especially whether or not the L2 was acquired simultaneously along with the L1 from birth, in early childhood (between the ages of four and seven), or after age 7, ages that are well within the putative critical period for language acquisition. These researchers also found that the continual availability of input plays a crucial role in determining the outcome of language contact for childhood bilinguals. As a result, these findings have had an important impact on the field of bilingual studies by challenging commonly-held assumptions regarding the nature of the critical period for language learning, such as the assumption that critical period effects are largely due to the learner's age of onset of second language acquisition rather than other factors.

Silva-Corvalán (1994) found that bilinguals who were either born in the United States or emigrated prior to 6 years of age showed signs of influence from English in their use of Spanish. She noted that in their Spanish grammar, heritage bilinguals simplified syntactic forms, overgeneralized regular forms, used periphrastic forms not found in monolingual Spanish and showed evidence of transfer from English to Spanish. However, Silva-Corvalán argued that cross-linguistic transfer was limited to lexical forms as well as the weakening of pragmatic rules in Spanish, and did not involve direct syntactic transfer from English to Spanish. For example, in monolingual Spanish, speakers tend to use post-verbal subjects with unaccusative verbs that introduce a new topic, as shown in (4a). However, heritage bilinguals tended to use English-like preverbal subjects, as in (4b).

(4) a.   *Estaban peleando y entonces llegó la policía.* General Spanish
         Ø   *Estaban peleando y   entonces llegó   la   policía*
         They were   fighting   and then   arrived the police
         'They were fighting and then arrived the police.'
    b.   *Estaban peleando y entonces la policía llegó.* Group 2
         Ø   *Estaban peleando y   entonces la   policía llegó*
         They were   fighting   and then   the police arrived.
         'They were fighting and then the police arrived.'   (Silva-Corvalán 1994)

Silva-Corvalán argued against the hypothesis that such examples constitute wholesale transfer from English to Spanish because although her participants tended to use more preverbal subjects, they did not do so exclusively, indicating that they did not transfer English SVO word order rules to Spanish. Rather, she claimed that such sentences reflected the relaxation of discourse-pragmatic constraints in Spanish due to contact with English.

Heritage learners of Spanish also differ from native speakers in their production of tense, agreement, and mood morphology (Silva-Corvalán 1994; Montrul 2002, 2009; Montrul and Perpiñán 2011). The simple past in Spanish has two different aspectual forms, as shown in (5). The preterit is used with actions that are seen as punctual whereas the imperfect is selected to express actions that occurred for an unspecified duration or were habitual:

Simple past tense in Spanish
(5) a.   preterit   *canté*   'I sang'
    b.   imperfect *cantaba* 'I used to sing/ I was singing'

This aspectual difference between events is also expressed lexically, or in the inherent meaning of the verb. For example, verbs such as *to know* lend themselves to an unbounded interpretation (e.g. it is ungrammatical to say *They are knowing the answer*), whereas other verbs like *to win* are almost always bound by a definite time reference. Verbs can be placed along a spectrum according to whether they refer to a state of being which is usually interpreted as holding for the length of an individual's existence (individual-level predicates such as *John is smart*), temporal states that are assumed to end (stage-level predicates such as *John is hungry*), or as different levels of more time limited events as shown in (6). The eventive verbs can be further subdivided into verbs which are activities without a specific goal such as *walk*, accomplishments which include a termination point (*draw a picture*), and achievements whose ending point is instantaneous (such as *win*) (Montrul 2002).

(6)   States   know   stative
           Activities   walk   eventive
           Accomplishments draw a picture eventive
           Achievements   win   eventive

In Spanish, these lexical verb classes interact with the morphological distinction between the preterit and imperfect past tense forms. While states and activities tend to occur in imperfect aspect, accomplishments and achievements tend to be marked with the preterit aspect. Some stative verbs in Spanish such as *querer* 'to want' obligatorily shift in meaning in the preterit and acquire an eventive interpretation. Some examples of this shift are provided in (7).

(7)   Verb   Meaning in the preterit aspect
           saber 'to know'   'to find out'
           conocer 'to know' 'to meet someone for the first time'

In English, however, there is only one form of the simple past, e.g. *I sang*. English does not possess the grammatical means of expressing the aspectual distinction between actions captured by the preterit/imperfect contrast in Spanish. For ongoing actions in the past in English, the past progressive is used, e.g., *I was singing*. Depending on the context, a verb in the imperfect tense in Spanish such as *cantaba* could be translated in English as *I sang*, *I was singing*, *I used to sing*, or *I would sing*.

In Spanish, the indicative and subjunctive moods are morphologically marked, unlike in English. Mood selection in Spanish is complicated and governed by many factors. However, certain verbs and lexical expressions always select either the indicative or subjunctive mood, whereas others can vary according to the pragmatic context. For instance, predicates of desire, such as (8a) always select for the subjunctive mood in the embedded clause, whereas the indicative mood is selected by epistemic verbs such as (8b).

(8) a.   *Marianela quiere*   *que sus hijos*   <u>*habl-en*</u>   *español.*
           Maríanela want-PRS.IND.3SG   that her children   speak-PRS.SBJ.3PL   Spanish
           'Marianela wants her children to speak Spanish.'
   b.   *Marianela sabe*   *que sus hijos*   <u>*habl-an*</u>   *español.*
           Marianela know-PRS.IND.3SG   that her children   speak-PRS.IND.3PL   Spanish
           'Marianela knows that her children speak Spanish.'

Monolingual children acquiring Spanish begin marking verbs with the preterit aspect before the imperfect one, but both types of past tense verbs appear in their speech with verbs of a variety of aspectual classes by age 3 (Hernández Pina 1984; López Ornat, Mariscal, Fernández, and Gallo 1994; Ezeizabarrena 1996; Bel 1998, 2001). The subjunctive mood in Spanish is acquired later, and begins to appear at approximately 4 years of age but is not fully acquired until age 8 or later (Pérez-Leroux 1998; Montrul 2008).

Heritage Spanish speakers growing up in the US usually experience intensive exposure to English before the acquisition of Spanish tense, agreement, and mood morphology is mastered, resulting in non-native like production of these morphological distinctions. Silva-Corvalán (1994) found that Mexican-American bilinguals who were born in the USA or had moved there before age 11 substituted the preterit for the imperfect with stative and eventive verbs, whereas they used the imperfect rather than the preterit with stative verbs exclusively. A 2002 study by Montrul found that simultaneous English–Spanish bilinguals and early L2 child learners whose first language was Spanish differed from monolingual adults in their use of stative verbs in the preterit and their use of the imperfect to mark habitual aspect.

Montrul (2009) and Montrul and Perpiñán (2011) investigated knowledge of tense, agreement, and mood morphology in Spanish L2 learners and heritage speakers. They used two tasks which required participants to select the correctly inflected form in a written context, one which examined the preterit/imperfect contrast, and the other which tested knowledge of the use of the subjunctive versus indicative mood. The authors found that heritage learners were more accurate than L2 learners in choosing the correct aspectual form, but not in choosing the correct mood, a difference they attributed to the fact that aspect is acquired earlier than mood in Spanish.

Several studies have found that adult heritage speakers of Spanish use more overt subjects in their Spanish than monolingual Spanish speakers do (Silva-Corvalán 1994; Montrul 2004a, 2004b). This is presumably due to influence from English, a non-null subject language. Paradis and Navarro (2003) found that a bilingual child acquiring Spanish and English from birth used more overt subjects (and fewer null ones) in her heritage Spanish than a monolingual child would. The authors mention several factors which could account for this result, including cross-linguistic influence and patterns in the adult input. The child's mother spoke highly fluent but non-native Spanish, and her father spoke a Caribbean variety of Spanish, which is characterized by a higher incidence of overt subjects than other dialects (Toribio 2000). Silva-Corvalán and Sánchez-Walker (2007) also found that a Spanish–English bilingual child produced more overt subjects in his Spanish than monolingual children do, but attributed this finding to the preponderance of third-person singular verbs forms in the child's speech (which required disambiguation) rather than to language interference.

Ionin and Montrul (2010) and Montrul and Ionin (2010) examined the interpretation of Spanish generics by heritage adult speakers. Unlike Spanish, English has two ways of expressing plurality, one which contains a bare NP without a determiner (such as *tigers*) and has a generic reading as in (9a), which refers to tigers generally. The second type of plural construction includes a definite determiner (*the tigers*) and has a non-generic, specific reading (9b), and refers to a particular group of tigers.

(9) a.   Tigers eat meat. [+ generic reference, – specific reference]
    b.   The tigers eat meat. [– generic reference, + specific reference]
           (Ionin and Montrul 2010)

Spanish, in contrast, uses phrases with definite determiners such as (10b) to express both generic and specific reference, with the interpretation depending on the context. Omitting the definite determiner as in (10a) is ungrammatical, unlike in English.

(10) a.   *Tigres   comen   carne.
            Tigers   eat   meat
            'Tigers eat meat.'
     b.   Los   tigres   comen   carne. [+ generic reference, + specific reference]
            The   tigers   eat   meat
            'The tigers eat meat.'

Ionin and Montrul found that heritage learners of Spanish, unlike native speakers, accepted bare NP subjects such as (10a) in Spanish and preferred a specific rather than generic interpretation for sentences such as (10b) with definite determiners. They interpreted these findings to be evidence of grammatical transfer from English to Spanish. In a subsequent study, Montrul and Ionin (2010) compared the interpretation of generics in Spanish L2 learners to heritage learners using the same tasks, and found that proficiency level better predicted the participants' performance than age of acquisition for both types of learners.

Another area of grammar in which there are differences between heritage learners of Spanish and native speakers is the use of differential object marking or DOM (using the marker *a* with animate, specific direct objects). In such contexts, the use of the accusative marker *a* is obligatory in Spanish. For example, DOM is obligatory in (11), since the direct object *Julieta* is animate and specific:

(11)   *He visto a̲ Julieta* [+ animate, + specific direct object]
          Ø   he   visto   a̲   *Julieta*
          (I)   have.PRS.IND.3SG see.PST.PTCP ACC-marker Julieta
          'I have seen Juliet'

However, the marker is not obligatory in (12a), since the direct object is not specific, or in (12b), which has a non-human complement:

(12) a.   *Se buscan médicos* [+ animate, – specific direct object]
          Se   *busc-a-n*   *médicos*
          CL =   look_for-TV-PRS.IND.3PL   doctors
          'Doctors are needed.'
     b.   *Se cortan los árboles* [−animate, + specific direct object (no a-marker)]
          Se   *cort-a-n*   *los árboles*
          CL =   cut-TV-PRS.IND.3PL   the trees
          'The trees are cut down.'

Rodríguez-Mondoñedo (2008) found that monolingual children acquiring Spanish begin using differential object marking early in development, and that by age 3 it is largely acquired.

Montrul and Bowles (2009) found that adult heritage speakers of Spanish were very inaccurate both in producing sentences with DOM as well as in making judgments of its grammaticality. They found this to be true even in the case of heritage learners with high levels of proficiency, indicating that differential object marking is difficult for bilingual learners to acquire despite its early appearance in development.

Results from the aforementioned studies showed evidence of influence from the dominant L2 in the L1 of heritage learners of Spanish living in the United States. However, Hohenstein, Eisenberg, and Naigles (2006) found that there was also influence from the L1 to the L2 in the lexicon and at the lexical–syntactic interface in heritage speakers of Spanish. These authors compared the production of motion and path verbs in English and in Spanish by bilinguals who had acquired English early (before age 5) or late (after age 12). Hohenstein *et al.* asked their subjects to describe videos of events in English and Spanish which presented various paths of motion (e.g. *girl running down slide, girl running up hill*). They found bidirectional lexical influence; the bilinguals used more manner verbs in their Spanish than the monolinguals did and more path verbs in their English than the English-speaking monolinguals. However, at the lexical-grammatical interface (choosing whether to include modifiers and prepositions to express motion along with the verb) they found influence from the L1 to the L2 only.

1.10   Conclusions

In this chapter, we have considered how to best define bilingualism, as well as the need to construct better instruments so that we can accurately classify bilinguals for both research and educational purposes. We have also discussed whether comparing monolingual speakers to bilingual speakers is a fair way to assess their competence and proficiency and whether ultimate linguistic attainment can ever be the same for both populations, as well as the role that age plays in determining it.

Differences in developmental outcomes between monolinguals and bilinguals will continue to be explored in the next two chapters. As we will see in Chapter 2 and expand on in Chapter 3, we have gained new insights into the effect of age and variable input on development from recent cross-disciplinary research, including neurolinguistic investigation on the neural consequence of different types of bilingual exposure, as well as psycholinguistic research which compares grammatical outcomes for monolingual native speakers and heritage speakers of Spanish.

2 Bilingual brains, bilingual minds

In this chapter, we examine how bilingualism affects the minds and brains of users of more than one language. Recent research in this area suggests that the continual cross-linguistic interaction that bilinguals experience at the lexical, syntactic, and phonological levels discussed in Chapters 1 and 3 enhances cognitive abilities related to attentional focus and inhibitory control, referred to as executive function skills. In turn, executive function abilities have important consequences for the development of literacy and academic ability in bilingual children. In addition, we discuss findings regarding the neuroanatomical consequences of bilingualism, and what is known about how these relate to the linguistic and cognitive experiences of bilinguals. While we highlight research conducted on Spanish-speaking bilinguals, we also include important findings from studies investigating bilingual speakers of other languages.

2.1 Bilingualism from the perspectives of neuroscience, cognitive psychology, and linguistics

Scientists approach the study of bilingualism in the mind and brain from various disciplines, each of which uses its own methodologies and theoretical frameworks. Neuroscientists examine how multilingualism affects the structure or activation of brain regions by using magnetic resonance imaging to investigate the density of gray matter in monolinguals versus bilinguals, for instance Mechelli, Crinion, Noppeney, O'Doherty, Ashburner, Frackowiak, and Price (2004), or comparing patterns of activation in the brains of monolinguals and bilinguals using neuroimaging techniques such as fMRI, MEG, PET, and EEG. Cognitive psychologists and psycholinguists investigate how bilinguals process language in real time via methods such as eye tracking and reaction-time measures. For example, psycholinguists use reaction-time tasks to measure how quickly bilinguals can name cognates in their two languages compared to words that are non-cognates (Costa, Caramazza, and Sebastian-Galles 2000). Linguists study how bilingualism affects linguistic knowledge via phenomena such as code-switching and language change, using grammaticality judgments, phonemic discrimination tasks, natural speech analyses, and corpus studies (among other methods) to carry out their research.

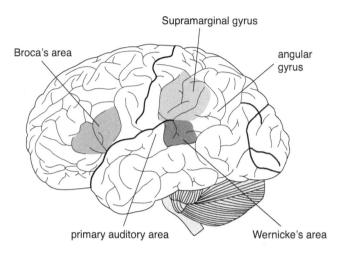

Figure 2.1 *Broca's and Wernicke's areas (from the Dana Foundation website)*

While each of these approaches has made important contributions to our knowledge of discrete aspects of bilingualism, how these perspectives connect to each other is not fully understood. For example, how can the study of the brain contribute to our understanding of linguistic primitives such as morphemes, for bilinguals and monolinguals alike? While there is psycholinguistic evidence that the mind encodes the morphological structure of words (e.g., Shapiro and Caramazza 2003; Rastle, Davis, and New 2004), we do not yet know how morphemes are represented at the neural level. This is not surprising given that, as Chomsky (2000: 14) points out, "the neural basis for the remarkable behavior of bees also remains a mystery." Yet most researchers assume that one day these connections will be identified and understood. Even those who claim that investigating computational properties of the human mind is unbiological in the sense that these computations could someday be performed by a computer rather than a human brain believe that "in finding the program of the human mind, one can expect biological and cognitive approaches to complement one another" (Block 1995: 390).

2.2   The representation of language in the brain

Research over the past two decades has helped clarify how language is processed in the brain and how it is represented at a neural level. Since the late nineteenth century, Broca's and Wernicke's areas on the left hemisphere have been implicated in speech comprehension and production, based on studies of patients who suffered from aphasia, or language loss, after brain injuries. These areas can be seen in Figure 2.1.

However, recent findings have made it clear that speech perception and production rely on many additional brain regions as well. Newer models of

(a)

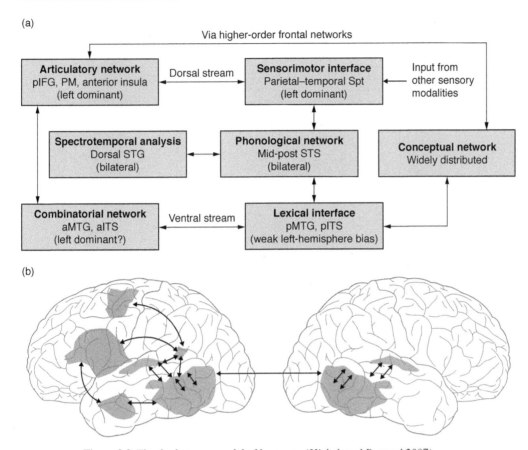

Figure 2.2 *The dual-stream model of language (Hickok and Poeppel 2007)*

speech processing include areas of cortical tissue linking Broca's and Wernicke's areas with the auditory and motor cortices. In one such model, Hickok and Poeppel (2007) proposed that there are dual pathways for speech perception, a dorsal and a ventral path involving both hemispheres, similar to models that have been proposed for visual processing (Milner and Goodale 1992). According to this model, depicted in the diagram in Figure 2.2, the earliest acoustic processing takes place bilaterally (in both hemispheres) in the superior temporal gyrus (STG), an area which houses Wernicke's area and the primary auditory cortex on the left hemisphere. Next, bilateral phonological processing occurs in the superior temporal sulcus (STS). Finally, speech processing follows two distinct pathways: the dorsal stream, which is strongly left-hemisphere dominant, connects sensory or phonological information to articulatory motor areas, enabling speech articulation and supporting phonological short-term memory (Hickok 2009); the ventral stream, which enables speech comprehension, matches sensory or phonological information to semantic–lexical representations.

Figure 2.3 *EEG recording (Wikipedia Commons)*

2.2.1   A brief introduction to neurolinguistic and neuroimaging methods

Advances in neuroimaging technology allow us unprecedented access to the workings of the bilingual brain. The methods used in most of the research discussed in this chapter include EEG, MEG, and fMRI. While all three are very safe, non-invasive methods, they differ considerably in terms of whether they can measure temporal changes in brain activity (EEG and MEG) or areas of the brain that become active as a result of experimental stimuli (fMRI). In a nutshell, EEG and MEG are very good for investigating when brain activity is taking place, and fMRI is better for discovering where it is occurring.

An electroencephalogram, or EEG, is a recording of the brain's electrical activity made with electrodes placed directly on the scalp. An image of a research participant wearing an EEG net can be seen in Figure 2.3.

Compared to other methods used for recording brain activity, EEG is relatively inexpensive, and since it tolerates movement it can be used with participants of all ages, including infants. It also provides excellent temporal resolution, meaning that it allows for fine-grained analyses of when different parts of the sentence are processed. The neural reaction to a particular experimental stimulus is called an Event-Related Potential (ERP), and this reaction produces a wave in the EEG recording with a characteristic amplitude and latency. Sentences which are semantically anomalous, such as the one shown in Figure 2.4, produce an effect known as the N400, or a negative peak seen 400 milliseconds after the stimulus is presented. This effect is illustrated in Figure 2.4, part (a), by the waveform

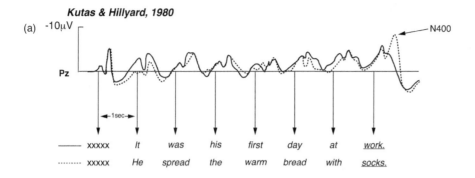

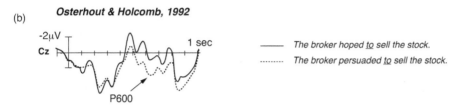

Figure 2.4 *N400 versus P600 effects (figure reprinted from Kuperberg 2007)*

accompanying the sentence *He spread the warm bread with socks* (Kutas and Hillyard 1980). In contrast, sentences which are ungrammatical produce an effect known as the P600, a positive waveform at around 600 milliseconds after the presentation of the syntactically unacceptable part of the sentence, such as the missing indirect object in the sentence *The broker persuaded to sell the stock* (Osterhout and Holcomb 1992) in Figure 2.4, part (b). P600 effects can also be produced by garden path sentences which are difficult to parse and require reinterpretation on the part of the listener/reader, such as *The broker persuaded to sell the stock was tall* (Osterhout and Holcomb 1992).

However, EEG suffers from the disadvantage of poor spatial resolution. Magnetoencephalography (MEG) is a method which measures the magnetic field produced by electrical activity in the brain, has better spatial resolution than EEG, and like EEG has excellent temporal resolution. However, MEG requires much more expensive equipment to operate than EEG, including a special scanner, as seen in Figure 2.5, as well as a room that is magnetically shielded.

fMRI (functional magnetic resonance imaging) has excellent spatial resolution, and can measure a region of interest in the brain with a few voxels (voxels are three-dimensional pixels). Unlike EEG or MEG, fMRI measures hemodynamic activity (oxygenated blood flow) in different regions of the brain, rather than electrical activity. Because the fMRI scanner uses a one-ton magnet to measure changes in blood flow, research participants lie on a gurney which is retracted into the scanner, as shown in Figure 2.6. In addition, participants must lie completely still while the scan is taking place.

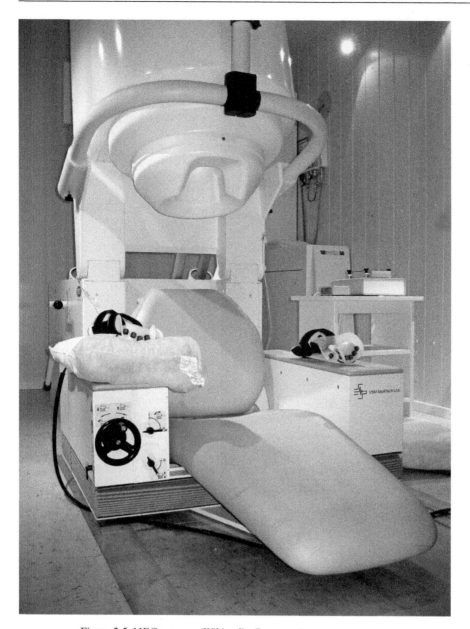

Figure 2.5 *MEG scanner (Wikipedia Commons)*

Because any movement can interfere with the fMRI signal, this method is
not well suited for use with infants and children (unless they are asleep). Other
disadvantages to using fMRI include the high cost of the scanner, which must be
housed in a magnetically protected room. In addition, unlike EEGs or MEG, the
fMRI scanner is extremely noisy when it is in operation, and as a result may not
be well suited to linguistic tasks which require good auditory input.

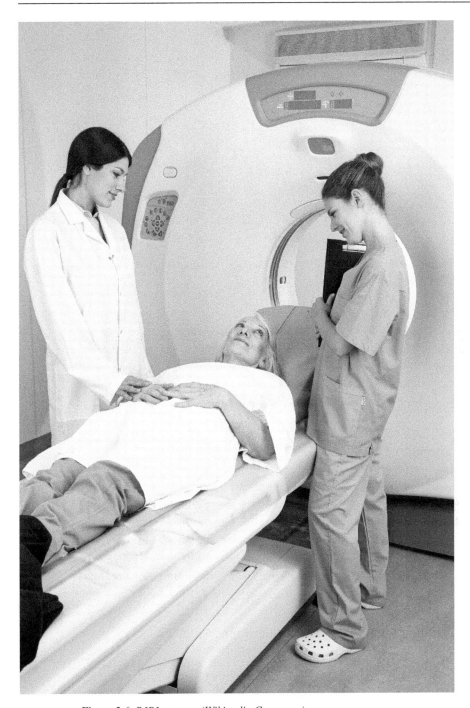

Figure 2.6 *fMRI scanner (Wikipedia Commons)*

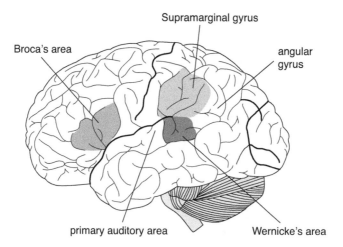

Figure 2.7 *The supramarginal and angular gyri, housed in the inferior parietal cortex (copyleft http://thebrain.mcgill.ca/)*

PET (Positron emission tomography) is a neuroimaging technique which uses a scanner to detect gamma rays emitted by a tracer containing a radioactive isotope which is injected into the participant's bloodstream. The data collected by the scanner allow a three-dimensional image to be created of brain activity during language tasks by mapping blood and oxygen flow to regions of the brain, as well as the metabolism of glucose by different brain areas.

2.3   The bilingual brain

Bilingualism influences the location and intensity of cortical activation during language processing and also changes the neural density of certain regions of the brain. The degree to which we see these effects in bilinguals is modulated by the age of acquisition of the second language, the degree of proficiency in both languages and the amount of continual exposure to each language. In the following sections, we review the evidence for bilingual–monolingual brain differences.

2.3.1   Neuroanatomical differences between bilinguals and monolinguals

Several studies have found that bilingual brains show greater density of gray matter than the brains of monolinguals in the inferior parietal cortex (Mechelli *et al.* 2004; Mechelli, Price, Friston, Ashburner 2005; Green, Crinion, and Price 2007), an area of the brain adjacent to Wernicke's area as well as the auditory and visual cortices. As shown in Figure 2.7, the inferior parietal cortex houses the supramarginal gyrus and the angular gyrus, and is involved in speech production (Geranmayeh, Brownett, Leech, Beckmann, Woodhead, and Wise 2012) and lexical learning (Lee, Devlin, Shakeshaft, Stewart, Brennan, Glensman, Pitcher, Crinion, Mechelli, Frackowiak, Green, and Price 2007) as well as semantic and phonological processing (Vigneau, Beaucousin, Hervé, Duffau, Crivello, Houdé, Mazoyer, and Tzourio-Mazoyer 2006). To examine the density of gray matter in certain areas of the brain, a technique called voxel-based morphometry is used which compares the density of brain regions voxel by voxel in scans obtained through structural magnetic resonance imaging.

The brain's gray matter contains neurons (as opposed to white matter, which mostly consists of myelinated connective tissue), and its global density is correlated with the normal working of cognitive abilities such as semantic memory and short-term memory (Taki, Kinomura, Sato, Goto, Wu, Kawashima, and Fukuda 2011). Gray-matter density in particular regions of the brain is correlated with expertise in specific domains, such as navigational abilities in taxicab drivers (Maguire, Gadian, Johnrude, Good, Ashburner, Frackowiak, and Frith 2000), keyboarding skills in musicians (Gaser and Schlaug 2003), mathematical thinking in professional mathematicians (Aydin, Ucar, Oguz, Okur, Agayev, Unal, and Ozturk 2007), and mindfulness meditation abilities in expert meditators (Hölzel, Carmody, Vangel, Congleton, Yerramsetti, Gard, and Lazar 2011).

Mechelli *et al.* (2004) analyzed the gray matter density of bilinguals and monolinguals and in groups of bilinguals with varying degrees of proficiency. In two studies, they compared gray matter density in twenty-five English-speaking monolinguals with twenty-five bilinguals who had learned a second language before age 5 and thirty-three bilinguals who had learned a second language after age 10 and who had been using both languages with regularity. In a second study of Italian–English bilinguals, they also examined how language proficiency and age of acquisition correlated with gray matter density in the inferior parietal cortex. Mechelli *et al.* found that bilinguals who had acquired their second language early in development and were highly proficient in both languages had the greatest density of gray matter in this region, and bilinguals who learned the second language later in life and had low proficiency had the least.

Green *et al.* (2007) discovered that Chinese–English bilinguals had greater gray-matter density than English monolinguals in the posterior supramarginal gyrus, which is a subregion of the same area of the brain where Mechelli *et al.* (2004) found greater gray-matter density in bilinguals. The posterior supramarginal gyrus is implicated in lexical learning and may underlie the ability to pair word sounds with meanings (Green *et al.* 2007). In monolinguals, denser gray matter in this area of the brain is correlated with larger vocabulary size, but not greater verbal fluency (Lee *et al.* 2007). In light of Lee *et al.*'s findings, Green *et al.* (2007) suggested the increase in gray-matter density discovered in bilinguals might be the result of bilinguals having a larger combined vocabulary than monolinguals do in each language.

Bilingualism has also been found to improve subcortical auditory processing. Krizman, Marian, Shook, Skoe, and Kraus (2012) used EEG to compare the

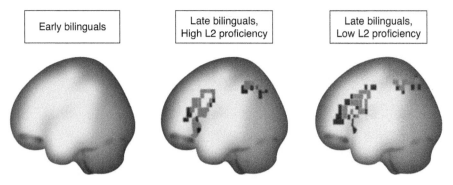

Figure 2.8 *Neural activation during grammatical processing in early versus late bilinguals (from Perani and Abutalebi 2005)*

response in the auditory brainstem to the fundamental frequency of speech sounds in Spanish–English bilingual adolescents and in English-speaking monolinguals. They found enhanced auditory perception of the sound [da] in the bilingual participants relative to the monolingual ones, especially when the target sound was presented against a competing auditory background of babbling speakers rather than in a quiet condition. In addition, the bilingual participants in Krizman *et al.*'s experiment outperformed the monolinguals on tasks measuring selective visual and auditory attention. The researchers noted that this enhanced auditory ability is also found in musicians with extensive training (ibid).

2.3.2   Cortical activation during linguistic tasks in bilinguals

Recent research has revealed that bilingualism affects the extent to which language areas of the cortex are activated during language processing. Both children and adults show greater right hemisphere involvement at early stages of L2 acquisition, and greater left hemisphere activity as proficiency increases (Paradis 1996; Perani, Paulesu, Galles, Dupoux, Dehaene, Bettinardi, and Mehler 1998; Fabbro 2001a; Indefrey 2006; Leonard, Torres, Travis, Brown, Hagler, Dale, Elman, and Halgren 2011). In addition, bilinguals show more extensive cortical activation during language tasks in both hemispheres than monolinguals do, and these effects are modulated by age of acquisition, proficiency, and continued exposure. The general finding is that bilinguals show *less* cortical activation (both in terms of intensity of activation and how widespread the areas activated are) in languages in which they have high levels of proficiency, have acquired early in life, or have been exposed to more (Kim, Relkin, Lee, and Hirsch 1997; Abutalebi, Cappa, and Perani 2001; Wartenburger, Heekeren, Abutalebi, Cappa, Villringer, and Perani 2003; Perani and Abutalebi 2005; Liu, Hu, Guo, and Peng 2010). Languages in which bilinguals are less proficient, which they have acquired late or to which they are not exposed as much cause activation in a larger area of cortex. This difference is illustrated in Figure 2.8, which depicts patterns of

(a) 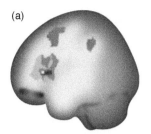   (b)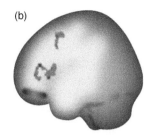

Figure 2.9 *Activation during lexical retrieval in Spanish–Catalan bilinguals (Perani et al. 2003)*

activation during grammatical processing in early bilinguals, late bilinguals with high L2 proficiency, and late bilinguals with low L2 proficiency, as revealed by fMRI scans.

The extent of cortical activation in multilingual speakers is also affected by how much the speaker is currently exposed to each language. Perani, Abutalebi, Paulesu, Brambati, Scifo, Cappa, and Fazio (2003) found that, for early Spanish–Catalan and Catalan–Spanish bilinguals, the extent of cortical activation during a lexical processing task was influenced by the amount of current exposure that the bilinguals had to each language, as seen in Figure 2.9. Although these participants had learned both languages in early childhood (acquiring either Spanish or Catalan at age 3) and had high levels of proficiency in both languages, they had greater ongoing exposure as adults to one of the two languages, which was also their first language. fMRI scans showed that lexical processing in the second language in these speakers activated a greater area of cortex (a) than the language that was learned first and that they had more exposure to in their daily lives (b).

Most researchers assume that the increased activation seen in the less proficient language of bilinguals reflects greater processing demands faced by bilinguals in language tasks, due to frequency effects (less input in the weaker language) and to cross-linguistic competition from the stronger language (Liu *et al.* 2010; Jones, Green, Grogan, Pliatsikas, Filippopolitis, Ali, Lee, Ramsden, Gazarian, Prejawa, Seghier, and Price 2012). This analysis is consistent with the *neural efficiency hypothesis*, which was first developed to account for the finding that people with a higher IQ consume less cortical glucose than individuals with a lower IQ while performing various cognitive tasks involving attentional control and learning new skills (Haier, Siegel, Nuechterlein, Hazlett, Wu, Paek, and Buchsbaum 1988; Haier, Siegel, Tang, Abel, and Buchsbaum 1992). Subsequent research has discovered that there are also individual differences in cortical activation resulting from expertise and experience in a particular area, such as reading (Prat, Keller, and Just 2007; Prat and Just 2011), navigation in taxicab drivers (Grabner, Stern, and Neubauer 2000) and motor skills in athletes (Del Percio, Rossini, Marzano, Iacoboni, Infarinato, Aschieri, and Eusebi 2008). Across these domains, individuals display less cortical activation in performing tasks in which they are experts than while performing novel or less familiar activities.

2.3.3   Other neurolinguistic effects of bilingualism

There is evidence that bilingualism has a different impact on discrete areas of linguistic competence, and that these effects are influenced not only by age of acquisition but also by proficiency and exposure to both languages.

Syntactic and semantic effects

Several researchers have argued that grammatical processing is more susceptible than semantic processing to age-of-acquisition effects in differing patterns of cortical activation. In a study of the English L2 of heritage speakers of Chinese, Weber-Fox and Neville (1996) found that Chinese–English bilinguals were less accurate than monolingual English speakers in judging the grammaticality of English sentences that tested knowledge of phrase structure, the specificity constraint, and the subjacency constraint, which is a syntactic constraint on movement. Deficits occurred across all sentence types with ages of acquisition of English as early as 4 to 6 years and, in the case of the subjacency constraint, as early as 1 to 3 years of age. Age of acquisition was a stronger predictor of performance than years of experience. Further, ERP data from the same participants revealed that patterns of brain activation for syntactic violations also differed from that of monolinguals even in individuals who had acquired English as early as 1 to 3 years. In contrast, only participants who had acquired English after age 11 exhibited distinct ERP reactions to semantic violations.

Wartenburger, Heekeren, Abutalebi, Cappa, Villringer, and Perani (2003) examined the effects of age of acquisition and language proficiency in an fMRI study of three groups of Italian–German bilinguals: early high-proficiency acquirers, late high-proficiency acquirers and late low-proficiency acquirers. They found that during grammatical processing in L2, both late acquisition groups showed significantly more activation of Broca's area, whereas during tasks involving semantic processing, the high-proficiency groups had comparable patterns of activation, regardless of age of acquisition. Wartenburger *et al.* argued that their results supported the hypothesis that the mechanisms underpinning grammatical learning and processing are served by the implicit (procedural) memory system, whereas semantic learning relies on explicit (declarative) memory and knowledge (Ullman 2001, 2004).

Neurolinguistic effects of bilingualism on morphological processing

Behavioral and neurophysiological evidence suggest that age at which a second language is acquired affects the processing of its morphology in bilinguals from a very early point in development. Lehtonen, Hultén, Rodríguez-Fornells, Cunillera, Tuomainen, and Laine (2012) used EEG and behavioral measures to compare morphological processing in Finnish-speaking monolinguals and in bilingual Finnish–Swedish speakers who had learned both languages before age 7, had balanced proficiency and continual exposure to both languages.

Finnish is a highly inflected language with rich nominal morphology, and mono-lingual Finnish speakers show a change in neural activation (N400) that reflects the morphological complexity of a word. Furthermore, in these speakers there was greater activation for low-frequency highly inflected words than for high-frequency highly inflected ones, suggesting that some commonly used, highly inflected words may be stored as a single unit because they are more accessible. In contrast, bilingual English–Finnish speakers did not show greater activation for high-frequency inflected words, suggesting that in bilinguals they may not be stored as a single unit, but rather must be processed by decomposing the word into its morphological pieces. This suggests that the greater exposure that monolin-guals have compared to bilinguals enables them to store complex morphological forms more efficiently for retrieval (i.e., as a single form).

Zawiszewski, Gutiérrez, Fernández, and Laka (2011) compared ERP responses to ergative case violations in Euskara L1 and early child L2 speakers. They found that bilingual adult L1 Euskara speakers and early L2 speakers who had learned Euskara at age 3 showed different ERP responses than Euskara L1 speakers towards sentences with ergative case violations such as (2), in which the subject is missing ergative case. (1) shows the grammatical counterpart of sentence (2).

Grammatical
(1)   *Goizean ogia erosi dut <u>nik</u> dendan.*
        Goiz-ean   ogia   erosi   dut   <u>ni-k</u>   denda-n.
        morning-in bread.DET bought have I-ERG shop-in
        'This morning I bought bread in the shop.'

Ungrammatical
(2)   *Goizean ogia erosi dut <u>ni</u> denda-n.*
        Goiz-ean   ogia   erosi   dut   <u>ni</u>   denda-n
        Morning-in bread.DET bought have I-Ø shop-in
        'This morning I bought bread in the shop.'

The early L2 speakers also performed significantly worse than the L1 speakers on a task requiring them to judge the grammaticality of sentences with ergative case violations.

Neurological effects of bilingualism on phonological processing

Behavioral studies have demonstrated that infants begin life with the ability to perceive any phonemic contrast, regardless of whether it forms part of their native phonemic repertoire or not. For example, children acquiring Spanish can initially perceive the contrast between /v/ and /b/, even though this sound contrast is not used in Spanish. However, by the end of their first year, babies develop specialized perception of the phonemic contrasts of their native language, and lose the ability to detect non-native contrasts (Werker and Tees 1984; Kuhl, Williams, Lacerda, Stevens, and Lindblom 1992). At the neurological level, children and adults have been found to show a negative mismatch response when detecting phonemic contrasts (Näätanen 2001; Friederici, Friedrich, and Weber 2002, Dehaene-Lambertz and Gliga 2004). In infants under 1 year of age, a positive response to phonemic contrasts has been found that changes to an adult-like negative response at around 1 year of age (Rivera-Gaxiola, Silva-Pereyra and Kuhl, 2005; Shafer, Yu, and Datta 2011).

Children who are bilingual from infancy must fine-tune their phonemic inventory in two native languages instead of one, and to accomplish this, they must learn to discriminate between their languages as well as to distinguish the phonemes of their native languages from other sounds. Monolingual newborns can distinguish between languages of different rhythmic classes, i.e., languages with syllable-based prosody such as Spanish and stress-based prosody such as English, but cannot distinguish between two languages of the same rhythmic class, such as Spanish vs. Catalan or English vs. Dutch. By 4 and a half months, Spanish–Catalan bilingual children – as well as monolingual children learning these languages – can distinguish between their languages, despite sharing a rhythmic class (Ramus, Nespor, and Mehler 1999). At 8 months, bilingual infants can perceive more fine-grained phonological contrasts in their two languages, such as the vowel distinction /e/-/ɛ/ in Spanish and Catalan (Albareda-Castellot, Pons, and Sebastián-Gallés 2011) and Spanish and English (Sundara and Scutellaro 2011).

In an EEG study comparing phonemic discrimination in infants who were Spanish–English bilinguals from birth with English monolinguals, Shafer *et al.* (2011) found that the bilingual infants had a negative response with a higher amplitude wave than the monolinguals at 6, 14, and 29 months, but that this difference disappeared at around 30 months. They interpreted this result to indicate that, initially, phonemic perception required greater effort for the bilingual children than for the monolingual ones. An fMRI study comparing Spanish–English sequential bilingual children and monolingual children found different patterns of cortical activation in the two groups during speech perception, even though the groups behaved similarly at the behavioral level (Archila-Suerte, Zevin, Ramos, and Hernández 2013). The bilingual children were L1 speakers of Spanish who had begun learning English at age 5. Whereas the monolingual children (age 6 to 10 years) and the younger bilinguals (age 6 to 8) showed activation in brain areas associated with phonological processing (bilateral superior temporal gyrus), the older bilingual children also showed activation in a network of areas related to attentional control and working memory (bilateral middle frontal gyrus and bilateral inferior parietal lobule). In the monolingual children, the younger group (6 to 8 years) showed more intense activation and recruited more areas for processing native speech than older monolingual children (9 to 10 years) and monolingual adults, both the older and younger bilingual children showed more activation during speech processing than bilingual adults, and the older bilingual children recruited more brain areas for processing speech sounds than either young bilingual children or bilinguals adults. Archila-Suerte *et al.* (2013: 61) interpret their results as evidence that while younger inexperienced bilingual children assimilate L2 speech via the bilateral STG, older more experienced bilingual children increase their attention to sounds and make use of their working memory to retain phonological information via the bilateral inferior parietal lobe and middle frontal gyrus. Activating a network of executive functions helps older bilingual children enhance their perception of non-native sounds.

There is ample behavioral evidence that L2 phonological acquisition is much more difficult for older children and adults than for young children. At beginning stages of second language acquisition, adults transfer phonological patterns from the L1 to the L2 (Flege and Davidian 1984), then go on to develop a second language phonological system which usually is heavily influenced by the L1. While many studies have shown that age of acquisition (AoA) is a critical factor in deciding how native-like the phonology of an L2 speaker is, learning a second language early does not guarantee native-like articulation. Research has shown that even children who acquire two languages from birth can develop a discernable "foreign" accent in one of their languages if they use it less than the other (Flege 1988) or do not develop a high level of proficiency in it (Archila-Suerte *et al.* 2012). Archila-Suerte *et al.* (2012) compared performance by monolingual English speakers (n = 28) and bilingual Spanish–English speakers (n = 70) on phonemic discrimination task in which they had to distinguish between four English vowels. The bilingual participants were divided into three categories by age of acquisition of English, and each category was further separated into two groups according to whether they had high or low proficiency in English: early bilinguals (AoA less than 5 years), intermediate bilinguals (AoA 6 to 9 years), and late bilinguals (AoA 10 to 24 years). While none of the bilingual groups perceived the phonemic contrasts in exactly the same way as the monolinguals, both age of acquisition and proficiency level had an effect on their ability to discriminate between the four English vowel contrasts, as shown in Figure 2.10.

An fMRI study by Archila-Suerte *et al.* (2012) found neurophysiological correlates to the behavioral effects produced by age of acquisition and language proficiency in patterns of cortical activation during the same English vowel discrimination task. While bilinguals with an early AoA recruited areas associated with auditory processing during the task (the superior temporal gyrus and inferior frontal gyrus), bilinguals with high proficiency in the L2 (regardless of AoA) also showed activation in the frontal and parietal lobes, brain regions associated with paying attention and perceiving phonetic change (ibid).

Cortical activation during lexical processing in bilinguals

Several studies have found that lexical processing is less affected by age of acquisition and proficiency effects than syntax, morphology, and phonology. English–French bilinguals with high proficiency in their L2 (French) and who had acquired French after 5 years of age demonstrated similar patterns of activation in both their languages during a word repetition task and word retrieval

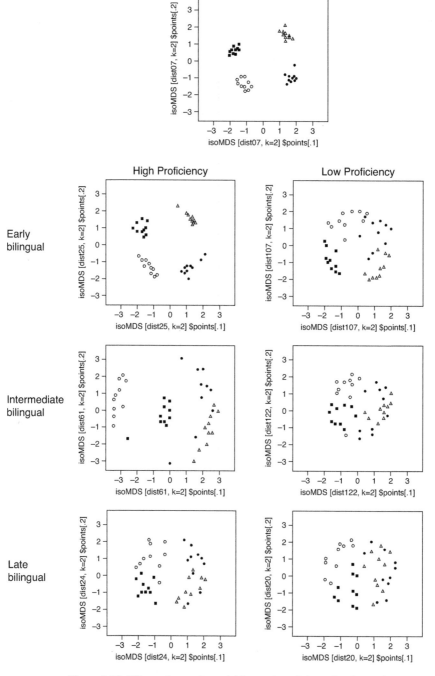

Figure 2.10 *Effects of age of acquisition and proficiency levels on phonemic discrimination in English (Archila-Suerte* et al. *2012)*

tasks in PET studies (Klein, Zatorre, Milner, Meyer, and Evans 1994; Klein, Milner, Zatorre, Meyer, and Evans 1995). This was also found to be the case in Chinese–English bilinguals with high proficiency in their second language, English, despite the script differences between the languages (Chee, Tan, and Thiel 1999). In an fMRI study, Chee *et al.* found identical areas of cortex activated in a word generation task in two groups of Chinese L1 bilinguals: a group who had learned English before age 6, and a group who had learned English after age 12, despite differences in the age of acquisition of their participants' second language.

2.4   Cognitive consequences of bilingualism

Se pelean en mi mente (They fight in my mind) – Camarón de la Isla, 1974

In addition to the neural effects of bilingualism discussed in the previous section, using more than one language changes the lexical and syntactic processing of both languages in bilinguals. The differences between language processing in monolinguals and bilinguals lead to important cognitive consequences for bilinguals, including enhanced performances on measures of executive function and working memory relative to monolinguals. The next section discusses recent research findings regarding the impact of bilingualism on language processing and cognition, and what the sources of these effects may be.

2.4.1   Lexical processing in bilinguals

Research on lexical processing in bilinguals suggests that the lexicons of bilinguals are highly interconnected. Furthermore, bilinguals' lexicons are accessed non-selectively, meaning that in retrieving a word from one language, bilinguals also activate words from the non-target language. While some tasks administered in a bilingual person's dominant first language can show evidence of selective access of the L1, there is strong evidence for non-selectivity: "the presence of nonselectivity at all levels of planning spoken utterances renders the system itself fundamentally nonselective" (Kroll, Bobb, and Wodniecka 2006: 132). There is evidence from a variety of studies supporting the hypothesis that lexical access is non-selective in bilinguals, including research on auditory word recognition (Spivey and Marian 1999; Lagrou, Hartsuiker and Duyck 2011), visual word recognition (Dijkstra and Van Heuven 2002; Duyck 2005; Boukrina 2012), cross-linguistic lexical priming (Altarriba 1992; Costa, Miozzo, and Caramazza 1999) and translation tasks (De Groot 1993; De Groot, Dannenburg, and Van Hell 1994). Non-selectivity even occurs across modalities, in accessing the lexicons of bilinguals who use spoken and signed languages (Morford, Wilkinson, Villwock, Piñar, and Kroll 2011). There is also evidence of non-selectivity in phonological access (Costa, Colome, Gomez, and Sebastian-Galles

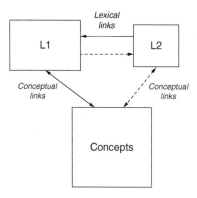

Figure 2.11 *Kroll and Stewart's Revised Hierarchical Model (from Kroll and Tokowicz 2005)*

2003), and syntactic processing in bilinguals (Meijer and Fox Tree 2003; Hartsuiker, Pickering, and Veltkamp 2004; Desmet and Declercq 2006; Dussias and Sagarra 2007).

The influential *Revised Hierarchical Model* (Kroll and Stewart 1994) proposed that a bilingual has two separate lexicons which are linked to a common conceptual store that is shared across languages. According to this model, translation equivalents in the two languages are directly connected, and in beginning L2 acquirers' access to concepts is mediated by the L1, as shown in Figure 2.11. In more proficient L2 learners, meaning is accessed by the L2 lexicon without going through the L1.

The *Revised Hierarchical Model* (RHM) has been very useful in conceptualizing bilingual lexical processing, and has spurred a great deal of investigation in this area. Some of the more recent research results, however, are challenging for the RHM's assumptions that the lexicons of the L1 and L2 are divided into separate stores, and that L2 words are strongly tied to semantic equivalents in the L1 (Brysbaert and Duyck 2010). As Brybaert and Duyck (2010: 364) remark, the words from the two languages of a bilingual behave "very much as though they are words of the same language, interacting with each other as part of the word identification process." The *Bilingual Interactive Model* (BIA) (Dijkstra, Van Heuven, and Grainger 1998; Van Heuven, Dijkstra, and Grainger 1998) and the BIA+ (Dijkstra and Van Heuven 2002) – seen in Figures 2.12 and 2.13, respectively – are adaptations of an existing connectionist model of monolingual language processing (McClelland and Rummelhart 1981) with added nodes for the second language of a bilingual.

The revised BIA (BIA+) includes semantic and phonological and visual input, as well as a task decision component to capture the fact that language access and inhibition can be influenced by the type of task that bilingual participants are asked to perform or the context in which they are speaking. According to this model, lexical items from both languages that match orthographic or phonological input are activated; for example, the word *pan* would activate homograph counterparts

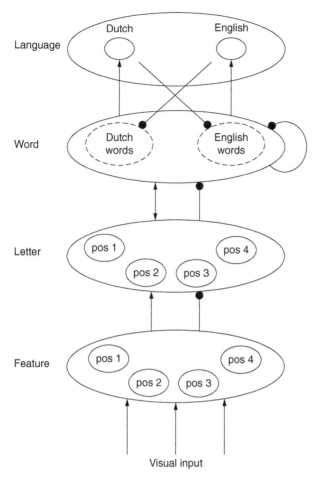

Figure 2.12 *The Bilingual Interactive Activation Model (BIA) (Van Heuven, Dijkstra and Grainger 1998)*

in both Spanish (*bread*) and English (*cooking instrument*). Lexical items from the two languages are tagged to different language nodes, and words tied to the same node (L1 or L2) increase activation in other words of the same node while concurrently inhibiting words tied to the other language node, thereby facilitating the selection of words from the correct language.

As an aside, while most models of bilingual processing assume that there is a common conceptual store shared across a bilingual's languages, there is evidence that at least some concepts are language-specific from research on bilingualism and linguistic relativity. Speakers of languages with grammatical gender such as Spanish where *la taza* 'the mug' is feminine, whereas *el vaso* 'the glass' is masculine, attribute male or female voices or characteristics to objects depending on their grammatical gender (Sera, Berge, and Castillo 1994). Bilingual children (Bassetti 2007) and adults (Forbes, Poulin-Dubois, Rivero,

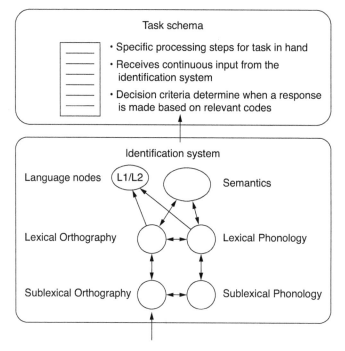

Figure 2.13 *The Bilingual Interactive Activation Plus Model (Dijkstra and Van Heuven 2002)*

and Sera 2008) who speak two languages with grammatical gender attribute voices and qualities consistent with the gender in each language, even if the genders of objects do not coincide across the languages. However, if only one of the languages has grammatical gender, speakers attribute gendered qualities consistent with the grammatical gender of language A to the words of language B, even though they do not have grammatical gender in language B (Forbes *et al.* 2008).

Along with the evidence for bilinguals' non-selective access to their lexicons, research has uncovered differences between bilinguals and monolinguals in lexical processing speed and facility. Bilinguals perform more slowly than monolinguals in picture-naming tasks (Gollan, Montoya, Fennema-Notestine, and Morris 2005; Gollan, Fennema-Notestine, Montoya, and Jernigan 2007; Bialystok, Craik and Luk 2008; Gollan, Montoya, Cera, and Sandoval 2008; Bialystok 2009), even when tested in their dominant language (Gollan and Acenas 2004; Ivanova and Costa 2008; Gollan *et al.* 2008). Bilinguals also experience tip of the tongue (TOT) states more often than monolinguals when retrieving words that are non-cognates, but perform similarly to monolinguals when retrieving cognates (Gollan and Acenas 2004). Gollan and her colleagues have proposed the *Weaker Links Hypothesis* to account for the disadvantage that bilinguals seem to experience in accessing their lexicons (Gollan and Acenas 2004; Gollan *et al.*

2005). According to this hypothesis, because bilinguals hear the words of each language less frequently than monolinguals do, the lexical connections between sound and meaning should be weaker in bilinguals than in monolinguals.

In contrast, the *Inhibitory Control Model* (Green 1998) posits that the bilingual disadvantage in lexical access stems from bilinguals' need to inhibit one of their languages during production, and from the fact that the inhibitory cost is higher for a bilingual's dominant language. According to this influential model, lemmas (lexical concepts attached to a particular syntactic configuration) compete from both of a bilingual's languages for selection during language comprehension and production. Lemmas in each language are tagged as belonging to one language or the other, and when a bilingual uses one of his/her languages, the lemmas tagged as belonging to the other language are actively suppressed, or inhibited.

The nature of this inhibitory mechanism is under debate, as well as whether or not there is a single locus for inhibitory control of a bilingual's languages (Kroll *et al.* 2006). As Gollan *et al.* (2008) noted, while the *weaker links hypothesis* provides an alternative mechanism to inter-linguistic competition in explaining slower lexical access in bilinguals, the two hypotheses are not mutually exclusive. However, the *Inhibitory Control Model* has the advantage that it can also account for the cognitive advantages demonstrated by bilinguals in non-verbal tasks involving inhibition, a subject which will be discussed further in Section 2.4.3.

Abutalebi and Green (2007) have proposed that cognitive inhibitory abilities in bilinguals rely on several different brain systems, principally the prefrontal cortex, but also including the inferior parietal cortex, the anterior cingulate cortex, and the basal ganglia. Their model can be seen in Figure 2.14.

Abutalebi and Green (2007) argue that this system of connected regions controls the language choice by regulating a single network which is shared by both of a bilingual's languages. Further, they suggest that the operation of the system depends in part on the bilingual person's degree of proficiency in the L2.

2.4.2   Syntactic processing in bilinguals

Studies of bilingual syntactic processing suggest that bilinguals and monolinguals do not parse sentences identically. Given evidence that monolingual speakers employ distinct strategies during sentence interpretation depending on their language (Bates, Devescovi, and D'Amico 1999) researchers investigated bilinguals' use of competing language-specific strategies to interpret sentences. Findings indicated that the direction of transfer in parsing strategies depended on age of acquisition of the L2, based on comparisons of strategy use in early and late bilinguals (Liu, Bates, and Li 1992). Some early bilinguals transferred parsing strategies from L1 to L2 as well as from L2 to L1 whereas others used language-specific strategies for Chinese (animacy), and English (word order). In contrast, the late bilinguals only showed evidence of transferring strategies from their L1 to their L2.

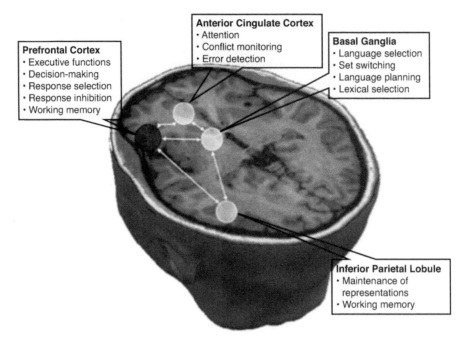

Figure 2.14 *The neural underpinnings of inhibitory control (Abutalebi and Green 2007)*

Research on the processing of sentences with ambiguously attached relative clauses has found evidence not only of transfer from L1 to L2 in late bilinguals, but also influence from the L2 to the L1 for late bilinguals immersed for many years in the L2 (Dussias and Sagarra 2007). In sentences with ambiguously attached relative clauses, there are cross-linguistic differences in speakers' preferences for which part of the sentence is modified by a sentence-final relative clause. For example, in the sentence *Brian knows the sister of the doctor who lives in Madrid*, the person who lives in Madrid could be the doctor or her sister. In English, speakers prefer the interpretation of the sentence in which *who lives in Madrid* refers to the doctor, whereas in Spanish, the preference is for *who lives in Madrid* to modify the sister (Cuetos and Mitchell 1988; Fernández 2003). An experiment on the attachment preferences of beginning French L2 learners whose first language was English found that they preferred the relative clause to modify the second noun in French, following an English-like pattern (Frenck-Mestre and Pynte, 1997). However, a series of experiments by Dussias (2001 2003, 2004) found differences in parsing preferences between Spanish–English bilinguals who had learned both languages before age 6 and were highly proficient in both languages and bilinguals who had acquired either Spanish or English as an L2 later in life. Whereas the early bilinguals did not show a preference for attaching the relative clause to either noun in either Spanish or English, the late L2 Spanish learners preferred the English-like interpretation in both languages (attachment to the first noun), whereas the late English L2 learners followed monolingual-like preferences for each language (the first noun in Spanish and the second in English). Dussias and Sagarra (2007) found that amount of exposure to the L2 changed the parsing preferences of highly proficient bilinguals. In an eye tracking experiment, they discovered that Spanish L1–English L2 bilinguals who had been immersed in an English-speaking environment for an average of seven years had English-like attachment preferences for sentences such as (4), namely they preferred attaching the relative clause to the second NP.

English

(3)   An armed robber shot the sister of the actor who was on the balcony.

Spanish

(4)   *Un ladrón armado le =*   *disparó   a   la   hermana   de-el*
           A robber armed CL.3SG.DAT =   shot   to   the   sister   of-the
           actor   que   estaba   en   el   balcón.
           actor   who   was   on   the   balcony
           'An armed robber shot the sister of the actor who was on the balcony.'

In contrast, Spanish L1–English L2 bilinguals with little exposure to an English-speaking environment preferred attaching the relative clause to the first NP, as did monolingual Spanish speakers.

A study with Dutch L1–English L2 bilinguals by Desmet and Declercq (2006) showed that attachment preferences for relative clauses can also be primed cross-linguistically. The participants in this study were native Dutch speakers living in Belgium who had studied English as a second language. In their experiments, subjects were asked to judge whether an ambiguous relative clause in English attached to the first or second noun after hearing a Dutch sentence in which the relative clause was clearly modifying either the first or second noun. The subjects followed the attachment patterns of the priming sentences in Dutch for the English targets.

Priming has also been used to detect which circumstances favor cross-linguistic influence in the syntax of adult bilinguals. Meijer and Fox Tree (2003) investigated cross-linguistic syntactic priming by presenting bilinguals with a target sentence in one language (Spanish or English) followed by a prime sentence in the other language and a distracter task. In the critical condition there was a switch in syntactic structure between the target and the prime sentence; the switch was in the order of the objects. For example, a switch would change *the waitress will bring the noisy customers a tray of drinks* into *the waitress will bring a tray of drinks to the noisy customers*. Participants were asked to recall the original target sentence aloud. The subjects were more likely to produce a syntactic switch during recall if a switch was presented in the prime sentence, thus providing evidence for syntactic influence between the languages.

Loebell and Bock (2003) also examined whether German L1–English L2 bilinguals were sensitive to priming across their languages. The participants were native speakers of German who had been living for at least two years in the United States and rated themselves as highly fluent in both languages. The researchers presented the participants with a prime sentence in one of the two languages, then asked their participants to translate the sentence into the other language. The sentences were either dative sentences, which exhibit the same word order in both languages, or passive sentences, which have a verb-final word order in German (6) but not in English, as seen in (5).

English
(5)   The floors are cleaned daily by the janitor.

German
(6)   *Die Böden werden täglich von dem Hausmeister gereinigt.*
         The floors are   daily by the janitor   cleaned.
         'The floors are cleaned by the janitor daily.'

The participants then described a picture in the other language. The results demonstrated that dative sentences served as a prime in either language, while the passive transitive sentences did not. Hartsuiker, Pickering, and Veltkamp (2004) further corroborated these conclusions by demonstrating that Spanish L1–English L2 bilinguals produced more passive sentences in English directly after hearing an unrelated passive sentence in Spanish. In Spanish and English passives have the same word order, in contrast with German and English. These findings suggest that bilinguals' languages are only susceptible to cross-linguistic priming for structures that share a common word order (Desmet and Duyck 2007).

Compared to the extensive work that has been done to model bilingual lexical processing, there is far less research on how to model the interaction between the grammars of a bilingual. De Bot (1992) developed the model of bilingual language processing (including grammatical processing) seen in Figure 12.5, based upon Levelt's (1989) model of monolingual speech processing.

While this model allows for a shared conceptual store and lexicon across languages, it is unclear how it could account for the strong evidence for cross-linguistic syntactic interaction found in recent research (Hartsuiker and Pickering 2008). Hartsuiker, Pickering, and Veltkamp (2004) proposed the model shown in Figure 2.16, in which in an English–Spanish bilingual, English (on the left) and Spanish lexical entries for the words *hit, chase, golpear* 'hit' and *perseguir* 'chase' would share nodes for "verb," "active," and "passive" across languages, thereby accounting for the fact that passive or active constructions can prime each other across languages.

However, this model does not account for the fact that active/passive sentences can produce different syntactic configurations across languages, and that cross-linguistic grammatical priming is only found when languages share a common word order for a syntactic representation (Bernolet *et al.* 2007; Salamoura and Williams 2007); this is true for typologically related and unrelated pairs, such as Korean and English (Shin and Christianson 2009). Further investigation is needed to devise a model of bilingual syntactic processing which takes into account cross-linguistic differences in the configuration of syntactic structure (word order and

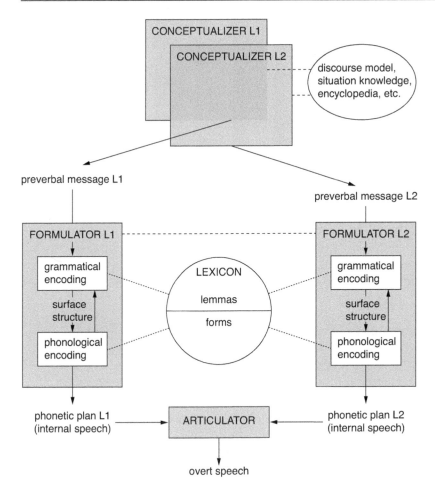

Figure 2.15 *De Bot's (1992) Bilingual Production Model (from Hartsuiker and Pickering 2008)*

branching direction, for example, which would need to be addressed in models of Quechua–Spanish or Basque–Spanish bilingualism).

2.4.3   Language separation, competition, and control

Children and adults who are bilingual from an early age are faster and more accurate than monolinguals in non-verbal measures of attentional control, also called executive function or executive control (Bialystok, Craik, Green, and Gollan 2009). This advantage emerges in infancy and persists throughout the lifetime (Kovács and Mehler 2009), and seems to protect older bilingual adults against the onset of dementia (Bialystok 2007). Age and proficiency levels in both languages affect the extent to which bilinguals exhibit these advantages (Bialystok and Baruc 2012). Children who have become bilingual through immersion in

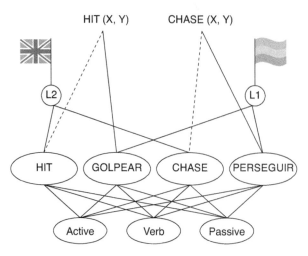

Figure 2.16 *Integrated syntactic and lexical network for bilingual lexical entries (Hartsuiker and Pickering 2008)*

school also show some of the enhanced executive function skills relative to monolinguals after three years of immersion, but to a lesser extent than children who have grown up bilingual from birth (Nicolay and Poncelet 2012).

Executive function skills are thought to be important for working memory, attention, focus, self-monitoring, motor skills, and social abilities. Executive function skills are highly correlated with academic achievement across subject disciplines, and are a better predictor of performance than IQ.

There are several tasks which are commonly used to assess executive function skills, including the *Stroop* task, the *Simon* task, the *Flanker* task, and the *Wisconsin card-sorting* tasks. All of them measure the ability of the person taking the test to inhibit a response to a given stimulus. For example, in the *Stroop* task, the test taker is asked to name colors that are written in the same color as their meaning as well as colors that conflict with the meaning of the word (e.g., the word *brown* written in white ink). Articulating the word *brown* under these conditions involves actively suppressing the word *white*, and causes a slower reaction time in subjects than a word whose meaning matches the color of the ink in which it is written.

Some of these tasks have been adapted for use with children, as exemplified by the Wisconsin card-sorting task. In this assessment, children are asked to play a "color game" or a "shape game" (i.e., match the all the rabbits by shape, or match all the blue cards by color) while ignoring the competing category.

Bilinguals have been found to perform these tasks significantly faster than monolinguals (Bialystok, Craik, Klein, and Viswanathan 2004; Bialystok, Craik, and Luk 2008; Costa, Hernández and Sebastián-Gallés 2008, Yang, Yang and Lust 2011), an advantage which many researchers have attributed to the role that cognitive inhibition plays in separating the languages of a bilingual. According to this hypothesis, bilinguals' continual need to monitor their language choice and suppress the non-selected language strengthens their executive function skills relative to monolinguals, who have no need to regulate their language choice. Support for this position comes from the considerable evidence that language processing is non-selective in bilinguals, suggesting that at all times both of the languages of a bilingual are competing for activation. Further support comes from a meta-analysis of neuroimaging studies which have found that during tasks in which they switch from one language to another, bilinguals' brains show activation in regions which are implicated in nonverbal executive control (Luk, Green, Abutalebi, and Grady 2012). In one such study of language switching in Spanish–English bilinguals, Hernandez, Dapretto, Mazziotta, and Bookheimer, (2001) found that bilinguals showed increased activity in the right dorso-lateral pre-frontal cortex, an area associated with executive function in a between-language switching task (English versus Spanish) but not in a within-language naming task (Spanish and Spanish).

2.4.4 The effects of bilingualism on cognitive development and literacy

Bilingualism affects cognitive development in children in ways that have important implications for academic outcomes, particularly the acquisition of literacy. The following sections will review research suggesting that bilingual children have enhanced abilities relative to monolingual ones in measures of phonological awareness, literacy development, and metalinguistic awareness.

Literacy and phonological awareness in bilingual children

Learning to read is a significant achievement that profoundly alters the brains and cognitive abilities of the literate (Dehaene, Pegado, Braga, Ventura, Nunes Filho, Jobert, Dehaene-Lambertz, Kolinsky, Morais, and Cohen (2010). At the neural level, the brains of literate and illiterate people have different patterns of activation in the visual cortex and language areas of the left hemisphere when they are shown printed text (Szwed, Dehaene, Kleinschmidt, Eger, Valabrègue, Amadon, and Cohen 2011). In particular, in literate people an area of the visual cortex on the left hemisphere referred to as the *visual word form* area is activated by written words regardless of the language in which they are read. The uniformity of cross-linguistic responses during reading suggests that this region becomes specialized for processing letter–sound (or character–sound) correspondences.

The cognitive changes brought about by literacy include reorganized and enhanced phonological representations for spoken language in the literate (Castro-Caldas, Petersson, Reis, Stone-Elander, and Ingvar, 1998), such as the ability to repeat nonsense words, as well as the ability to process complex sentences more efficiently (Petersson, Reis, Askelöf, Castro-Caldas, and Ingvar 2000). Literate people also show enhanced abilities in visual processing relative to illiterate ones in tests of recognizing contour integrations as well as horizontal checkerboards, presumably because of their experience in processing horizontally presented words. However, there are also cognitive costs associated with becoming literate. As more of the visual cortex is recruited for representations of written letters or script, people who are literate become less skilled at recognizing faces and at judging the mirror symmetry of two objects than those who are illiterate (Dehaene *et al.* 2010).

At the cognitive level, learning to read enhances auditory and spoken phonological representations in the literate. This is because literacy develops expertise in phonological awareness, a set of abilities that begin to develop as soon as a child is exposed to written text that is read aloud and is taught the alphabetic principle and the connection between sounds and letters (Morais, Cary, Alegria, and Bertelson 1979). Phonological awareness refers to a person's ability to recognize the patterns governing the sound structure of words in his/her language and to manipulate these sounds. In pre-literate children, it is an important predictor of reading readiness, as well as eventual literacy attainment (Adams 1990; Griffin, Burns, and Snow 1998; Whitehurst and Lonigan 1998). For children acquiring alphabetic languages such as Spanish and English, there are several stages in the development of phonological awareness which begin with the recognition of spoken words, i.e., the fact that sentences contain words. The second stage is the ability to recognize the syllables in a word, such as the three syllables in the word *pa/ta/ta* 'potato.' The following stage is the child's awareness of onset and rimes in syllables, as well as the ability to recognize rhymes (e.g., *vaso* 'glass' and *caso* 'case'). The onset of a syllable consists of the initial consonants of the syllable, and the rime is the vowel and any subsequent consonants. For example, in the proper noun *Luis* (which in Spanish has only one syllable), *L-* is the onset and *-uis* is the rime. The fourth stage in phonological awareness is the recognition of individual phonemes within a word, for example, that fact that the word 'stop' has four phonemes: /s/ /t/ /o/ and /p/, whereas 'shoe' only has two: /š/ and /u/. The final stage consists of phonemic manipulation, or the ability to add or delete a phoneme, creating a new word with parts of a word. For example, adding the phoneme /s/ to 'top', creates 'stop', and deleting the phoneme /f/ changes the word 'floss' into 'loss'. Some phonemes may be easier for children to learn to manipulate than others. In a study of phonological awareness in Spanish-speaking children enrolled in preschool and kindergarten, Jimenez González and Haro García (1995) found that the manner of articulation of a consonant facilitated its identification; children were more successful at isolating continuant consonants (such as /s/) than stops (e.g., /t/).

Research suggests that bilingual children can transfer phonological awareness skills from one of their languages to the other. Durgunoğlu, Nagy, and Hancin-Bhatt (1993) found that phonological awareness ability in Spanish predicted reading skills in English in Spanish–English bilingual children, a result which they interpreted to mean that phonological awareness is a metalinguistic ability that applies to both of a bilingual child's languages. Their study followed thirty-one Spanish L1–English L2 children in a bilingual first-grade classroom who were provided with reading instruction only in Spanish. Children with strong phonological awareness skills in Spanish scored significantly better in reading English words and pseudo-words than those with poor phonological awareness abilities.

Further studies have supported this hypothesis, finding that phonological awareness skills are transferable from the L1 to the L2 of bilingual children, as well as from the L2 to the L1 (Quiroga, Lemos-Britton, Mostafapour, Abbott, and Berninger 2002; Lindsey, Manis, and Bailey 2003; Branum-Martin, Mehta, Fletcher, Carlson, Ortiz, Carlo, and Francis 2006; Gottardo and Mueller 2009; Kuo and Anderson 2010).

Furthermore, bilingual children outperform monolingual ones on some measures of phonological awareness, but this advantage depends on whether they are acquiring languages with the same script (as in Spanish and Quechua, Basque or English) as well as whether they have received reading instruction in that language. Bialystok, Majumder, and Martin (2003) conducted a cross-sectional study which compared the development of phonological awareness in monolingual children with bilingual children in grades K–2 who were acquiring Spanish and English, French and English, or Mandarin and English. In their first experiment, they compared the performance of thirty-six French–English bilingual children with monolingual English-speaking children in a phoneme substitution task in English, and found no significant difference in performance between monolinguals and bilinguals. In a second experiment, they administered the same task to French–English bilinguals in both French and English, and found that bilingual children performed identically to monolingual children in the language in which they received literacy instruction.

In a third experiment, Bialystok *et al.* (2003) compared phonological awareness skills and vocabulary size in eighty-nine children in the first and second grades from three groups: English-speaking monolinguals, bilingual Chinese–English children, and Spanish–English bilinguals. The tasks that they administered included a vocabulary test (PPVT-R), a sound–meaning rhyming task (*which word sounds like 'dog': 'log' or 'puppy'?*), a phoneme segmentation task in which children were asked to count the sounds in a word with poker chips, a phoneme substitution task, a word identification task (which asked them to identify real words), and word attack (which asked them to identify pseudo-words) They found that in the vocabulary task, monolinguals and Spanish–English bilinguals did not differ significantly in performance, but the Chinese–English bilinguals performed significantly worse than monolinguals. In the phoneme segmentation task, Spanish–English bilinguals performed best, followed by monolinguals and Chinese–English bilinguals. For the remaining tasks, there were no significant differences between the three groups.

Luk and Bialystok (2008) investigated whether phonological awareness and word identification abilities are language-dependent skills for bilingual children acquiring languages with different writing systems. Their participants were fifty-seven Cantonese–English bilingual children who were six years old, and who were living in Canada. The children were given tasks measuring their abilities in English and Chinese syllable deletion, English and Chinese phoneme-onset deletion, English phoneme counting, tone awareness in Chinese, English word identification, and Chinese character identification. The results showed that measures of phonological awareness correlated strongly across languages, but measures of word identification in both Chinese and English did not, indicating the need to develop language-specific reading skills for languages with different writing systems.

Furthermore, bilingualism seems to enhance literacy for children acquiring two alphabetic scripts such as Spanish–English and Euskara–Spanish bilinguals, who have higher levels of literacy than matched monolingual peers. This advantage does not extend to bilingual children acquiring an alphabetic and a non-alphabetic script, such as Chinese and English (Bialystok *et al.* 2003).

The advantages in phonological awareness and literacy that bilingualism confers are thought to stem from enhanced metalinguistic abilities; bilingual children have been shown to outperform monolingual children in several studies of metalinguistic awareness (Ben-Zeev 1977; Galambos and Hakuta 1988; Galambos and Goldin-Meadow 1990). In one such study, bilingual children attending an immersion school performed better than monolingual ones in tasks such as applying morphological rules to pseudo-words, as well as distinguishing between sentences that are grammatically incorrect, such as *Where does a horse likes to run?*, from those that are semantically anomalous, such as *Where does a horse like to sail?* (Bialystok and Barac 2012). Bialystok and Barac (2012) found that while proficiency level in the language of testing predicted performance on measures of metalinguistic awareness ability in that language, length of time spent in the immersion program predicted scores on tests of executive function.

2.4.5 Language loss, aphasia, and atypical development in bilinguals

Evidence from bilinguals who have suffered from language attrition or aphasia can offer insight into the circumstances that contribute to differences in language outcomes for monolingual and bilinguals. Such research can also make important contributions to understanding the plasticity of the brain and the cognitive systems that underpin the development of language and its ultimate attainment more generally, by disentangling factors such as language proficiency and age of acquisition that are confounded in monolingual speakers. In the following sections we review research on language loss in bilinguals, as well as recent work investigating the effect of bilingualism on selective language impairment in children.

Selective language impairment in bilingual children

Selective language impairment (SLI) is a language disorder which is independent of non-verbal cognitive or motor problems. Children are diagnosed with SLI when their expressive and receptive language abilities are substantially below the normal range for their age group and IQ level; children in this category generally score in the lowest 10 percent on a standardized measure of language ability (Bishop 2006). In contrast, these children have normal scores on non-linguistic tests of ability, including non-verbal IQ, motor and social development.

Children with SLI are often late talkers whose first words do not appear until 2 years of age or later, and may have difficulty articulating speech sounds. They also have a limited vocabulary, both in reception and production, as well as poor performance on tasks requiring the repetition of words or sentences, reflecting a weak short-term verbal memory. The disorder also manifests itself as a difficulty in producing inflectional morphology, such as verbal inflection and clitics in Spanish (Merino 1983; Restrepo 1998; Restrepo and Kruth 2000) and plural -s or 3rd singular -s in English (Wexler, Schütze, and Rice 1998; Wexler, Schaeffer and Bol 2004). Some examples of plural nouns produced by monolingual Spanish-speaking children diagnosed with SLI are provided in (7) (from Grinstead, Cantú-Sánchez, and Flores-Ávalos 2008):

(7) a.   *flors*
          flor-s   (Target form: *flor-es*)
          'flowers'
    b.   *árbols*
          árbol-s   (Target form: *árbol-es*)
          'trees'

About 5 to 10 percent of school-aged children are diagnosed with SLI, and boys are more often affected than girls. Because SLI runs in families, the disorder is assumed to have a genetic component (Bishop 2002), and monozygotic twins share SLI diagnoses more often than dizygotic twins do. While some researchers have suggested that SLI might be attributable to a mutation in a single gene (FOXP2), this hypothesis has been discredited since further research has revealed that FOXP2 it is not a gene for language alone, but rather a gene that is implicated in the regulation of many other genes, including some which are important for the development of language systems in the brain (Fisher 2005). Other researchers have argued that SLI reflects an underlying auditory processing disorder. Benasich and Tallal (2002) found that infants' ability at 6 to 9 months to detect differences in brief, rapidly presented tones was a strong predictor of the likelihood that they would be diagnosed with SLI at age 3, suggesting that auditory processing plays an important role in SLI.

Although there are no studies comparing the incidence of SLI in bilingual and monolingual children, we would expect the disorder to affect roughly the same percentage of children in each population (Jacobson 2012). While bilingualism does not exacerbate SLI (Paradis, Crago, and Genesee 2005/2006; Jacobson 2012), being bilingual can make the accurate diagnosis of SLI more difficult. Unfortunately, there is a significant risk of misdiagnosing children who are normally developing bilinguals as suffering from SLI (Ortiz, Robertson, Wilkinson,

Liu, McGhee, and Kushner 2011), given that some of the linguistic markers of SLI used for clinical diagnosis, such as non-target verbal inflection in Spanish, are also characteristic of bilingual children undergoing first language loss (Anderson 1999a, 1999b, 2004). In order to avoid such confusion, it is important to screen a bilingual child for language disorders in both of his/her languages (Kohnert 2010).

In addition, current best practices recommend speech therapy in both of the languages of a bilingual child with SLI, something that was not done in the past in the United States: "Over the past decade bilingual clinical researchers have advocated replacing the question 'Which language should we support in intervention with bilingual children?' with 'How can we best support both languages needed by bilingual children with SLI?'" (Kohnert 2010: 13). Despite recommendations to the contrary, in the US most bilingual children with language impairments continue to be treated in one language only (Jordaan and Yelland 2003; Ortiz *et al.* 2011; Kohnert 2010).

Language attrition in bilingual children and adults

Research on first and second language attrition in children and adults examines how the factors that allow language to be acquired can also permit it to be lost. The critical variables include access to language learning mechanisms (whether innate or learned), availability of sufficient language input, age of acquisition, and the extent of cross-linguistic influence. In the following sections, we will review findings regarding attrition in children and adults, as well as theoretical models that can elucidate these results.

Theoretical models of language attrition

Attrition can be defined as the non-pathological loss of language structures that were previously acquired (Köpke 2004). As the language of a bilingual speaker is lost, its structures become vulnerable to restructuring and influence from the other language, whether because of lack of use or competition from the other language, or both factors (ibid). Studies of L1 and L2 attrition in children and adults have found that age plays a critical role in the extent to which a language can be lost; the severity of attrition in young children is much greater than in older children and adults (Köpke and Schmid 2003). In both child L1 and L2 attrition, several researchers have suggested that the lexicon is more vulnerable to loss than morphosyntax, which in turn is more susceptible to attrition than other aspects of syntax such as word order (Cohen 1975, 1986, 1989; Olshtain 1989; Kaufman and Aronoff 1991; Kuhberg 1992). However, a few studies have found evidence that there is greater morphosyntactic than lexical attrition in L2 speakers with low levels of proficiency (Moorcroft and Gardner 1987; Tomiyama 2008).

Many have also reported ordering effects in the progression of attrition within these domains, finding that certain areas of morphosyntax seemed more resilient than others to loss, and that recently acquired structures were the first to be lost in attrition (Cohen 1975, 1989; Hansen and Chen 2001; Hayashi 1999). These ordering effects are often interpreted as supporting the *Regression Hypothesis*, which posits that during attrition, dementia and aphasia, linguistic elements are lost in the reverse order in which they were acquired (Jakobson 1968).

However, as Bardovi-Harlig and Stringer (2010, 2013) noted, most studies supporting the *Regression Hypothesis* have not controlled for frequency effects; however, input frequency could also explain the order in which lexical items or grammatical structures are lost, since those that are acquired late tend also to be low in frequency. A study which did examine frequency effects in the attrition of numeral classifiers in L2 Japanese found that frequency predicted the order in which the classifiers were lost more accurately than the order in which they are acquired by L2 learners (Hansen and Chen 2001). Bardovi-Harlig and Stringer (2013) suggested that the *Activation Threshold Hypothesis* (Paradis 1993, 2004, 2007), can better account for ordering effects in L2 attrition than the Regression Hypothesis, since frequency effects find a natural explanation in the Activation Threshold Hypothesis (ATH). The ATH postulates that the activation threshold of a lexical item is determined by the neural impulses necessary to activate it. Both frequency and recency of activation can speed activation and lower the activation threshold; according to this analysis, linguistic structures that have not been activated often or for a long time will have a higher activation threshold and will be more difficult to retrieve. According to Bardovi-Harlig and Stringer, several other findings from studies of second language attrition also find a natural explanation under the assumptions of this model (Paradis 2007), including evidence that high-frequency items in the L2 can replace those in an L1 undergoing attrition, that comprehension is more resilient to loss than production, since comprehension requires less neurological activation, and the prediction that pragmatic and conceptual knowledge can also undergo attrition.

First language attrition in children and adults

Two factors have been identified as critical in determining the extent of L1 attrition in bilingual children: the age of exposure to the second language, and the degree to which the child maintains use of the L1. First language attrition has been found to be more pervasive in children who are schooled in the majority L2 and not in their L1 (Guiberson, Barrett, Jancoset, and Yoshinaga Itano 2006) and in children who acquired their L2 at an earlier age (Silva-Corvalán 1994). Behavioral and neuroimaging studies have found that a native language can be completely replaced by a second language during childhood if a child is cut off from exposure to his/her first language. A case study of an adopted child who moved from China to Canada at age 17 months found that within four months, she could no longer understand or produce many Cantonese words (Nicoladis and Grabois 2002). In a case study of a 9-year-old Russian-speaking child adopted by an English-speaking family in the USA, Isurin (2000) found that the child's ability to produce vocabulary in Russian declined steeply a year after she moved to the USA and lost contact with Russian, but was not as rapid or severe a loss as that reported by Nicoladis and Grabois in their younger subject.

Ventureyra, Pallier, and Yoo (2004) conducted a study of phonological attrition in Korean L1 speakers using a task which asked the participants to perceive a three-way phonemic contrast that exists in Korean but not French. Their participants were eighteen Korean L1–French L2 speakers who had been adopted by French-speaking families between the ages of 3 and 9 years and were subsequently cut off from all contact with Korean after moving to Europe. They found that the participants showed only a small advantage (marginally significant in one condition) in perceiving the phonemic contrast relative to monolingual French speakers who had never been exposed to Korean.

This behavioral evidence is corroborated by neuroimaging research indicating that first language attrition can lead to complete loss of the L1 in cases where the child no longer has contact with the first language. Pallier, Dehaene, Poline, LeBihan, Argenti, Dupoux, and Mehler (2003) conducted an fMRI study of eight Korean children adopted by French families who moved from Korea to France when they were between 3 and 8 years old and lost all contact with Korean. The adoptees were tested in early adulthood, after having spent most of their lives in France. In a language recognition task, the participants were unable to distinguish sentences in Korean from others in Japanese, Wolof, Swedish, and Polish. They were also unable to identify which of two spoken Korean words was the correct translation of a written French word. During an fMRI task, the same participants listened to 128 sentences in French, Korean, Japanese, and Polish. They found that for the adopted group, there was no difference in cortical activation when they were listening to Korean versus the two languages to which they had never been exposed (Japanese and Polish). However, when the adoptees listened to French, they showed a similar cortical response as a control group of French L1 speakers, but showed activation in a more extensive area of cortex.

Interestingly, in cases where children have ceased to speak an L1 but have ongoing contact with it by overhearing it spoken by family members, there is evidence that they have residual phonological knowledge of the first language even after years of disuse. Au, Knightly, Jun, and Oh (2002) compared the production of Spanish consonants in two groups of English-speaking adults; one group had been exposed to Spanish for several hours a week between birth and six years but had not been re-exposed to Spanish until high school (at 14 years of age), whereas the second group had been exposed to Spanish for the first time in high school. They found that native speakers of Spanish rated the production of Spanish consonants by the group that had been exposed to Spanish early in life as more target-like than the group who had begun acquiring Spanish in high school. In a related study, Oh, Jun, Knightly, and Au (2003) compared the performance of three groups of English-speaking adults enrolled in beginning Korean classes on the same phonemic discrimination task used by Ventureyra et al. (2004), a group who had spoken Korean as children, a group who had overheard Korean as children but had only spoken a few words or phrases, and a third group of novice learners. While the groups who had overheard Korean and the childhood speakers performed better on the task than the novice learners, only the childhood speakers were able to discriminate between all the consonants in the three-way distinction. In later research, Oh *et al.* (2010) found that English-speaking adults who had been adopted from Korea as infants (before age 1) and who had no subsequent contact with Korean outperformed novice learners on a phoneme identification task after only two weeks of relearning Korean in a beginning university class. As the researchers note, because they did not test the participants before the beginning of the study, it is possible that the adoptee participants simply retained knowledge of these phonemic contrasts in Korean rather than relearning them. However, Bowers, Mattys, and Gage (2009) had similar findings in a study of adults who had spent several years in childhood living in countries where their parents worked as missionaries and who learned Zulu or Hindi as an L2 but did not continue to speak these languages as adults. The childhood learners found it easier to relearn phonemic contrasts in Zulu or Hindi than adults who had never been exposed to them. These results suggest that continued exposure to a language even in the face of complete disuse may preserve some knowledge of the language, at least at the phonological level.

Most children who are immersed in a second language in childhood experience some degree of L1 attrition, even if it is not as drastic as in the cases of the adoptees investigated in the aforementioned studies. The extent of first language attrition in such children depends on factors such as the amount of continued exposure to the L1 that the child receives, whether the child is a simultaneous or sequential bilingual, whether the L1 or the L2 (or both) are languages used by the majority of speakers in the larger community, and whether the child receives schooling in his/her L2 only or in both the L1 and L2.

For example, most Spanish-speaking children growing up in the United States receive instruction in school only in English, which is also the dominant language of the wider speech community. Although many children in this situation continue to receive input in their L1 at home, as English becomes their preferred language they rapidly lose proficiency in Spanish and begin to show signs of L1 attrition such as increased production of grammatical errors and greater substitution of nonspecific, deictic terms such as demonstrative pronouns (*eso, esa,* 'that one, neutral and feminine, respectively') and adverbs (*aquí* 'here', 'there') for more specific lexical items (Anderson 1999a; Guiberson *et al.* 2006).

The age at which the child is immersed in the L2 is also an important predictor of the extent to which the child's L1 will undergo attrition; the earlier L2 immersion occurs, the more likely that the L1 will undergo attrition (Seliger and Vago 1991; Silva-Corvalán 1994; Köpke and Schmid 2003). There may also be some late-developing areas of the L1 grammar which are never acquired in a native-like way in children who are immersed in an L2 early in life, making it important to distinguish between non-target uses of the L1 which result from attrition and those that have not been fully acquired (Montrul 2002, 2004b,

2008). Montrul and Potowski (2007) studied the comprehension and production of Spanish grammatical gender in school-age bilingual children who were L1 speakers of Spanish and were enrolled in a dual-immersion school in the United States. They found that bilingual children who had learned Spanish and English simultaneously produced more errors in tests of Spanish grammatical gender than sequential bilinguals who had begun learning English at age 4. The authors suggested that children who learned Spanish and English simultaneously from birth may never have received sufficient early input in Spanish to fully acquire grammatical gender. Polinsky (2011a: 306) pointed to the importance of comparing early bilinguals immersed in an L2 with age-matched monolingual speakers of the L1 in order to distinguish between incomplete acquisition and L1 attrition:

> Incomplete acquisition: If a child and an adult deviate from the baseline in the same way, it can be assumed that the feature has not been acquired. Attrition: If a child performs as his or her age-matched baseline control but the adult does not, the feature can be assumed to have been acquired but may have subsequently been lost or reanalyzed.

Longitudinal studies can also help distinguish such cases of L1 attrition from incomplete acquisition by tracking changes over time in first language knowledge in bilingual children and by establishing a "peak of attainment" of the L1 (Bardovi-Harlig and Stringer 2010, 2013). Austin, Blume, and Sánchez (2013) conducted a longitudinal study of thirteen Spanish-speaking children growing up in the USA who were being schooled mostly in English, their L2, with a few hours of instruction per week in Spanish. Austin *et al.* compared the development of grammar in three areas in which Spanish and English have different morphosyntactic characteristics: subjects in *wh*-questions, which occupy a postverbal position in Spanish and a preverbal one in English; sentential negation, which occurs before an inflected verb in Spanish but after such a verb in English; and negative polarity items (NPIs), expressions which must be licensed by negation and which have different distributions in Spanish and English. They found that whereas interrogative and negative polarity item (NPI) structures in the children's Spanish showed evidence of attrition over the course of two years, negative sentences did not. The utterances in examples (8)–(9) illustrate the contrast between the acquisition of negation, which developed strongly in both languages, and the acquisition of NPIs and interrogatives, structures which showed progress in English over the course of two years, but which underwent attrition in Spanish (Austin *et al.* 2013). The production of sentences with correct negation in Spanish increased from 80 to 100 percent over two years, and in English, the children correctly produced 60 percent of the sentences requiring negation at the beginning of the study, and 100 percent by the end. Examples of utterances produced by the children with correct negation in each language are provided in (8).

(8) Negation (correct in Spanish and English):

    a.   *No   com-e   pastel.*

            Not eat-3SG.PRES cake.

            'He does not eat cake.'

    b.   He doesn't like apple pie.

In contrast, the correct production of NPIs in Spanish began at 30 percent and ended at 20 percent after two years. In English, the children's production of correct NPI structures increased from 30 to 90 percent over the course of two years. An example of an incorrectly produced NPI in Spanish can be seen in (9b), in which the child used the phrase *ni un* ('not one') instead of the target-like *ningún* 'none.'

(9) Negative polarity items (incorrect in Spanish, correct in English):

    a.   *No le   gust-a   ni   un pastel.*

            Not CL like-3SG.PRES not a   cake.

            'He doesn't like any cake.'

    b.   She said she doesn't like any bread.

In the development of *wh*-questions in the same children, Austin *et al.* found a contrast over time between the acquisition of these structures in Spanish and in English. In Spanish, the correct production of *wh*-questions over the course of two years went from 30 to 50 percent, whereas in English the percentage of correctly produced *wh*-questions increased from 30 to 80 percent during the same time. The authors concluded that differences in functional feature strength between English and Spanish in interrogative and NPI sentences as opposed to negation could account for the finding that negation in Spanish was less vulnerable to attrition than interrogatives and NPIs.

    Bilingual adults experience less extensive first language loss than bilinguals whose L1 attrition begins in childhood (Seliger and Vago 1991). For adult bilinguals, a number of studies also point to continued L1 exposure as an important predictor of first language attrition, but the evidence is more equivocal than it is for children (Schmid 2002, 2007). Behavioral studies have also shown the degree of L1 attrition in adults to be related to literacy in the L1 and the age of acquisition of the L2 (Sharwood Smith 1983; Olshtain 1989; Köpke 2004). While the lexicon has been found to be most susceptible to first language loss in adults, L1 attrition can also occur in morphosyntax, syntax, semantics, and phonology. Studies of bilingual adults have reported attrition in L1 knowledge of binding in Turkish speakers of English as an L2 (Gürel 2004), L1 attrition in the morphosyntax and syntax of Dutch L1 speakers living in Canada (Keijzer 2010), phonological attrition of the German L1 of bilinguals living in a Dutch L2 or English L2 environment (Hopp and Schmid 2013), and semantic attrition in the Russian L1 of adults who learned English late as an L2. In adult bilinguals, L1 grammatical attrition has been argued to be most likely to occur in areas of syntax which involve discourse–syntax interfaces, following the predictions of the *Interface Hypothesis* (Sorace 2000, 2005, 2006; Tsimpli, Sorace, Heycock, and Filiaci 2004). As discussed at greater length in Chapter 3, the areas of gram-mar involving interfaces between syntactic and semantic or pragmatic knowledge seem to be more vulnerable to attrition and cross-linguistic influence in bilinguals (for example, the use of overt subjects in pro-drop languages) than the narrow syntax (e.g., word order).

Second language attrition in children and adults

As was the case for L1 attrition, second language attrition in children can be much more extensive than L2 attrition in adults, especially for children who are not literate in their second language. In the case of pre-literate children, severe L2 attrition is possible even in children who obtain a near-native degree of proficiency in the second language. Berman and Olshtain (1983) and Olshtain (1989) studied thirty bilingual children between the ages of 5 and 14 who were L1 speakers of Hebrew and had acquired a native-like level of English as an L2 after living in the USA for two or more years. They found that the children's English underwent lexical, morphosyntactic, and syntactic attrition after the children moved back to Israel. However, the attrition experienced by children who were 5 to 8 years old at the beginning of the study was much more extensive than that of the older children (8 to 14 years old). While the younger children lost the irregular forms of nouns and past tense verbs, and overregularized words such as *men* to *mans* and *slept* to *sleeped*, the older children retained the target-like morphological forms (Olshtain 1989). The younger children also transferred more grammatical properties of Hebrew to their English than the older ones did, such as word order in noun phrases, e.g., *you can't play with shoes soccer* (Berman and Olshtain 1983). As Berman and Olshtain noted, literacy most likely played a role in these findings. Whereas the younger children did not become literate in English before moving back to Israel and therefore were cut off from all contact with English, the older children had learned to read in English and continued to get exposure to their L2 through reading.

Rapid L2 attrition has also been documented in young children acquiring a second language in an immersion school setting. For the participants in Cohen's (1975, 1986) study of three children in the second grade acquiring Spanish as an L2 in an immersion school, there was notable L2 attrition after three months of summer vacation. When the children were recorded before the vacation, their speech contained utterances that used grammatical gender, present and present progressive morphology, as well as the *ser/estar* copular distinction. After three months, two of the children's Spanish had undergone attrition in these areas.

Compared to the considerable research on the linguistic effects of adult L1 attrition, there are surprisingly few linguistic studies of adult second language attrition which have collected and analyzed original data (Bardovi-Harlig and Stringer 2010). Some of these studies have examined L2 attrition in adults in naturalistic learning environments (Hansen 2001), whereas others have examined adult L2 attrition after formal study (Bahrick 1984; Nagasawa 1999; Mehotcheva 2010). The populations of adult L2 attriters that have been studied are quite diverse compared to the participants of child L2 attrition studies, who are generally children who have moved with their parents from one country to another. Adult second language attriters include university students who have learned a second language, adults who have lived for a time in a country where the L2 is spoken, and people who for work reasons have needed to become proficient in a second language.

Despite the heterogeneity of L2 attriters that have been investigated, there are a number of general research findings which are applicable to both children and adults whose L2 is undergoing attrition (Schmid and Mehotcheva 2012; Bardovi-Harlig and Stringer 2013; Tomiyama 2000). First, bilinguals who have attained a high degree of proficiency in the L2 are likely to experience less attrition than those with a lower level of proficiency in their second language (Bahrick 1984; Mehotcheva 2010). Second, the L2 lexicon and grammar soon begin to show signs of attrition if contact with the second language is cut off or even reduced (Unsworth 2013). Third, after an initial period in which attrition occurs rapidly, it then levels off (Bahrick 1984). Fourth, younger children experience greater L2 attrition than older children or adults, a correlation which may be modulated by literacy in the L2 (Berman and Olshtain 1983; Olshtain 1989). Finally, productive skills are more affected by L2 attrition than receptive language skills (Cohen 1975, 1989; Weltens 1987; Tomiyama 2000).

Aphasia in bilingual speakers

Aphasia, the loss of language after a stroke or other injury to the brain, does not always affect all the languages of bilingual speakers in the same way (Paradis 1995). The three most common patterns of recovery are parallel, in which both languages are recovered at the same time, selective recovery, in which one of the languages is recuperated and the other is not, and successive recovery, where one language improves more quickly than the other (Fabbro 2001a).

Research on the patterns of language loss and recovery in bilingual patients suffering from aphasia has provided important insights into the organization of more than one language in the brain. In addition to experiencing the aphasias that affect monolingual speakers in one or both of their languages, there are some types of aphasia that are unique to bilinguals. These include pathological mixing, in which the bilingual patient produces utterances with elements from both languages even when asked to use one language only or when speaking with someone who does not understand one of their languages (Fabbro 2001b). Pathological mixing is found in fluent aphasics, and has been hypothesized to stem from more general lexical retrieval problems (Fabbro 1999). Pathological switching, which is when a bilingual aphasic switches back and forth uncontrollably between utterances in more than one language, and pathological mixing are associated with damage to the prefrontal cortex (Fabbro, Skrap and Aglioti 2000), the left inferior parietal lobe and the basal ganglia (see Abutalebi and Green 2007 and references therein), brain areas associated with inhibitory control, language control, and motor control, and which have been hypothesized to form part of the bilingual language control system in healthy individuals (Abutalebi and Green 2007 (see Section 2.4.1).

Some bilingual aphasics also display translation disorders which can be dissociated in their languages, for example, a bilingual aphasic may have difficulty translating from language A to language B, but not vice versa (Fabbro and Paradis 1995). These disorders suggest that there are specific neural systems underlying translating abilities in each direction, a hypothesis that has yet to be tested in healthy bilinguals (Fabbro 2001b).

2.5   Conclusions

In this chapter, we reviewed recent research on the neural and cognitive consequences of becoming bilingual for users of more than one language. Bilingualism has been found to produce changes in brain structure, including greater gray-matter density for bilinguals relative to monolinguals in the posterior supramarginal gyrus, a region of the left hemisphere implicated in lexical acquisition (Mechelli et al. 2004; Green et al. 2007). Early bilinguals have also demonstrated enhanced subcortical auditory processing abilities when compared to monolinguals (Krizman et al. 2012). In addition, bilinguals show activation of more extensive cortical areas during language tasks than monolinguals; this effect is modulated by age of acquisition, level of proficiency, and degree of continued exposure to both languages (Perani and Abutalebi 2005).

There is extensive evidence that the languages of a bilingual are highly interconnected at the phonological, lexical, and syntactic levels (Costa et al. 2003; Meijer and Fox Tree 2003; Kroll et al. 2006, inter alia). Furthermore, research has found that bilinguals' need to continually regulate their languages and actively suppress their non-active language leads to a lifelong enhancement of executive function skills (Bialystok et al. 2009; Kovács and Mehler 2009; Bialystok, 2007). In addition to these cognitive benefits, bilingualism also confers a few disadvantages to multilingual speakers, including more tip-of-the-tongue-states, slower lexical retrieval, and smaller vocabularies in each language relative to monolinguals (Gollan et al. 2004; Bialystok 2009). Taken together, these studies indicate that being bilingual produces significant changes in the minds and brains of multilingual speakers. In several important respects, the languages of a bilingual are not equivalent to two monolingual language systems stored in a single brain (Grosjean 1989).

3   Bilingual development and bilingual outcomes

3.1   Introduction

In order to understand current views on language development in the bilingual child it is necessary to understand the evolution and development of bilingual studies. Definitions of bilingual development have been shaped in the past and continue to be shaped now by the relative weight assigned to one of many factors involved in bilingual development such as the language component investigated. In the present chapter, we will focus on two major language components that have been at the center of varying lines of research on bilingual development: the development of the bilingual lexicon and the development of bilingual syntax. We will also focus on how theories of lexical and syntactic development in bilinguals have reflected our understanding of linguistic and cognitive processes that take place in the bilingual mind and on how they have shaped our views of language acquisition. Theoretical developments in these two major components have also had important consequences for how we view the emergence of new varieties of language and the societal use of language.[1]

Inquiry into lexical and syntactic development in bilinguals evolved as independent lines of research and to a certain extent they were isolated from each other. It is only in recent times, and partly due to new theoretical developments in linguistic theory (Chomsky 1995, 1998, 2001), that they have begun to be perceived not only as complementary areas of research but as part of a more general line of inquiry that aims at developing a complex and rich model of how languages are represented in the mind of the bilingual speaker.

In this book, we espouse a view of language that assumes the existence of different language components: a lexicon, a phonological component, a syntactic component, and an interpretive component (Chomsky 1995). Regarding the syntactic component, we assume a generativist view of syntax according to which knowledge of syntax involves knowledge of (a) basic syntactic operations that allow the formation of syntactic expressions (Merge, Agree and Move), (b) structural configurations that are crucial in determining the grammaticality

---

[1] In this chapter we will focus on the relationship between semantic and functional features and on how they guide the development of the bilingual lexicon in regard to semantic content and functional categories.

of expressions (c-command, relativized minimality), and (c) basic units in the lexicon that are labeled functional features (Ouhalla 1991; Chomsky 1995, 1998, 2001; Muysken 2008).

Functional features are a limited set of minimal units that have values such as +/–definite, +masculine, +feminine, or +/–past. Functional features play an important role in triggering syntactic operations that create new phrases or relations between constituents. They are assumed to be stored in our lexicon along with lexical items (Chomsky 1995, 1998). When they are relevant to a syntactic operation or they trigger it, they are labeled uninterpretable features and must be erased before the syntactic expression that contains them is decoded by the interpretive component of language. If they are interpretable, they contribute to the meaning of the expression and must not be erased before reaching the interpretive component. An example of an uninterpretable feature that must be erased before it is interpreted is the EPP feature. EPP is a formal feature that captures the universal principle originally labeled Extended Projection Principle, according to which all sentences must have a subject (Chomsky 1981). The EPP is a feature in the functional head T (tense) that in a language such as English triggers a subject movement to the specifier of Tense Phrase (TP), resulting in the preverbal nature of English subjects in active and passive sentences as shown in (1):

(1) a.   <u>Mary</u> opened the window
    b.   <u>The window</u> was opened by Mary.

Another example of an uninterpretable feature in some languages is gender. In Spanish there is agreement in gender between nouns and determiners and modifiers and this agreement takes place as a syntactic operation as shown in (2):

(2)   *El libro famoso*
        El   libr-o   famos-o
        The.M   book.M   famous-M
        'The famous book'

Because it triggers a syntactic operation, gender in Spanish can be considered an uninterpretable feature. In a language such as English, gender is not activated and is neither an interpretable nor an uninterpretable feature.

Given the importance of uninterpretable features in determining cross-linguistic differences, the question arises of how these features are stored and accessed in the mind, in particular in the bilingual mind. If we assume that functional features are stored along with lexical items in our lexicon, the word *libro* 'book' in Spanish is stored along with its syntactic features (Chomsky 1995, 1998) including gender and its phonological representation (Jackendoff 2002). In bilinguals these associations are expected to be found in two lexicons. Under this view, for a Spanish–English early bilingual child, the acquisition of a lexical item such as *libro* 'book' in Spanish would imply the acquisition of the masculine value of the gender feature associated with it, while its English counterpart *book* would not be characterized by an association of this type.

Acquisition of the values of functional features that are relevant in each of the languages makes possible the development of differentiated syntactic representations in the bilingual mind. If we take, for example, a feature such as gender in Spanish, it would be activated along with the phonological representation of the word *libro*, and along with its phonetic expression and the relevant semantic representation. In the case of its English equivalent, *book*, the activation of gender features should be null, if the two lexicons are distinct and lack associations between them. This should be the case if we assume that no cross-linguistic influence takes place in the bilingual mind and that acquisition of functional features is related to acquisition of lexical items. Current developments in the study of bilingual acquisition of the lexicon might lead us to think that there is a more complex picture of how the activation of lexical items and functional features takes place in the bilingual mind. If we adopt views of lexical selection in bilinguals that give inhibition of the unselected language a strong role, we might start to see potential accounts of conflicting data that show evidence for autonomous development of syntax and at the same time evidence of cross-linguistic influence in bilingual representations. We will see this in detail in the next section.

The evidence for autonomous development comes from previous research that has shown that an important part of the inventory of lexical items developed by young bilingual children is a set of functional features whose values may differ in both languages (Meisel 1986; Paradis and Genesee 1996). Work by Liceras, Spradlin, and Fernández Fuertes (2005) and Liceras, Fernández Fuertes, Perales, Pérez-Tattam, and Todd Spradlin (2008) has shown that Spanish–English bilingual children are able to distinguish between gender assignment to nouns in Spanish and its consequent triggering of agreement with other Determiner/Noun phrase (DP/NP) constituents and the lack of grammatical gender feature assignment in English nouns. Liceras *et al.* (2008) show a basic asymmetry in Spanish–English bilingual children's preferences for language choice regarding determiners in DP-internal code-switching. Early bilingual children exhibit a strong preference for production of definite articles in Spanish and nouns in English. Liceras *et al.* (2008) show that early bilingual children prefer expressions such as the ones in (3) over those in (4):

(3)   *La chair / La girl*
        L-a   chair   / L-a   girl
        DET-F (SP) chair (EN) / DET-F (SP) girl (EN)
        'The chair / The girl'

(4)   *The silla / The chica*
        The sill-a   / The chic-a
        DET chair-F (SP) / DET girl-F (SP)
        'The chair / The girl'

Liceras *et al.* (2005) propose that this preference is due to the fact that, once the functional features of the two systems are activated, bilingual children select the determiner with the richer array of uninterpretable features. For this language pair, the Spanish determiner is specified for gender, a feature that involves agreement between different syntactic constituents. Liceras *et al.* analyze gender as an uninterpretable feature on the basis of its relevance for the syntactic operation Agree. As the determiner in Spanish has one more functional feature, it is richer in uninterpretable features than the English determiner. Liceras *et al.* (2005) consider that the preference for forms like (3) follows from the *Grammatical features spell-out hypothesis* (Liceras *et al.* 2003). According to this hypothesis, "in the process of activating the features of the two grammars, the child who will rely on the two lexicons, will make code-mixing choices which will favor the functional categories containing the largest array of uninterpretable features (Chomsky 1998, 1999)" (Liceras *et al.* 2005: 227). This basic asymmetry is evidence that early bilinguals are able to distinguish between the specification for gender features in the Spanish DP and the lack of such specification in the English DP.

Studies such as those by Liceras *et al.* open up the possibility of exploring stronger links between acquisition of the lexicon and acquisition of functional features. In this line of research it is very important to proceed cautiously given that acquisition of lexical items may differ crucially from acquisition of functional features in that the former involves explicit aspects related to conscious learning subserved by declarative memory as well as implicit aspects involving unconscious acquisition subserved by procedural memory (Ullman 2005; Paradis 2009). The relationship between the acquisition of functional features and explicit learning of lexical items has not yet been explored in depth and remains an open field. In this chapter we will provide a general overview of how theories of lexical and syntactic development have evolved and where the common areas and patterns of research interest lie.

Earlier studies of bilingualism focused on the development of two lexicons in the bilingual mind and studies of bilingual populations who speak Spanish and other languages were at the forefront of this line of research (Caramazza and Brones 1979). This type of approach tended to focus on the study of cognates. Cognate studies were privileged gateways to understand the organization of the lexicon as a unitary system or as multiple systems. This line of research was pioneered by authors such as Caramazza and Brones (1979), De Groot and Nas (1991), and Sánchez-Casas, Davis, and García-Albea (1992) *inter alia* and has continued in recent work by Heredia (1996), Schwartz and Kroll (2006), and Antón-Mendez and Gollan (2010), to mention a few. Some of the initial proposals focused on cognates as a way of testing the unitary nature of the lexicon, while other models such as the *Revised Hierarchy Model* (RHM) proposed by Kroll and Stewart (1994) (see Chapter 2) were characterized by assuming the existence of two separate lexicons. Kroll and Stewart (1994) also assumed a conceptualization of the structure of the lexicon in hierarchical terms. The RHM proposes that there is a direct connection between the two lexicons of a bilingual individual and at the same time there is a connection between these lexicons and a conceptual level. According to the RHM, the strength and directionality of the connections between lexical elements in the two lexicons changes with increased proficiency in the second language in successive bilinguals. In this model, in the mind of a native speaker of English who is acquiring Spanish as a second language, a word like *libro* 'book' is strongly connected to its English counterpart *book* at the initial stages of the acquisition of Spanish and less strongly connected to the conceptual level. The RHM as a model made predictions about the strength of the connections between lexical items from the two lexicons but without taking into account the syntactic context as well as the possible associations between meaning and grammatical features.

In current terms the study of bilingual lexical acquisition has shifted towards a model that no longer proposes that words from the two lexicons are always in competition when a bilingual individual tries to access the lexicon for comprehension or production purposes. Instead, the new proposals focus on the idea that some lexical items compete within the same language while others compete across languages (Brysbaert and Duyck 2010).

In a parallel fashion to the development of bilingual lexical acquisition studies, in the area of bilingual syntax development, research on bilingualism in Spanish and other languages has contributed enormously to our understanding of how syntax is represented and accessed in the bilingual mind. While originally unitary syntactic systems were proposed for early stages of bilingual acquisition (Leopold 1949/1970; Volterra and Taeschner 1978), proposals in favor of two autonomous syntactic systems were developed on the basis of studies such as Meisel (1986) and Paradis and Genesee (1996). These studies provided strong empirical evidence of independent development of word order properties (Meisel 1986) and of functional categories (Paradis and Genesee 1996). An example of independent development in Spanish bilinguals comes from Spanish–Euskara bilingual children. Austin (2010) has shown independent development of Euskara and Spanish morphology in Euskara–Spanish bilingual children. Austin (2010) shows a higher frequency of uninflected verb forms known as root infinitives in the Euskara oral production of bilingual children. The bilingual child with the highest percentage of root infinitives in Spanish had 7 percent and the child with the highest percentage of root infinitives in Euskara had 80 percent. This is evidenced in the speech of a Euskara–Spanish bilingual child (age 2;01) who exhibits uninflected forms in Euskara and inflected forms in Spanish as shown in the following examples:

Euskara

(5)   *Jat-en   Pinotxo*
           Eat-IMP Pinocchio-Ø
           'Pinocchio (is) eating.'   (GG 2;01; Austin 2001)

Spanish

(6)   *Es   el   caballo, ese*
           Is   the   horse,   that_one
           'That one is the horse.'

As Austin (2010) notes, in this child's Euskara utterance, the participle *eating* is morphologically marked for progressive aspect but lacks the inflected auxiliary required in Euskara main clauses. In the Spanish utterance the verb is correctly inflected. Austin (2010) attributes the difference between the development of Spanish and Euskara found in the speech of Euskara–Spanish bilingual children to a higher level of morphological complexity in Euskara than in Spanish. Austin defines morphological complexity as the number of morphemes that an inflected verb contains in Euskara. In Euskara transitive sentences, the auxiliary verb is marked for subject and object morphology (ergative and absolutive markings) and that is not the case in their Spanish equivalents that show only subject morphology. This is shown by the contrast between the following examples:

Euskara
(7)   *Nereak ardoa erosi du.*
           Nerea-k   ardoa-Ø   erosi du.
           Nerea-ERG wine-ABS buy   AUX.PRS.ABS.3 SG.ERG.3 SG
           'Nerea has bought the wine.'   (Austin 2010: 49)

Spanish
(8)   *Nerea ha comprado el vino.*
           Nerea-Ø   ha   comprado el   vino.
           Nerea-NOM AUX.1 SG.PRS.NOM bought   the   wine
           'Nerea has bought the wine.'   (Austin 2010: 49)

Austin's work shows that morphosyntactic development might differ in crucial ways in the two languages of the bilingual child.

The view that autonomous development in bilingual acquisition is possible is a prevalent one in the field of bilingualism studies. However, the pervasive nature of cross-linguistic influence has also required a principled explanation of its nature and of the factors that favor it. This has resulted in the need to identify the locus of cross-linguistic influence.

Two major streams of thought have emerged with respect to this view. One line of thought identifies the locus of cross-linguistic influence at the interface between the computational component[2] and the articulatory/perception system (Bullock 2009) and/or at the interface between the computational component and the semantic/pragmatics system (Hulk and Müller 2000; Sorace 2000; Müller and Hulk 2001). An example of how the interface between syntax and pragmatics in child bilingualism shows cross-linguistic influence has been explored is a study conducted by Paradis and Navarro (2003) on the overt realization of subjects in Spanish–English bilingual children. Spanish is a null subject language in which null subjects occur as continuing topics and overt subjects express new referents or in some pragmatic contexts contrastive focus or emphasis. The following

---

[2] By computational system we understand the set of syntactic operations, functional features and categories that allow the formation of sentence structure (Chomsky 1995).

examples from Paradis and Navarro (2003) illustrate these differences. The cases of a null subject as a continuing topic and an overt subject expressing a new referent are illustrated in the following example from Paradis and Navarro (2003). The child (E) is talking about a trip to Barcelona and is asked by the mother who they traveled with. E uses a null subject in the expression *no sé* 'I don't know' whose subject is a first-person speaker. In the next sentence, *papá se va a Barcelona* 'Dad leaves for Barcelona,' E introduces a new referent in this context by means of the overt subject *papá* 'Dad.' At the end of the excerpt, when asked who is going to Barcelona, the child has a first-person null subject in the sentence *que me voy a Francisco* 'I leave for Francisco' that refers back to the child as a speaker:

(9)   *MOT: *¿y con quién fuimos?*
        %eng: who did we go with?
        *CHI: *no sé.*
        %eng: I don't know.
        *CHI: *papá se va a Barcelona.*
        %eng: Dad leaves for Barcelona.
        *NAC: *¿quién se va a Barcelona?*
        %eng: who leaves for Barcelona?
        *CHI: *que me voy a Francisco.*
        %eng: I leave for Francisco.   (Paradis and Navarro 2003: 390–391)

The following is an example of a contrastive overt subject also from Paradis and Navarro, this time uttered by the child's father:

(10)   *CHI: *oto [= otro] pato [= plato].*
        %eng: another plate.
        *FAT: *no, eso no es un plato.*
        %eng: no, that is not a plate

Paradis and Navarro (2003) analyzed the distribution of null and overt subjects in the spontaneous speech of a Spanish–English bilingual child (1;09 to 2;06) and compared it to the distribution found in the spontaneous production of two Spanish monolingual children. While the child data analyzed showed consistent use of null subjects, as expected in Spanish oral discourse, they also showed a somewhat higher rate of overt realization of subjects in the bilingual child data than in the monolingual children's data. Furthermore, the bilingual child data had a significantly higher percentage (26 percent) of overt subjects with "low informative" value than one of the monolingual children (10 percent). Paradis and Navarro (2003) propose cross-linguistic influence from English as a possible explanation for this difference in distribution, given that overt subjects in English are not subject to pragmatic constraints in the same way as overt subjects are in Spanish.

A different line of thought in bilingualism studies focuses on convergence, i.e., the emergence of new matrices of functional features due to processes of re-assembly of features from the two languages to which the bilingual is exposed (Lardiere 1998, 2003, 2005; Sánchez 2003, 2004). Evidence in favor of reassembly processes comes from studies of older children and adult second language acquirers as well as from the study of creolization processes (Lefebvre 1988; Lardiere 1998; Lardiere 2003; Sánchez 2003, 2004; Siegel 2004; Lardiere 2005).

An example of cross-linguistic influence at the morphosyntactic level can be found in the Spanish of older Quechua–Spanish bilingual children (10 to 12 years of age). In a story retelling task Sánchez (2004) found that Quechua–Spanish bilingual children exhibit evidential uses of pluperfect forms in their Spanish that correspond to the reportative past in Quechua. In Quechua, there are two different forms of past tense morphology (attested and reportative past tense suffixes). The following sentences illustrate the contrast:

Quechua

(11)   *Huwanmi Mariyata qhawarqan.*
         Huwan-mi   Mariya-ta   qhawa-rqa-n.
         Huwan-EVID.ATT   Mariya-ACC   see-PST.ATT-3 SG
         'Huwan saw Mariya.'   (Attested information, Sánchez 2004: 149)

(12)   *Huk punchaysi kasqan huk viejacha.*
         Huk punchay-si   ka-sqa-n   huk viejacha.
         One day-EVID.REPORT be-PST.REP.3 SG one old woman
         'One day there was an old woman.'   (Hearsay information, Sánchez 2004: 151)

In (11) the morpheme *-rqa* is an attested past morpheme that shows agreement with the clausal-level attested evidential/focus morpheme *-mi*. This contrasts with (12), where the suffix *-sqa* encodes past tense and a reportative value of evidentiality, which means that the information conveyed by the sentence is hearsay.

In Spanish, on the other hand, past tense morphology is associated with perfective or imperfective aspect, as shown by the following examples:

(13)   *Compr-é.* (past perfective)
         buy-PST.PRF.1SG
         'I bought.'

(14)   *Compr -a   -ba.* (past, imperfective)
         Buy   -TV -PST.IPFV.1SG
         'I used to buy (habitual).'

In (13) the suffix *-é* encodes past tense and perfective aspect, while in (14) the suffix *-aba* encodes past tense and imperfective aspect. Using a story retelling task, Sánchez (2004) found evidence of imperfective past tense forms conveying reportative evidentiality in the Spanish spoken by Quechua–Spanish bilingual children who are dominant in Quechua. The following sentences illustrate the contrast between the input provided in a story-retelling task and a segment of the short narrative produced by a Quechua–Spanish bilingual child in which past imperfective and pluperfect forms express the hearsay nature of the information conveyed. Notice also the discourse marker *dice* '(he/she) says' as a marker of clausal-level evidentiality:

Input
(15)   *Un día una viejita estaba sembrando maíz*
          Un   día   una   viejita   est-a-ba   sembrando   maíz
          One   day   an   old lady be-TV-3 S.PST.IPFV sowing   corn
          'One day, an old lady was sowing corn'

(16)   *y se encontró un pajarito amarillo.*
          y   se   encontr-ó   un   pajar-it-o   amarillo.
          and   CL =   find-3 S.PST.PFV a   bird-DIM-M   yellow
          'and (she) found a little yellow bird.'   (Sánchez 2004: 154)

Bilingual Spanish
(17)   *Había una viejita dice.*
          Hab -í   -a   una   viej   -it   -a   *dice.*
          Be -TV -PST.IPFV.3 SG   a   woman-DIM   -F   say
          '(There) was an old woman, (they) say.'

(18)   *Había sembrado maíz*
          Ø   Hab -í   -a   sembrado   maíz.
          Ø   Have -TV PST.IPFV.3 SG   sowed   corn
          '(S/he) had sowed corn.'

(19)   *Ella sembraba maíz.*
          Ella sembr -a   -ba   maíz.
          She   sow   -TV PST.IPFV.3 SG   corn
          'She sowed corn.'

(20)   *Le había encontrado un pajarito amarillo.*
          Le   hab -í -a   *encontrado* un pajarito #amarillo.
          CL.3 SG.DAT =   have-TV-PST.IPFV.3 SG   found   a   birdy   yellow
          '(She) found a yellow bird for him/her.'   (Sánchez 2004: 157)

Sánchez (2004) concludes that it is possible for tense, aspect, and evidentiality features to be reassembled due to a process of functional convergence by which: "the common specification for equivalent functional features in the two languages spoken by the bilingual who lives in a language contact situation, takes place when functional features not present in one of the languages are activated by input and production in the other language" (Sánchez 2004: 147). From a syntactic development perspective, autonomous development of syntax and cross-linguistic influence (at the interfaces or due to feature reassembly) in bilinguals are coexisting theories that have emerged from the study of bilingual populations with diverging levels of dominance in each of the languages, differences in frequency of exposure and activation for production and comprehension purposes in both languages. While it has been shown that autonomous development of syntax is possible when input and activation for production and comprehension in two languages are available to the bilingual child, it has also been shown that, in certain language contact situations with different levels of input and output frequency in two languages, there is evidence of cross-linguistic influence. Cross-linguistic influence may result in feature reassembly or in differences in constraints at the interface of syntax and the pragmatic component (Döpke 2000).

Given the two lines of development in the theories of lexical access and theories of syntactic development in bilingualism studies introduced above, a more encompassing approach to bilingual development has to emerge, one that takes into account how the complex network of the bilingual lexicons is stored and accessed and how activation of certain areas of the lexicon is related to the development and the mental representation of grammar. This is especially true in the present context in which research on the bilingual representations of the lexicon and of the syntactic component has evolved into new perspectives that incorporate other very important factors such as the relative frequency of exposure to input in each of the languages (Hauser-Grüdli *et al.* 2010), the quality of input and the level of dominance in each of the languages, and the frequency and quality of activation of lexical and functional items for comprehension and production tasks (Montrul and Foote 2012; Hopp 2013).

In addition to these factors, there are also a series of complex processes such as code-switching, transfer, and cross-linguistic influence that take place in the bilingual mind during processing and may have lasting effects in the mental representation of two languages in a bilingual individual (Sorace and Serratrice 2009). These processes are also affected by differences in the level of lexical and syntactic development in bilingual individuals, the frequency and quality of input in each of the languages as well as frequency and type of activation. Research on bilingualism in Spanish and other languages has shown that these processes may have a long-lasting effect that results in grammatical changes in contexts of language contact and heritage bilingualism (Silva-Corvalán 1994; Cuza and Frank 2011; Montrul 2004b, 2009; Montrul, Bhatt and Bathia 2012).

In this chapter we provide an overview of how studies on bilingualism in Spanish and other languages have contributed to our understanding of language development in bilinguals from a cognitive and linguistic perspective. In the first section of this chapter, we will provide a general overview of how studies on the bilingual acquisition of two lexicons have shaped our understanding of bilingual development evolving from a view in which two separate lexicons were assumed to a more complex view of how lexical networks interact.

In the second section, we present a general overview of studies on bilingual development of syntactic representations. While initially it was assumed that bilinguals possessed a single underlying syntactic representation for the two languages they speak (Leopold 1949/1970; Volterra and Taeschner 1978), later research showed that bilingual individuals develop two autonomous syntactic representations for each of the languages they speak (Meisel 1986; Paradis and Genesee 1996). In the last couple of decades, there have been multiple proposals that view cross-linguistic influence in bilinguals as the product of how the computational system interacts with other components such as the conceptual and the pragmatics component (Müller and Hulk 2000; Sorace 2000) in the bilingual mind. Cross-linguistic influence that takes place at the interface between syntax and pragmatics may initially affect language production in a first generation of bilinguals. This production in turn becomes a significant part of the input that bilinguals share with other bilinguals and with younger generations leading to potential language change. In this section, a parallelism is drawn between recent findings on how bilinguals access their lexicons and recent findings on how they store and access functional features, the minimal units in syntax.

In the third section we discuss the effects that processes such as convergence, cross-linguistic influence, code-switching, and language transfer have had on the grammar of Spanish speakers and how they contribute to intergenerational language change and to the emergence of new varieties of Spanish in different contexts of language contact.

Finally, in the fourth section, we discuss how societal attitudes affect the outcome of language contact in terms of language choice and the availability of code-mixing and code-switching. We focus on bilingual communities in three areas of the Spanish-speaking world: the Andean regions of South America, Spain, and the USA.

3.2   Lexicon storage, access, and activation in bilinguals

One of the areas in which most progress in bilingualism studies has been made is lexical storage and access. While some initial work focused mainly on bilingual aphasic populations and on issues such as lateralization (Paradis 1985, 1990), the issue of storage and access in non-aphasic bilingual populations evolved and progressed as new research on models of production and comprehension in monolinguals also evolved (Levelt 1992; Hermans *et al.* 1998). While initial debates focused on the separate (McCormack 1977; Snodgrass 1984) versus unified nature of lexicons in the two languages spoken by a fluent bilingual (Kolers 1966; Caramazza and Brones 1980; Brown, Sharma, and Kirsner, 1984; Kirsner *et al.* 1984; Scarborough *et al.* 1984; Gerard and Scarborough 1989), subsequent proposals focused on hierarchical models of lexical organization in sequential bilinguals.

Of particular importance in supporting a hierarchical view of how the lexicon is organized was Kroll and Stewart's work (1994). Their proposal of a *Revised Hierarchical Model* of lexical organization was very influential in incorporating factors such as language fluency and dominance into a model of lexical organization in bilinguals. Assuming previous proposals, they adopt a distinction between a common conceptual level of organization, which accounts for evidence of shared conceptual knowledge, and a lexical level that is language specific and accounts for previous findings showing lack of interference across lexicons in bilinguals. Both levels are active in bilingual memory. Kroll and Stewart's work is based on two very important assumptions about how the lexicon is organized. One of them is the notion that there is a level of conceptual organization that is connected to the lexicon of each of the languages. The other assumption is that access to the lexicon can be tested through two different routes: one is a relationship between images and concepts and the other one is through translation from L1 to L2 and vice versa.

This model was created for sequential bilinguals. In it, both the L1 and the L2 lexicons are linked to a common conceptual level. The strength of the links between the L1 and L2 lexicons and between the L2 lexicon and the conceptual level might differ according to the levels of dominance and fluency of the sequential bilingual in the second language. In sequential bilinguals with low levels of proficiency in the second language the links between L1 and L2 lexicons are stronger than those between the L2 lexicon and the conceptual level. The lower the dominance in the L2, the more bilinguals rely on the relationship between the L2 and the L1 lexical levels. This is shown by an asymmetry in translation time in tasks involving the presentation of lexical items according to semantic categories or in randomized lexical form. L2 to L1 translation tasks showed greater category interference than L1 to L2 translation tasks.[3]

Heredia (1997) provides examples of how the notion of a common conceptual level of representation works. Spanish words such as *mesa* 'table' have been shown to be conceptually related to English words in Spanish–English bilinguals in experiments in which presenting a semantically related word from the other language, *chair*, for example, results in faster responses than if the word is not semantically related. This common conceptual level is accompanied by a lexical level of organization that is language specific. According to Kroll and Stewart (1994), "Words in each of a bilingual's two languages are thought to be stored in separate lexical memory systems, whereas concepts are stored in an abstract memory system common to both languages" (Kroll and Stewart 1994: 150). While there have been many critiques to the RHM based on the fact that the model seems to account better for bilinguals with lower levels of dominance in their second language (Heredia 1997) and on the fact that the model does not look at competition that is constrained by the actual needs of language processing for production or comprehension, the RHM has been very useful in providing some understanding of the relationship between a conceptual level and the lexicon at earlier stages of acquisition in a second language.

In light of the previously mentioned critiques, a different line of research that focuses on access to the lexicon during sentence processing emerged (Schwartz and Kroll 2006). Unlike previous studies that focused on isolated word translations, Schwartz and Kroll (2006) examined second language speakers'

---

[3] An alternative model to Stewart and Kroll's (1994) Revised Hierarchical Model is the BIA Model+ initially proposed by Dijkstra and Van Heuven (2002) and later refined by Brysbaert and Duyck (2010).

performance in word recognition in high- and low-constraint sentential contexts. In two experiments, they used a reading task that tested cross-language activation of cognates and homographs. The first experiment involved Spanish–English bilinguals who were highly proficient in both languages and who lived in a bilingual community and the second one involved Spanish–English bilinguals with lower levels of proficiency in English and who lived in a Spanish-dominant community.[4] Participants were tested on sentences with cognates and homophones in two conditions: high and low levels of semantic constraint. The following sentences illustrate these two types:

High constraint

(21)   Before playing, the composer first wiped the keys of the <u>piano</u> at the beginning of the concert.   (Schwartz and Kroll 2006: 203)

Low constraint

(22)   When we entered the dining hall we saw the <u>piano</u> in the corner of the room.   (Schwartz and Kroll 2006: 203)

In sentence (21) there are many cues that constrain the options the reader has when s/he reaches the cognate word, while in sentence (22) there are fewer contextual clues that restrict the options. Schwartz and Kroll's (2006) findings demonstrated that high-constraint sentences had a negative effect on cross-language activation but low-constraint sentences did not create such an effect. On the other hand, in low-constraint sentences they found evidence of cross-language activation in both groups of participants.

In addition to findings that suggest that on-line constraints have an important role in cross-language activation, recent research (Schwieter and Sunderman 2008) has proposed that other factors in addition to language dominance may play a role in the way in which lexical items are activated in the mind of a bilingual individual. While previous work by Green (1985, 1998), Costa, Santesteban, and Ivanova (2006), and Kroll, Bob, Misra, and Guo (2008) *inter alia* have shown that inhibitory control is a fundamental mechanism that determines how successive bilinguals access the lexicon in their two languages, there have been other proposals that favor language-specific mechanisms for lexical selection (Gerard and Scarborough 1989). Schwieter and Sunderman (2008) have provided evidence from Spanish–English bilinguals in favor of robustness of lexical representations as a factor that might influence the functionality of a language-specific mechanism of lexical selection. Schwieter and Sunderman (2008) conducted a study in which a verbal fluency test was used to measure lexical knowledge in the L2 Spanish of English learners. An experimental picture-naming task involving language switches was used to determine accuracy in lexical access in each of the languages and to determine whether there were stark differences in switching times that could indicate stronger suppression of the L1 than of the L2. Their

---

[4] This group was actually trilingual since they were also speakers of Valenciano, a language spoken in Catalonia, Spain.

results show that bilinguals with higher levels of accuracy in lexical access exhibited lower levels of asymmetry in switching times between languages than those bilinguals with lower levels of accuracy. The study highlights the role of lexical robustness in favoring language-specific selection.

Another important aspect of research on lexical storage and access is the issue of whether lexical items are in some way tagged as belonging to one or the other language. Assigning lexical items to a specific vocabulary network has played a very important role not only in theories of lexical development, lexical storage and access but also in theories of code-switching (Belazi, Rubin and, Toribio 1994; MacSwan 2000), theories of language activation in bilinguals (Grosjean 1998) and theories of cross-linguistic influence at early stages of bilingual acquisition (Meisel 1986; Paradis and Genessee 1996; Müller and Hulk 2001). These theories assume that lexical items (irrespective of whether they are stored as lexical categories or functional categories) are assigned to one of the two lexicons available to a bilingual speaker. One proposal in particular, Belazi *et al.*'s (1994) *Functional Head Constraint* (FHC) formalized the notion of this assignment by proposing the existence of a language feature. According to the FHC code-switching between a functional category and its complement must obey the *Functional Head Constraint* that requires that both the functional category and the head of the complement share the language feature (i.e., the functional category and the head of the complement should be in the same language).

Research on the organization of the lexicon and access to it as well as on the tagging of lexical items generates important questions that need to be addressed by current and future research on how languages develop in bilingual individuals. Some of the main questions that emerge are: (a) how is lexical storage related to the storage and organization of the functional features in the lexicon? (b) are functional features tagged as belonging to a language-specific lexicon? and (c) is it possible for the same functional features to be associated with separate lexicons? In the next subsection, we will present some of the main proposals on bilingual syntactic development and their commonalities with research on bilingual lexical development in order to understand the possible avenues needed to tackle the aforementioned questions.

3.3   Syntactic development in bilinguals

In a similar fashion to research on lexical storage and access, research on bilingual syntactic development has evolved from the debate between shared systems versus independent ones to a more complex approach to what are the constitutive primary elements of syntax. Initial hypotheses such as Leopold's (1949/1970) and Volterra and Taeschner's (1978) proposed that bilinguals from birth initially had a common syntactic representation for both languages that became differentiated over time. Later research has shown that bilingual children develop different syntactic representations for each of the languages they speak at rates of development similar to their monolingual peers and that these representations are clearly differentiated even by young children (Meisel 1986; Paradis and Genesee 1996). One of the crucial matters that we will discuss in this section is the notion of syntactic representation that different studies have assumed in the past and how changes in our analysis of syntactic differences have brought us closer to a better understanding of why it is possible to find at the same time evidence of independent autonomous syntactic systems and evidence of cross-linguistic influence in bilingual child and adult syntax.

If one assumes a general computational system composed by basic operations such as Merge, Agree, and Move (Chomsky 1995), then bilingual children should not differ in their capacity to apply these operations once they have acquired a significant part of their lexicon. However, current understanding of the locus of syntactic variation across languages and dialects takes it to be a subcomponent of the lexicon known as functional features (Ouhalla 1991; Roper and Green 2007; Muysken 2008; Adger and Smith 2010). The inventory of functional categories and features is limited and the selection of values of functional features varies cross-linguistically. Most researchers assume that the selection of functional features that are responsible for major syntactic configurations across human languages is triggered by exposure to lexical elements in the input (Ouhalla 1991; Paradis and Genesee 1996). Under this assumption the question of unitary versus separate syntactic systems becomes less a matter of syntactic operations since these are universally available to all speakers and more a matter of whether functional features are associated with lexical items in two separate lexicons. For instance, in the case of gender features discussed above, Spanish lexical items are associated with gender features while English lexical items are not.

In this regard, the possibility of further exploring the extent to which there are similarities and differences in the bilingual acquisition of lexical items and functional features, as well as their assembly and mapping onto morphology, opens up a fruitful research agenda. Preliminary work trying to disentangle differences between lexical borrowing and syntactic transfer in sequential bilinguals (Marian and Kaushanskaya 2007) has shown differences according to categories in the way in which cross-linguistic influence takes place. Nouns are more susceptible to be the target of borrowing while verbs tend to be more prone to undergo what Marian and Kaushanskaya (2007) term *syntactic transfer*. This implies that verbs might undergo changes in argument structure or functional features such as tense, aspect, or mood that are relevant for syntax.

The study of how strongly functional features are linked to the semantic content and the phonological form of lexical items in the two languages spoken by a bilingual individual across their lifespan is also a matter of past and current exploration, especially with respect to the memory systems that subserve the storage and usage of the lexicon (Ullman 2001, 2004; Paradis 2003). Proposals such as Ullman's (2001) declarative/procedural model for second language acquisition as well as Paradis' *Activation Threshold Hypothesis* (1993) can be viewed as complementary to already existing theories of how processing might affect bilingual first language acquisition (Müller and Hulk 2000; Hulk and Müller 2001). In this section, we will present a brief overview of the history of the study of cross-linguistic influence in bilingual acquisition from a perspective that assumes functional features as the locus of cross-linguistic variation.

3.3.1   The Unitary System and Separate Development hypotheses

Until the 1980s, most researchers on infant bilingualism claimed that their subjects initially had one grammatical system that eventually developed into two. This position is known as the *Unitary System Hypothesis*. One of its earliest proponents was Leopold (1949/1970), who conducted a longitudinal study of the language development of his German–English-speaking daughter, Hildegard. He argued that there was initially a "hybrid" stage at which his daughter could not distinguish between her languages and used "one medium of communication." Leopold based this claim on the fact that, early on, Hildegard produced utterances, which mixed German and English words, as seen in (23):

(23) a.   *All babies Bett.*
            'All babies <u>sleep</u>.'   (Hildegard 1;11)
      b.   *Three meows lost Handschuhe.*
            'Three meows lost <u>gloves</u>.'   (Hildegard 2;01)
      c.   *I can't give you any Kuß because I have a Schmutznase.*
            'I can't give you any <u>kisses</u> because I have a <u>cold</u>'   (Hildegard 3;03)
      d.   *Look how many Platz there is; is this viel?*
            'Look how many <u>spaces</u> there is; is this <u>a lot</u>?'   (Hildegard 3;09, all
            examples from Leopold 1949/1970)

As noted by Meisel (2004), these examples show some forms of language mixing that are not consistent with the view that there is a unitary syntactic system. If we look carefully at these sentences, we can see that they consist mostly of English sentences in which some lexical items in German have been inserted. As noted by Meisel (2004), it is not clear whether, at early stages of acquisition, bilingual children's mixing of lexical items is in anyway similar to adult code-switching given that the latter requires a higher level of competence in both languages (Poplack 1980; Toribio 2001). However, as we saw above, work by Liceras *et al.* (2008) has shown that early bilingual children have a preference for functional features from one of the two languages in Determiner + Noun mixed utterances. This clearly indicates that there is evidence that simultaneous bilingual children do distinguish between functional features from each of the two lexicons.

A more complex conceptualization of an initial unitary system was put forth by Volterra and Taeschner (1978). Volterra and Taeschner conducted a longitudinal study of two Italian–German bilingual children. They proposed a three-stage model of a unitary system for bilingual development. One of the children was studied between the ages of 1;05 and 3;06, and the other from 1;02 to 2;06. These authors claimed that in the first stage, the bilingual child has one grammar and one lexicon with lexical items from both languages. In the second stage, the child has two lexicons, but only one syntactic system. At this point, the authors reported, the children mixed their languages within utterances, as in examples (24a–d):

(24) a.　*Spetta <u>lass zu</u> Lisa <u>komm ida</u>, bene? Bene.*
　　　　'Wait, <u>let closed</u>, Lisa <u>comes back</u> OK?'　(Lisa 2;05)

　　b.　*Mami vuole <u>Strickzeug</u>, vuole <u>Arbeit</u>, si?*
　　　　'Mommy want <u>knitting</u>, wants <u>work</u> yes?'　(Lisa 2;07)

　　c.　*Giulia <u>gemacht</u> a caseta per a <u>böse</u> Wolf.*
　　　　'Giulia <u>made</u> a little house for the <u>bad</u> wolf.'　(Giulia 2;02)

　　d.　Mami *ich will* prendere *ja?*
　　　　'Mommy, <u>I will</u> take it, <u>yes</u>?'　(Giulia 2;05)

The third stage is reached when the child "speaks two languages differentiated both in lexicon and in syntax" (Volterra and Taeschner 1978: 312). This position has been challenged by work arguing that bilingual children develop separate systems by the time they begin producing complex sentences (Lindholm and Padilla 1978; Meisel 1986, 1994; De Houwer 1990; Paradis and Genesee 1997, and others). These authors defend the hypothesis that a bilingual child's languages develop separately on several grounds, a position known as the *Separate Development Hypothesis*. First, they argue that mixed utterances should not be used as evidence for or against grammatical fusion given that code-switching requires a highly developed competence in both languages (Meisel 1996, 2004). Another important aspect that must be taken into account is the level of productivity of mixing. As De Houwer (1990) notes, Leopold used his daughter's mixed utterances as proof of an initial hybrid grammatical system, but he could just as easily have used the much higher percentage of non-mixed utterances to argue against this conclusion. More recently, Ezeizabarrena and Aeby (2010) have provided evidence from Euskara–Spanish bilingual children data (longitudinal and cross-sectional) that shows that intrasentential code-switching utterances exhibit very low frequencies. Longitudinal data from two children, Mikel (1;07–3;06) and Kerman (2;00–2;09), both bilingual from birth, show that production of code-switching utterances such as the ones in (25) and (26) constitutes at most 5 percent of the total files recorded.[5]

(25)　　*Nun　da <u>mi</u> <u>león?</u>* (M 2;11)
　　　　Where is　<u>my</u> <u>lion</u>
　　　　'Where is my lion?'　(M 2;11; Ezeizabarrena and Aeby 2010: 66)

---

[5] It is quite possible that these percentages might be different in communities with more extended code-switching practices.

(26)   *No sé   hau ala este.*
         Not know this or this
         'I don't know this or this (one).'   (M 1;11; Ezeizabarrena and Aeby
         2010: 66)

In addition to low frequency, several arguments have been postulated against the *Unitary System Hypothesis*. One is considering cases such as the ones found by Volterra and Taeschner (1978) as instances of grammatical transfer from the child's dominant language to the weaker one (Meisel 1989). In current terms, some cases of grammatical transfer could also be understood as cases in which values for functional features in one of the languages are shared in both languages, as shown in examples (17)–(20) of shared evidentiality values presented in the previous section (Sánchez 2003, 2004).

When levels of dominance in each of the languages are similar, language development in bilingual children proceeds along the same paths as in monolinguals (De Houwer 1990; Ezeizabarrena 1996; Paradis and Genesee 1997, among others). Further evidence for the *Separate Development Hypothesis* includes the finding that bilingual children are sensitive to the context in which their languages are spoken (Lanza 1992; Genesee *et al.* 1995), and that they have metalinguistic awareness of speaking two codes from an early age.

It is not the case, however, that a bilingual child's grammars are completely autonomous as well as separate. Recent work in the field has focused on how to explain instances of cross-linguistic influence in the syntax of young bilingual children, that is, when and why cross-linguistic influence appears in development (Schlyter 1994; Gawlitzek-Maiwald and Tracy 1996; Döpke 1998; Müller 1998; Yip and Matthews 2000; Müller and Hulk 2001; Paradis and Navarro 2003; Kupisch 2003; Serratrice, Sorace, and Paoli 2004; Zwanziger, Allen and Genesee 2005; Kupisch 2007). In the next section we present the areas in which most evidence of cross-linguistic influence has been found in bilingualism in Spanish and other languages.

3.3.2   Autonomous development and cross-linguistic influence in bilinguals

In this section we will focus on two areas in which evidence of autonomous development and of cross-linguistic influence has been abundant: differential acquisition of morphology, in particular of inflectional morphology, and the acquisition of syntactic structures that are at the interface with other components such as the semantics/pragmatics components. These two areas are of great importance in the study of cross-linguistic influence in bilinguals, especially in light of our previous discussion about storage and access to the lexicon.

The acquisition of morphology is revealing of the relationship between the acquisition of functional features and their morphological counterparts, especially in the case of bound morphemes as they are acquired as part of the lexicon. Of particular interest is the acquisition of verbal inflection in Spanish and other languages since the levels of complexity in the mapping of functional features and bound morphemes might result in differences in the two languages acquired by a bilingual individual. In fact, if one assumes that cross-linguistic variation lies mostly on feature specification at the representational level, it is conceivable that some aspects of the evidence of cross-linguistic influence in simultaneous and sequential bilinguals can be better accounted for as a result of varying degrees of activation of functional and lexical features in their mapping onto phonological and morphological forms first at the processing level and possibly at the representational level (Sánchez 2003; Lardiere 1998, 2003, 2005).

Cross-linguistic influence in the way in which syntactic features are represented in the mind can also be explained in terms of the complex relationship that is established between core aspects of syntax and the interpretive component (Hulk and Müller 2000; Sorace 2000; Müller and Hulk 2001; Paradis and Navarro 2003; Serratrice *et al.* 2004; Serratrice 2007; Sorace and Serratrice 2009) especially during processing. The complex relationship between lexical access and syntactic parsing in bilinguals for comprehension and production purposes may have long-lasting effects on the mental representation of their two languages. As proposed for sequential bilinguals by Sorace and Serratrice (2009), there are many factors that are at the basis of what they term the vulnerability of the syntax–pragmatics interface. Following Chomsky (1995) and Jackendoff (2002), they define an interface as a component that links either (a) sub-modules of language, or (b) language and non-linguistic cognitive systems (Sorace and Serratrice 2009: 197). In their view the syntax–pragmatics interface is prone to vulnerability due to at least four variables: underspecification, cross-linguistic influence, quantity and quality of the input, and processing limitations. In the approach we will present here, we take the evidence of cross-linguistic influence as the phenomenon to be explained and we try to identify previous work that has shown how processing and shared parsing strategies in bilinguals are some of factors that may result in cross-linguistic influence at the representational level.

Evidence of differential development and cross-linguistic influence at the morphological level

Examining evidence of cross-linguistic influence in the acquisition of verbal morphology in bilinguals has as its goal to examine the commonalities of research on the acquisition of the lexical items and of functional features linked to those lexical items. Of course, any type of relationship that is established between these two lines of research has to take into account important differences between lexical items and grammatical features as proposed in the declarative/procedural model of the role of memory in second language acquisition (Ullman 2005). In Ullman's (2005) model, lexical items are acquired in the L1 and the L2 by declarative memory, which according to Ullman (2005: 143): "underlies the learning, representation, and use of knowledge about facts (semantic knowledge) and events (episodic knowledge)." Ullman proposes that knowledge learned in declarative memory is available to conscious awareness and "at least partly (but not completely; Chun 2000) explicit" (Ullman 2005: 143). On the other hand, according to Ullman, "the procedural memory system is implicated in the learning of new, and in the control of long-established, motor and cognitive skills and habits, especially those involving sequences" (Ullman 2005: 146). In Ullman's (2005) proposal the declarative and procedural systems interact in a dynamic way that allows for cooperation between systems as well as competition. According to Ullman's DP (declarative/procedural) model, the declarative memory system underlies the mental lexicon, whereas the procedural memory system subserves aspects of the mental grammar. Ullman proposes that:

> The procedural system network of brain structures subserves the implicit learning and use not only of motor and cognitive skills but also aspects of a rule-governed combinatorial grammar. The system is expected to play computationally analogous roles across grammatical subdomains, including morphology, syntax, and possibly phonology.   (Ullman 2005: 149)

While these two systems differ, the fact that they interact in cooperative and competitive ways is relevant to our examination of the evidence of cross-linguistic influence in verbal inflection in bilinguals. Even though the model is intended to account for cases of second language acquisition, its approach to the relationship between two types of memory systems and the acquisition of the lexicon and of grammatical regularities can be extended to bilingual acquisition.

In this subsection, we present some studies that have revealed evidence of differential development and cross-linguistic influence in bilinguals and we will try to explore the relationship between the activation of lexical items (subserved by declarative memory) and the activation of functional features of lexical and morphological items (presumably subserved by procedural memory).

Several researchers have noted that there is a lead–lag pattern in the development of inflection in simultaneous bilingual children acquiring a language with rich inflection and another with impoverished inflection (Ezeizabarrena 1997; Deuchar and Quay 2000; Fernández et al. 2008, among others). This has been especially noted for bilingualism in Spanish and languages such as English with an impoverished verbal paradigm.

In a longitudinal case study of a child acquiring Spanish and English, Deuchar and Quay (2000) found that by age 1;11 their subject produced language-specific verbal and nominal morphology in each language, with verbal morphology appearing earlier in Spanish than in English. In their view, the question of why verbal morphology would appear earlier in Spanish than in English could be accounted for as corresponding to more morphological evidence in the Spanish input than in the English input. This view, however, does not fully answer the question: to what extent is the different rate of acquisition of morphology in each of the languages evidence of acquisition of formal syntactic features?

Differences in rates of acquisition related to verbal morphology have been identified in studies of L1 acquisition. Legate and Yang (2007) point out that there are developmental differences across languages with respect to the length of the root infinitive stage in children that crucially depend on the richness of verbal morphology. Spanish-speaking children have a very short root infinitive period, if they have one at all, because they acquire a language with rich verbal inflection and that reinforces the hypothesis that the language has a [+Tense] value, while English-speaking children exhibit evidence of a longer root infinitive period and take longer to establish the hypothesis that English is a [+Tense] language because English is a language with very poor verbal morphology. Legate and Yang (2007) assume a UG-based probabilistic model of language acquisition that incorporates variability in the selection of hypotheses. In their model, children develop hypotheses that are either reinforced or discarded. They assume the following formulation of such process:

(27) For an input sentence **s**, the child
    a.   with probability **P**i selects a grammar **G**i,
    b.   analyzes **s** with **G**i,
    c.   if successful, reward **G**i by increasing **P**i
                otherwise punish **G**i by decreasing **P**i

From this perspective the lead–lag pattern observed in Spanish–English bilingual children can be accounted for as a result of the frequency with which Spanish input provides verbal morphology in sentences that are analyzed as having Tense and therefore the probability of such analysis being correct increases. What this means in terms of the relationship between acquisition of lexical items and functional features is that acquisition of finite verbs is highly relevant for the acquisition of a syntactic property in Spanish but may be less so in English. Therefore, while in Spanish acquisition of finite verbs is at the intersection of the acquisition of lexical and syntactic properties, it is less relevant in English. The lead–lag pattern shows that autonomous development might be sensitive to the type of interaction between lexical items (verbs in this case) and functional features in each of the languages. While in Spanish there are high levels of interaction between verbs and functional features such as person and tense, in English that is not the case resulting in differential rates of acquisition of morphology.

Further support for the autonomous nature of acquisition of lexical items that are relevant for the acquisition of syntactic properties comes from work by Fernández *et al.* (2008). They also found evidence of earlier acquisition of Spanish rich verbal morphology than of weak English verbal morphology in their study of Spanish–English bilingual twins. In their view, the lead–lag pattern can be better explained as the by-product of the different role that morphology has in both languages. While in Spanish agreement morphemes have semantic content and are pronominal elements that are part of the numeration required in the computation of the sentence, in English, agreement morphemes do not have semantic content and are only phonological spell-outs. The following sentences in Spanish and English from (Fernández *et al.* 2008) illustrate the contrast:

(28)   *Vamos*
         V   -a   -mos.
         go -TV -PRS.IND.1 PL
         'We go.'

(29)   *We go.*   (Fernández *et al.* 2008: 54)

In the Spanish sentence, the verbal inflection *-amos* provides information on person and number and is relevant for the interpretation of the subject and for the computation of the sentence. Therefore, it must be selected as part of the set of elements that are merged in the syntax. In the English sentence, the pronoun *we* provides the information on person and number and is merged with the rest of the sentence. The verb is not inflected. In English, in the present tense verbs are inflected only in the third-person singular as in:

(30)   She go-es.

Despite the inflection, the pronoun is required for the sentence to be grammatical. Fernández *et al.* (2008) take this to be evidence of the different role that verbal morphology plays in both languages.

Following Rivero (1997, 1999), Chomsky (2001) and Fernández *et al.* (2008) assume that "operations which belong to core grammar – the computational component – are less marked than the operations which take place at the periphery – the interface levels – " (Fernandez *et al.* 2008: 53). Given that Spanish agreement morphemes are part of the numeration and of core grammar, they are less marked and should therefore be acquired earlier than English weak agreement (singular morpheme *-s*). Thus, the implementation of the agreement morphemes in English would be more marked than the obligatory presence of subject pronouns in English or the implementation of agreement morphemes in Spanish. What this means in terms of how lexical and functional items are acquired is that not all inflectional items are processed in a similar manner. English morphology taken as a syntax–phonology interface phenomenon is not of the same nature as Spanish verbal morphology, which is an important part of the numeration. This indicates that the nature of the morphemes is also relevant in order to understand whether differences in acquisition are likely to take place in bilinguals. In terms of the parallelism between acquisition of lexical items and acquisition of grammatical features, Fernández *et al.*'s findings point in the direction of the need to study the differences in bilingual acquisition between verbs with syntactically relevant morphology and morphology that is at the syntax–phonology interface.

In addition to the differences with respect to the type of morphological items acquired in each language, it is also important to recognize the differences across languages in the levels of morphological complexity that a bilingual child finds. In a study on the distribution of imperatives in two Euskara–Spanish bilingual children (Mikel and Jurgi), Ezeizabarrena (1997) finds some differences in the development of Euskara and Spanish imperatives. Euskara has synthetic (31a) and periphrastic (31b) finite forms of the imperative as well as infinitival forms (31c):

(31) a. *Ato-z.*
          come-IMP-2 S
          'Come.'
     b. *Etor   zaitez.*
          come ABS.2 S
          'Come.'
     c. *Etorri.*
          come-INF
          'Come.'   (Ezeizabarrena 1997: 300)

Spanish, on the other hand, has a second-person finite form, (32a), that may (32a) or may not – as in (32b) – coincide with the third-person indicative in the singular, and under the scope of negation has imperative forms that coincide with the subjunctive forms, as shown in (32c). This last form is more complex than the ones found in Euskara because it involves a different morphological pattern that emerges only in the scope of negation:

(32) a. *Canta*
          Cant-a.
          Sing-IMP.2 SG
          'Sing.'
     b. *Ven*
          V-en.
          Come-IMP.2 SG
          'Come.'
     c. *No vengas / no vienes*
          No   veng -a   -s   / no   vien -e-   s.
          NEG come -TV.SUBJ -2 SG / NEG come -TV.IND 2 SG
          'Do not come. / No come.'   (Ezeizabarrena 1997: 300)

For both Mikel and Jurgi the first imperative forms in Euskara are the simple forms and the infinitival forms. At 2;00 (Mikel) and 2;08 (Jurgi) there is an increase in finite forms (synthetic and periphrastic). Thus, while the acquisition of imperatives in Euskara does not show evidence of major difficulties, in Spanish the children exhibit some difficulties acquiring the inflected forms of the imperative in negative contexts such as (32c), which coincide with the subjunctive form. The following examples illustrate these difficulties:

(33) a. *No la ata (= ates)*
          No   l-a   at-a   (= at-e-s)
          Not CL-F.ACC   tie-TV.IND.3 SG(= tie-TV.SBJ-2 SG)
          'Do not tie it.'   (M; 2:03)
     b. *No (l-o)   quit-a-s   (= quit-e-s)*
          Not (CL-M.ACC) take-TV.IND.2 SG   (= take-TV.SUBJ-2 SG)
          'Do not take it away.'   (M; 2:04)

This difficulty shows the lead–lag pattern in two languages with rich inflection. It might be indicative of the fact that the level of complexity of the particular morphological paradigms might be an important factor in generating the lead–lag pattern. This would be consistent with the idea that difficulties emerge in areas in which the mapping of functional features onto morphological forms is complex due to the fact that morphology in one of the languages has an even more complex set of morphological forms than the other language. This is the case in Spanish, which requires overt subjunctive morphology in the negative command context. These findings show some parallelisms with findings on the acquisition of the lexicon in that acquisition of one type of mapping in a language may lead to a more pronounced delay in the acquisition of another pattern in the other language. In the case discussed, acquisition of negative commands might take longer in these bilingual children than in their monolingual counterparts, an issue that remains to be explored.

On the other hand, the interface between the lexicon and morphology also shows evidence of cross-linguistic influence in the morphological component. Such evidence comes from a special type of noun-related morphology: case marking. Evidence from bilingualism in Spanish and languages with rich case morphological paradigms such as Quechua (Sánchez 2003) and Euskara (Austin 2007; Ezeizabarrena 2012) has shown that, depending on the type of access to input and activation of both languages, it is possible to observe changes in the morphological expression of rich case-marking languages.

Sánchez (2003) notes that second-generation Quechua–Spanish older bilingual children (9 to 13 years of age) exhibit dropping of accusative case marking in DPs. Quechua is a nominative–accusative language in which direct objects and, in some cases, other VP-internal DPs are marked for accusative case. In the speech of some bilingual children, the lack of accusative case marking coincides with the emergence of definite determiners, as shown in the following example:

(34)   *Chay niñito apuntaykan chay sapito.*
         Chay niñ -it -o apunta -yka -n chay sap -it -o.
         That boy -DIM -M point_out -PROG -3 SG that toad -DIM -M.
         'That boy points at that toad'   (Sánchez 2003: 92)

In this sentence, the canonical SOV word order of Quechua is altered in favor of SVO word order typical of Spanish and we see a demonstrative in both the subject and the object DPs, which is also atypical of monolingual varieties of Quechua, a language that favors determinerless DPs. The subject and the direct object have a Spanish noun, which in the case of *sapo* 'toad' appears to be a common borrowing from Spanish. Worth noticing is the fact that the direct object is unmarked for accusative case. The DP *chay sapito* 'that toad' should be *chay sapu-cha-ta/* that toad-DIM-ACC/ 'that toad.' Sánchez (2003) proposes that accusative case dropping seems to be favored by the emergence of a definite determiner in the speech of these bilingual children. In Sánchez's proposal the emergence of this determiner in the speech of these children who are second-generation bilinguals seems to correspond to a process by which convergence takes place in order to express definiteness morphologically in both languages. The mapping of definiteness onto the determiner results in the erosion of case marking and is reinforced by the fact that in Spanish no overt case marking of direct objects takes place.

Another study that notes case marking dropping in bilinguals is Austin (2007). Austin notes that Euskara–Spanish bilingual subjects omit the ergative case marker in Euskara to a greater extent than monolingual children. Euskara is a language with an ergative–absolutive case-marking pattern. Unlike Quechua, which assigns nominative case to subjects regardless of whether the verb is transitive or intransitive and assigns accusative case to the direct object, in Euskara the subject of transitive sentences takes the ergative case and the direct object and the subject of intransitive verbs take absolutive marking. Euskara–Spanish bilingual children drop the case marking assigned to the subject of transitive verbs.

As in the dropping of case marking described by Sánchez (2003), Austin proposes that this is the case because of cross-linguistic influence from Spanish, a language that lacks overt case marking on full DPs. In Austin's view, the grammar of Spanish reinforces absolutive case marking which is morphologically null in Euskara as the default option. The following examples illustrate the overextension of absolutive marking (null marking) in Euskara–Spanish bilingual children's speech:

(35)   *Ni(k) badaukat hau etxian*
         Ni(k)   badaukat   *hau   etxi-an*
         I-Ø   have-ERG.1 SG.ABS.3 SG   that-ABS   house-in
         'I have that at home.'   (LA 3;00; Austin 2007: 320)

Example (35) shows the dropping of ergative marking in favor of no marking that corresponds to absolutive marking in the adult Euskara grammar. According to Austin (2007), the fact that Spanish does not distinguish between absolutive and ergative case for subjects and does not overtly mark differences between nominative and accusative case in full DPs allows bilingual children to retain absolutive marking as the default case marker for all arguments. This phenomenon, according to Austin, lies at the syntax–morphology interface and is indicative that cross-linguistic influence is more likely to take place at the interfaces. However, it is important to highlight that in a subsequent study, Austin (2013) has argued that it is the inherent complexity of the case-marking system of Euskara that is the main factor in the delay found in bilinguals and that some form of a delay is also found in Euskara monolingual children.

Ezeizabarrena (2012) also notes some inconsistency in the marking of the ergative morphology in Euskara. She points out that there is an asymmetry in the acquisition of ergativity in the verbal and in the nominal domain in monolingual children. The latter is characterized by delay in comparison to acquisition of the first one. In her analysis this delay cannot be accounted for in terms of language-internal inconsistency or cross-linguistic influence. Furthermore, Ezeizabarrena points out that the delay lasts longer in child second language acquisition than in early monolingual and bilingual first language acquisition and that the type of input and the degree of exposure to the language play a significant role in this delay.

To summarize, in this section we have presented evidence of:

(a)   autonomous development in syntactically relevant morphology (lead–lag patterns due to the different roles that morphology plays in syntax in both languages and also possibly due to differential levels of complexity in morphological paradigms in each language) and

(b)   cross-linguistic influence evidenced by a lag pattern of case marking or case erosion (possibly due to cross-linguistic influence that debilitates the association between lexical items and case-marking endings). This debilitating effect of case marking may be due to differences between the acquisition of noun and verbal morphology.

One could always argue that differences in dominance are at play when evidence of cross-linguistic influence is found. However, cross-linguistic influence does not follow a uniform pattern nor does it emerge in all areas of morphosyntax at once. One way of looking at these different pieces of evidence is to think of the role that functional features play in the acquisition of lexical items with verbal morphology (verbs) and in the acquisition of lexical items with gender or case morphology (nouns) in each of the language pairs examined. In Spanish, verbal morphology is closely linked to functional features and this is less the case in English, therefore differences in the rate of acquisition are expected in Spanish–English bilingual children as well as robustness of the Spanish verbal morphology. At the same time, activation of case morphology can be understood as the morphological spell-out of a syntactic operation (Marantz 2000; Baker and Vinokurova 2010). If this operation is expressed by means of morphological patterns found in the other language, then erosion of case in second-generation bilinguals should not be surprising.

In this subsection we have presented evidence of autonomous development as well as of cross-linguistic influence in bilinguals at the morphological level. We have related evidence of autonomous development to the differential role that functional features linked to lexical items may have in the two languages represented in the bilingual mind. We have also related evidence of cross-linguistic influence in the case of morphological erosion of case-marking morphology to the fact that it is the spell-out of a syntactic operation but it is not the probe of such an operation. It would seem as though morphological markers are not all stored in an equal manner in the bilingual mind in terms of their association with the lexical items to which they are bound (verbs or nouns). In fact, in the case of nouns and case marking, we observe that some level of dissociation between the lexical root and the morphological marking takes place. Whether cross-linguistic influence at the level of morphological marking is due to the processing difficulties inherent in keeping two complex paradigms separate or due to convergence in feature–morpheme mapping strategies still remains a matter of further research.

Evidence of cross-linguistic influence at the syntax–discourse interface

In addition to the morphological evidence of cross-linguistic influence, there is also evidence of cross-linguistic influence at the syntax–pragmatics interface. Research on this type of cross-linguistic influence provides a better understanding of the cognitive skills and processing factors involved in generating separate mental representations for the two languages in bilingual populations.

The focus on cross-linguistic influence in bilingual speakers is represented in the work by Müller and Hulk (1999, 2000) and Hulk and Müller (2000). Their work represents a change of perspective in research on syntactic development in bilingual children. Hulk and Müller's work recognizes the previous findings in the literature supporting the autonomous syntactic systems hypothesis and at the same time it provides a framework for the understanding of instances of cross-linguistic influence found in bilingual children. Their proposal focuses on the idea that there are some conditions under which cross-linguistic influence takes place: (a) at the interface between syntax and pragmatics and (b) when there is a surface overlap of the two languages (Hulk and Müller 2000: 228). On the basis of several studies of German–Italian and Dutch–French bilingual children Hulk and Müller propose that when these two conditions are met, cross-linguistic influence is more likely to take place.

Other scholars have argued that overlap between syntactic constructions in the bilingual child's languages can lead to cross-linguistic influence by reinforcing a non-target analysis in one of the languages. For example, Döpke (1998) found that bilingual children acquiring German and English used SVO word order to a much greater extent than monolingual children acquiring German. Döpke claimed that the bilingual children's exposure to SVO word order in English encouraged them to overproduce SVO order in German, even in contexts which required SOV order. Hulk (1997) and Müller (1998) had similar findings for bilingual children acquiring Dutch–French and German–French, respectively; bilingual children in both studies produced a word order that was marginal or unacceptable in language A but that was acceptable in language B.

To explain this phenomenon, Müller suggested that transfer could be used as a relief strategy when a bilingual child is faced with several competing interpretations of a syntactic structure. Under these circumstances, bilingual children may overproduce one of the options provided by the ambiguous input if it coincides with a grammatical option in the other language.

Hulk and Müller (2000) and Müller and Hulk (2001) also invoked influence from German as an explanation for their finding that bilingual children acquiring German and either French or Italian dropped more object pronouns than monolingual children acquiring these Romance languages. However, they argued that the cross-linguistic influence is indirect in nature, and that input from German, in which object drop is grammatically acceptable, led the bilingual children to retain the option of pragmatically licensed empty objects provided by a *Minimal Default Grammar* (Roeper 1999) longer than a monolingual child acquiring French or

Italian would. Furthermore, Müller and Hulk claimed that these syntactic constructions involve a bilingual child's developing the C-domain of the sentence, namely the part of sentence structure that is related to sentence type (questions, assertions, subordination) and is discourse-oriented in that it hosts elements that are old information or new information. The C-domain is particularly vulnerable to cross-linguistic influence as it is an interface between syntactic and pragmatic operations (e.g., the expression of null vs. overt arguments depending on their information status as new or already established in discourse or as topics of discourse).

In support of this claim, Müller and Hulk cited research which found C-related constructions to have a protracted developmental course in monolingual and bilingual children as well as children with SLI, adult L2 learners and aphasic adults (Meisel 1992; Platzack 2001).

These findings are consistent with several recent studies on syntactic convergence in child and adult L2 grammars, which claim that interpretable features (which are found in the peripheral or interface areas of grammar) are most vulnerable to interference and attrition (Sorace 2003; Bullock and Toribio 2004; Montrul 2004a, 2004b; Sánchez 2004).[6] However, Unsworth (2003) did not find evidence of cross-linguistic influence in the distribution of root infinitives in German in a German–English bilingual child, despite the fact that root infinitives lie at the syntax–pragmatics interface. In fact, Hulk and Müller (2000) show convincingly that the condition that requires surface overlap in both languages does not hold in the case of root infinitives. Hulk and Müller (2000) follow Hoekstra and Hyams' (1998) analysis according to which root infinitives differ from finite sentences in that the latter have a C (complementizer) projection that hosts a temporal operator. This operator anchors the sentence in time. Root infinitives lack this C-projection and are therefore dependent on discourse for their temporal interpretation. In this respect root infinitives are ideal candidates for cross-linguistic influence at the syntax–pragmatics interface. On the other hand, while root infinitives do exist in the oral production of monolingual children of the two language pairs (French–Dutch and German–Italian) investigated in their study, root infinitives are very limited in adult language. For that reason they are not frequent in the input and do not constitute a case in which the child grammar will be compatible with the adult input in one of the languages. Hulk and Müller (2000) did not find evidence of cross-linguistic influence in the minimally different distribution of root infinitives in the French–Dutch and German–Italian bilingual children studied.

In the literature on Spanish–English child bilingualism, work by Paradis and Navarro (2003) has noted differences in the distribution of overt and null subjects in the speech of young children. Paradis and Navarro's study looked at the

---

[6] Not all researchers would agree with this generalization; Döpke (2000: 28) remarked that her
    data: "indicate that structural overlaps between languages can lead to variation in the acquisition
    paths at any level of the structural hierarchy" and not just in the C-domain.

distribution of null and overt subjects in the speech of one Spanish–English bilingual child and compared it to the distribution found in the speech of two monolingual children. They looked at two factors that could in principle account for cross-linguistic influence in the speech of the bilingual child: (a) the syntax–pragmatic interface nature of the distinction between null and overt subjects and (b) the nature of the input that the bilingual child received at home.

Paradis and Navarro (2003) base their study on Hulk and Müller's (2000) and Müller and Hulk's (2001) proposal according to which cross-linguistic influence tends to occur at the pragmatics–syntax interface. Paradis and Navarro argue that this proposal is particularly relevant since pragmatic factors affect the realization of overt arguments in languages that syntactically allow null subjects. Furthermore, as mentioned above, Hulk and Müller's (2000) and Müller and Hulk's (2001) proposal requires a surface overlap in a particular structure in the two languages spoken by a bilingual child that could generate a common syntactic analysis in a converging manner for both languages. In their study, Paradis and Navarro (2003) used spontaneous language data available from CHILDES for the two monolingual children, ages: 1;08–2;07 and 1;08–1;11 and a bilingual child (ages 1;09–2;06). They analyzed the frequencies of overt and null subjects in the speech of the bilingual and monolingual children and they also determine their distribution according to the following pragmatic conditions: (a) new information, (b) contrast, (c) query, (d) emphasis, (e) absent, and (f) low informativeness. They labeled *contrast* contexts those in which an overt subject disambiguates between two potentially competing referents or the subject was focused. *Query* referred to contexts in which the subject was questioned or was used in a response to a question. *Emphasis* contexts referred to overt subjects with more prosodic prominence, mostly pronouns. *Absent* contexts included those in which the subjects' referents are not visible during the speech utterance. *Low informativeness* contexts correspond to those cases with no clear pragmatic function. They also looked at the distribution of these variables in the speech of the children's parents. Their results showed a slightly higher overall percentage of overt subjects in the bilingual child (35 percent) than in the monolingual children (20 percent). They take this as apparent evidence for cross-linguistic influence but this evidence is partially confounded by the fact that the adult Spanish input received by the bilingual child corresponds to Caribbean Spanish which has been found to exhibit a higher frequency of overt subjects than other varieties of Spanish. Of interest is the fact that the bilingual child had higher frequencies of overt subjects in the low informativeness category than one of the monolingual children, and this type of subject was not found in the speech of the other monolingual child.

Liceras (2011) notes that Paradis and Navarro's (2003) results are better understood as the result of parent's input than as evidence of cross-linguistic influence. Liceras notes that the bilingual child's use of overt subjects corresponds to discourse pragmatic uses that differ from those of the monolingual children and that the bilingual child's mother (a non-native speaker) has a higher frequency of overt pronouns than the parents of monolingual children.

Another study on bilingual acquisition at the syntax–pragmatics interface is Pladevall's (2010). Pladevall conducted a study on the distribution of null versus overt subjects in children who are native speakers of English in the process of acquiring Spanish as a second language. This study looked at the distribution of overt versus null subjects in (a) main and subordinate sentences, (b) sentences with unaccusative verbs, (c) sentences with transitive verbs, and (d) sentences with unergative verbs. Bilingual participants in the study were grouped in three age cohorts: 5-, 10-, and 17-year-old children. Three groups of native speakers paired in age served as control groups. Using grammaticality and preference judgment experimental tasks, Pladevall's study uncovered acquisition of the strong pronominal agreement features in the verb that allow the raising of the verb to Tense and an expected distribution of overt and null subjects in the older group but some difficulties in the younger groups. This was evidenced in the preference for null subjects over overt subjects in the appropriate context. The following is an example of one type of item given to the children that corresponds to the choice of null vs. overt referential subjects in main sentences. Children were asked to choose between (a) and (b) as their preferred answer to the question:

(36)   *¿Qué decidistéis hacer ayer por la tarde?*
         ¿Qué decid -i -sté   -is   hac -e -r   ayer   por
         What decide -TV -PST.PFV -2 PL do -TV -INF yesterday in
         la   tarde?
         the afternoon?
     a. *Finalmente nosotros decidimos ir   al   parque.*
         Finally   we   decided to go to-the park
     b. *Finalmente decidimos   ir   al   parque.*
         Finally   (we) decided to-go to-the park   (Pladevall 2010: 194)

The expected answer was (36b). The group of 5-year-olds showed an average acceptance of the expected type of sentences of 85.71 percent, the 10-year-olds had an average of 84.61 percent, and the 17-year-olds an average of 97.91 percent.

There was also evidence of delay in the acquisition of postverbal subjects with unergative and unaccusative verbs. While unaccusative verbs require postverbal subjects, unergative verbs do not, except when they are focalized (Belletti 2001, 2004). The delay showed in the results of the two youngest cohorts. Children were asked to choose between options (a) and (b) as answers to the questions. In the case of the sentence below with an unaccusative verb and no focus on the subject a preference for a postverbal subject in sentences is expected. In the case of the sentence with an unergative verb with a focalized subject, a postverbal subject is also expected:

Unaccusative verbs
(37)   *¿Qué ocurrió   después del   accidente?*
         What happened after   of-the accident
         'What happened after the accident?'

a. *Mi padre vino a ayudarnos.*
   My father came to help-us
   'My father came to help us.'

b. *Vino mi padre a ayudarnos.*
   Came my father to help-us
   'My father came to help us.'

Unergative verbs

(38)   *¿Qué le ocurría a tu hermanito al empezar el cole?*

       ¿Qué le   ocurría   a tu   hermanito al
       What cl.3 SG.DAT happened a your brother   to-the

       empezar el   cole?
       begin.inf the school?

       'What happened with your brother when he started college?' (habitual)

a. *Lloraba mucho mi hermanito al empezar al cole.*
   Llor -a -ba   mucho mi
   Cry -TV -PST.IPFV.3 SG a-lot my

   herman -it -o al   empez -a -r el cole.
   brother -DIM -M to-the begin -TV -INF the school.

   '(He) cried a lot my little brother when (he) began school.'

b. *Mi hermanito lloraba mucho al empezar el cole.*
   Mi herman -it -o llor -a -ba   mucho al
   My brother -DIM -M cry -TV -PST.IPFV.3 SG a-lot to-the

   empez -a -r el cole.
   begin -TV -INF the school.

   'My little brother cried a lot when (he) began school.'

The 5-year-old and 10-year-old children had a 50 percent average of acceptance of the unexpected option with unaccusative verbs and 100 percent average of acceptance of the unexpected option with unergative verbs, while the 17-year-olds had 0 percent average in both cases.

In addition to evidence of cross-linguistic influence from the syntax–pragmatics interface, work on bilingualism in Spanish and English at the interface of syntax and lexical semantics has shown delays in bilingual acquisition. Two important studies that have shown some evidence of cross-linguistic effects at the syntax–lexico-semantic and pragmatics interface are Silva-Corvalán and Montanari (2008) and Fernández and Liceras (2010). Both studies focus on the acquisition of copular verbs in Spanish by Spanish–English bilingual children. The distinction between the two types of copulas in Spanish (*ser* and *estar*) may prove difficult to acquire by bilinguals given reinforcement of a single copula in English. Current analyses of the difference between the two Spanish copulas gravitate towards semantic distinctions between individual and stage-level predicates (Carlson 1977; Kratzer 1995) as the source of the choice between *ser* and *estar* (Schmitt and Miller 2007; Camacho 2012, among others; see Schmitt 1996 for a similar distinction in Brazilian Portuguese). This distinction is based on the notion that individual-level predicates denote properties that hold of the individual and not of a particular state of the individual, whereas stage-level predicates hold only of a particular state of the individual. The distinction has also been associated with a grammaticalized aspectual distinction (Luján 1981; Fernández Leborans 1999) that is at the core of the selection of different complements by each copula. While there are overlapping contexts in which *ser* and *estar* may select as complements projections of the same categories, such as adjectives, there are also contexts in which they are in complementary distribution, such as the use of *estar* but not *ser* with locative expressions or the impossibility of *estar* to select DPs. In some overlapping contexts, such as the selection of Adjectival Phrases, there are also differences regarding the restrictions imposed on the lexical properties of the adjectives that are related to differences between individual and stage-level predicates. The following examples illustrate the difference between these types of predicates:

Individual-level predicate
(39)   La   casa   es/*está   roja.
         The   house   be-individual level/be-stage level   red
         'The house is red.' (permanent property)

Stage-level predicate
(40)   La   casa   está/*es   roja.
         The   house   be-stage level/be-individual level   red
         'The house is red.' (temporary property)

The examples show the complementary distribution of the Spanish copulas according to the type of predicate they denote.

    In a study on the acquisition of copulas by a Spanish–English bilingual child (1;06 and 3;00), Silva-Corvalán and Montanari (2008) examined cross-linguistic influence from English into Spanish in the distribution of copular constructions. The focus of their study is the acquisition of syntactic and semantic contrasts in Spanish that are not grammatically expressed in English. Silva-Corvalán and Montanari (2008) provide a comparison of the frequency of distribution of the copulas *ser* and *estar* in the bilingual child and the adults he interacts with in Spanish in the context of English as a stronger language. The results show an autonomous development of copular constructions in Spanish and English, although some delay was found in the acquisition of *estar*, which the authors attribute to a possible influence from English. At 1:08, the child (N) utters questions with *ser* but lacks *estar* as an auxiliary in questions with verbs in progressive forms, as shown in the following contrast:

(41) N: ¿Qué es eso, Bibi?   (1;8.21)
            'What is that, Bibi?'

(42) N: ¿Qué Ø haciendo, Bibi?   (1;8.29)
            'What Ø you doing, Bibi?'   (Silva-Corvalán and Montanari 2008: 350)

During the twentieth month, both copulas (*ser* and *estar*) appear with a variety of nouns, and in the next month (1;09) there is an increase in locative questions that alternate a null copula and *está*:

(43) N: *¿Dónde (e?) / 'stá auto ə papi?* (1;09;16)
               'Where (is?) / is daddy's car?' (Silva Corvalán and Montanari 2008: 350)

There are, however, some instances of *ser* where *estar* is expected at later stages of acquisition as in (44):

(44) C: *¿Dónde pusiste tus calcetines?*
               'Where did you put your socks?'
     N: *Son en mi <u>drawers</u>.*
               'They're in my drawers.' (2;09;02; Silva-Corvalán and Montanari 2008: 355)

Despite the delays found in the use of *estar*, Silva-Corvalán and Montanari (2008) note that there is a clear separation between the type of adjectives that require *ser* and those that require *estar*. In fact there are few errors in copula choice before age 2;08. Interestingly, during the period studied, forty-nine out of the fifty-two adjectives are used with one of the copulas and not with the other despite the fact that thirty-four may occur with both copulas. Silva-Corvalán and Montanari (2008) argue that this is evidence in favor of an initial lexically based stage that allows the child to distinguish between the two copulas. The child later acquires more complex semantic distinctions that are the intersection of lexical semantics and syntax and allow the child to extend the uses of *ser* and *estar* to multiple syntactic contexts.

In a different type of study Liceras *et al.* (2012) explored cross-linguistic influence in the acquisition of the English copular *be* (as well as the omission/ production of subject pronouns in Spanish) in the grammar of two English–Spanish bilingual children. They analyze the omission of the English copula *be* with nominal predicates as well as with locative expressions. Previous work on monolingual acquisition of English by Becker (2000, 2004) had shown that there is a higher frequency of copular omission with nominal predicates than with locative predicates. They propose that the existence of a clear distinction between stage-level and individual-level predicates in Spanish could generate a positive influence in the realization of overt copulas in bilingual child English. In fact, their data show a higher frequency of overt expression of copulas with nominal predicates, which the authors analyze as the results of cross-linguistic influence from Spanish.

These studies point in the direction of a complex relationship between the acquisition of lexical items and their association with morphological and syntactic features as well as with their distribution at the syntax–pragmatics interface. In addition to work that has focused on the interfaces of syntax and the pragmatic and lexico-semantic components, more recent approaches to how cross-linguistic influence proceeds in bilingual acquisition have tried to incorporate evidence from lexical activation at the processing and representational levels by relating activation of certain lexical items to activation of functional features. Putnam and Sánchez (2013) propose a model for the study of the competence of heritage bilinguals that incorporates processing and the declarative/procedural differences along with functional features in order to account for the two main areas where cross-linguistic influence has been found. As Putnam and Sánchez (2013) propose, this type of model along the lines of previous proposals such as the *Activation Threshold Hypothesis* (Paradis 1993) might provide a better descriptive and explanatory framework of analysis than the discussion on whether bilinguals exhibit incomplete acquisition or attrition in subtractive environments experience. These are consistent with cross-linguistic influence at the processing level and also with more stable cross-linguistic influence at the representational level.

3.4   The effects of bilingualism on grammar

In the previous section, we provided evidence of cross-linguistic influence in the morphosyntactic component as well as at the syntax–pragmatic interface in bilinguals. In this section, we will discuss the effects of cross-linguistic influence processes such as transfer of L1 morphosyntactic properties to an L2, code-switching, and convergence in functional features in the two languages spoken by a bilingual individual. While in many cases, these processes might not result in long-term effects, in some cases they may show residual effects on the specification of feature values in the lexicon of bilingual individuals. In this section, we will illustrate how bilingualism in Spanish and other languages in different geographical contexts has contributed to shape new grammatical features that are at the basis of some aspects of dialectal variation. Before presenting the specific cases, we present a general outline of how these processes might have long-lasting effects on bilingual grammars.

3.4.1   Transfer, code-switching, and convergence, and their potential effects on bilingual grammars

Transfer, code-switching, and convergence have been the matter of extensive research (for previous references see Bullock, Hinrichs, and Toribio 2014; Treffers-Daller and Sakel 2012) and were first presented in the Introduction. They are mental processes that can only take place in the mind of a bilingual individual and, while historically they have been seen as the source of uneven development in bilinguals, our current understanding of them is that they are natural processes that are indicative of how the mind represents and processes language.

As mentioned in the Introduction, transfer is a concept traditionally associated with the literature on second language acquisition (Gass 1979; Zobl 1980; Odlin 1989; Gass and Selinker 1992; Eubank 1993; Schwartz and Sprouse 1996, among others). It originated in the behavorist framework as the transfer of forms, meanings, and their use from the L1 onto the L2 (Lado 1957; Gass and Selinker 1992). In current terms it has been reinterpreted as referring to transfer of some crucial aspects of the mental representation of one language onto the other, particularly transfer of the value specification of functional categories in the L1 to the L2 (Schwartz and Sprouse 1996). Some theoretical approaches to L2 transfer view it as an initial stage that is later overcome by full access to the language acquisition device that results in an end-state that does not diverge from that of monolingual grammar (Schwartz and Sprouse 1996). There are, however, alternative views according to which such access is not available to adult L2 learners (Clahsen and Muysken 1989; Hawkins and Chen 1997, among others). In the last decades a new approach has emerged that locates long-term residual transfer at the interface between syntax and other components (Sorace and Serratrice 2009). In this subsection, we will focus on cases of transfer of functional feature values and their mapping onto morphological expressions from the L1 onto the L2 that have been historically identified as the source of the emergence of new varieties of Spanish in bilingual contexts.

Code-switching is also a concept that has been explored in depth from multiple perspectives and has been defined in multiple ways (Bullock and Toribio 2009; Isurin, Winford, and De Bot 2009; Bhatt and Bolonyai 2011). In this section we will present some cases of code-switching, understood as the possibility of alternating lexical items and morphological expressions from the two linguistic systems known by the bilingual, that are revealing of how code-switching might affect language change in a language in contact with Spanish.

Convergence in bilingualism has been a matter of intense debate in the field of bilingualism. Like the other two terms, it has been defined from multiple perspectives (Muysken 2001; Toribio 2004) and it has been shown to be of great importance in the understanding of how processing in two languages might result in converging representations of some aspects of the grammar of the two languages in bilinguals. Muysken defines it as bidirectional influence in the grammar of two languages (Muysken 2001: 264). In this chapter, we will look at a definition of convergence that is restricted to the sharing of values for functional features in the two languages spoken by a bilingual individual and at the consequences of functional convergence for the emergence of new morphosyntactic characteristics in the context of bilingualism in Spanish and other languages.

3.4.2   Language contact and grammatical change

Several lines of research have explored the relationship between language contact and grammatical change. Our current understanding of this relationship has been shaped by pioneering research that established a correlation between language contact in the human brain and the emergence of temporary patterns that diverge from monolingual patterns in childhood (Hulk and Müller 2000; Müller and Hulk 2001; Meisel 2004), research that focused on social variables in language contact situations as the main forces that drive language change (Thomason and Kauffman 1988; Silva-Corvalán 1994; Thomason 2003), and research on code-switching practices that has deepened our understanding of knowledge of language in contact situations (Toribio 2001; Myers-Scotton 2002; MacSwan 2012). These different lines of analysis have led us to a view of bilingualism that recognizes the possibility of autonomous development in the two languages spoken by a bilingual and at the same time acknowledges the contribution of bilingualism in the emergence of new grammatical characteristics in the languages spoken by a bilingual individual.

In this respect, different social contexts might provide crucial elements to account for why autonomous development is more characteristic of certain bilingual communities while residual transfer is more pervasive in others and might lead to the emergence of new grammatical characteristics in bilingual populations. By looking at Spanish in contact with other languages in contexts in which Spanish is a socially dominant language and contexts in which it is a non-dominant language we might be able to develop some sense of how contact with different languages in diverging social contexts is involved in the emergence of new grammatical characteristics. In the next section we will provide examples of different types of cross-linguistic influence that illustrate transfer, convergence, and in some cases code-switching practices in three different regions of the Spanish-speaking world: the Andean region in Peru and Bolivia, the Basque region of Spain, and the United States.

In language contact situations in which two speech communities coexist new varieties of language emerge. In most communities bilingualism is characterized by a generation of sequential bilinguals that gives raise to simultaneous bilingualism. Due to political, social, and economic reasons, bilingual communities tend to be characterized by growing levels of instability in terms of the contexts of language use (Baker 2011). In this section we present an overview of some cross-linguistic influence phenomena at the individual level that have shaped the grammar of Spanish in bilingual communities. We focus on three major bilingual communities: Quechua–Spanish, Euskara–Spanish, and Spanish–English communities.

Quechua and Spanish in contact, cross-linguistic influence and grammatical change

The history of bilingualism studies in the Andes has been characterized by sociolinguistic and educational approaches in countries such as Bolivia, Ecuador, and Peru. The result of extended bilingualism has been studied from a historical perspective with evidence of language change dating back to the early times of the contact (Rivarola 1989; Escobar 2012). An example from a text from the Huancavelica area from the seventeenth century shows neutralization of gender and well as accusative clitic doubling in the written Spanish of a Quechua–Spanish bilingual individual:

(45)   *El   portugués   aunque   dice que dio   bastante*
        The portuguese even though says that gave a lot of
        información o   probanç-a-s, no opstante l-o
        information or   proof-F-PL,   however   CL- M.SG.ACC
        pueden dar   vuesas mercedes otra   mexor probanc-a;
        can   give your   graces   other better proof-F.SG
        ay   l-o =   remito la   cart-a.
        there CL-M.ACC = submit the letter-F.SG
        'Even though the Portuguese (man) says that he gave a lot of information
        and proofs, your graces could still give another better proof; here I submit
        the letter.'   (Rivarola 1989: 157)

As this seventeenth-century example shows, in this text there is one clear instance
of an accusative clitic-doubling structure represented by *Ay lo remito la carta*
'Here I submit the letter' that also shows neutralization of gender in the clitic.
The sentence *No opstante lo pueden dar vuesas mercedes otra mexor probanca*
'Your graces could still give another better proof' illustrates either accusative clitic
doubling with gender neutralization of the clitic *lo* or a case of substitution of the
dative clitic *le*. This early attested phenomenon is also found in many descriptions of contemporary varieties of the Spanish spoken by Quechua–Spanish
bilinguals.

In pioneering work by Escobar (1978), some of the major characteristics of the
emerging varieties of Spanish in contact with indigenous languages, in particular
with Quechua, in Peru were identified. In syntactic terms, these included DP
and clausal-level phenomena as well as significant areas of morphosyntax. In the
DP domain some of the phenomena mentioned by Escobar (1978) are: (a) the
existence of null determiners, (b) the overextension of possessive determiners,
(c) the order possessor–possessed in noun phrases. At the clausal level: (a) the use
of hearsay evidential markers, (b) null objects with fronted constituents (for topic
or focus reasons), (c) the neutralization of gender and case in pronominal clitics,
(d) the use of resumptive pronouns, among other phenomena. The following are
examples of each type of construction identified by Escobar (1978):

Null determiners
(46)   *María escribe Ø carta.*
        María writes   letter
        'María writes (a/the) letter.'   (Escobar 1978: 108)

Overextension of possessives
(47)   *Esta es su tienda de mi compadre.*
        This is his store of my godfather (of your children)
        'This is my child's godfather's store.'   (Escobar 1978: 108)

Order possessor–possessed
(48)   *De mi perro su hocico.*
        Of my dog   his muzzle
        'My dog's muzzle.'   (Escobar 1978: 108)

Use of evidential hearsay markers
(49)   *Extrañaba a   su   marido   dice.*
             Missed   to her husband says
             '(I heard she) missed her husband.'   (Escobar 1978: 109)

Null objects in fronted structures
(50)   *A   la   chica he   visto en misa.*
             To the girl   have seen in mass
             'The girl I have seen at mass.'   (Escobar 1978: 109)

Neutralization of gender and case in pronominal clitics
(51)   *A mi hija   todos l -o =   adoramos.*
             To my daughter all   CL-3 SG.M.ACC = adore
             'My daughter, we all adore her.'   (Escobar 1978: 110)

(52)   *A Florencio l-o =   has   dicho que no   venga.*
             To Florencio CL-3 SG.M.ACC = have said   that not come
             'You have told Florencio not to come.'   (Escobar 1978: 110)

Many of the grammatical features and syntactic structures presented by Escobar (1978) have been studied since his pioneering work and are currently being analyzed. In this section, we will focus on the grammatical consequences of cross-linguistic influence at the morphosyntactic level for Bilingual Spanish varieties in contact with Quechua in three phenomena noted by Sánchez (2015): (a) the emergence of non-argumental clitics, (b) evidentiality mapping on tense and aspect Spanish systems, and (c) aspectual markers and changes in argument structure.

One of the effects of cross-linguistic influence at the morphosyntactic level is the emergence of new non-argumental clitics in Quechua–Spanish bilinguals. Camacho, Paredes, and Sánchez (1995) and Kalt (2009) note a possessor clitic at different stages in the Spanish of Quechua speakers from southern Peru. The following example illustrates this type of clitic:

(53)   *[L-o]$_i$ =   amarran su pata [del   condor]$_i$*
             CL-3 SG.M.ACC = tie   his leg of-the condor
             como si estuviera montando.
             as   if was   riding
             'They tie the condor's leg as if it was riding.'   (Camacho *et al.* 1995: 135)

The clitic *lo* is coindexed with the genitive expression *del condor* 'of the condor,' not with the direct object constituent *su pata del condor* 'the condor's leg.' This possessor clitic is not found in general or monolingual Spanish:

(54)   **L-o = /*l-e =**   *toqué la mano del   niño.*
             CL-3 SG.M.ACC = / CL-3 SG.M.DAT = touched the hand of-the boy
             'I touched the hand of the boy.'   (Camacho *et al.* 1995: 135)

Camacho *et al.* (1995) show that the clitic *lo* is associated with the full genitive expression *del condor* 'of the condor' and not with the direct object DP as it can coexist with the *wh*-extraction of the possesed constituent, as shown in (55). This is consistent with a general pattern of doubling found in L2 Spanish:

(55)   *¿Qué l-o$_i$-*   *amarran t$_i$ [del condor]?*
         what   CL-3 SG.M.ACC$_i$ tie   t$_i$ [of-the condor]
         'What (part) of the condor do they tie?'   (Camacho *et al.* 1995:136)

The emergence of a possessor clitic in L2 Spanish can be understood as the result of transfer of L1 genitive features found in the DP structure of Quechua (Sánchez 1996) and their association to L2 pronominal clitics. This type of feature transfer and reassembly is possible because there is a similar structure involving non-direct objects in other varieties of Spanish (Camacho *et al.* 1995; Kalt 2012). As Kalt (2012) notes, in general Spanish there are some structures with oblique clitics that are characterized by a clitic-DP chain in which the DP is a possessor preceded by the prepositon *a* 'to' but not by the preposition *de* 'of.' This is shown in the contrast between (56) and (57):

(56)   *María l-e$_i$-*   *robó el   dinero a Juan$_i$.*
         María CL-3 SG.DAT stole the money to Juan
         'María stole the money from Juan.'

(57)   **María l-e$_i$*   *robó el   dinero de Juan$_i$.*
         María cl-3 SG.DAT stole the money of Juan
         'María stole Juan's money.'   (Kalt 2012: 174)

Kalt proposes, following Masullo (1992), that some oblique objects incorporate into the theta grid of the verb and can be clitic doubled if they are introduced by the preposition *a*, as shown in the following example:

(58)   *María l-e$_i$*   *puso azúcar al   café$_i$.*
         María CL-3 SG.DAT put   sugar in-the coffee
         'María put sugar in the coffee.'   (Kalt 2012)

In this example the oblique object *al café* 'in the coffee' has been incorporated into the argument structure of the verb and can be now doubled as a clitic on the verb.

Incorporation is blocked with possessives because the preposition *de* assigns structural case to its complement resulting in ungrammaticality. Camacho *et al.* (1995) and Kalt (2012) propose a reanalysis of the features of the clitic and the preposition *de* so that genitive features are now assigned to the preposition and the clitic. This is compatible with the idea that the genitive features found in the possessed constituent of possessor–possessed structures in Quechua, as the case marking suffix *-pa* shown in (59), can be spelled out as the preposition *de* deprived of its case-assigning features.

(59)   *Kuntur-pa   chaki-n.*
         condor-GEN   leg-3 SG
         'The condor's leg.'   (Camacho *et al.* 1995: 142)

This accounts for sentences such as (54) in the L2 Spanish of Quechua speakers. Camacho *et al.* (1995) propose that doubling in (54) and (55) is possible because the clitic is marked in the L2 for genitive features. In this analysis, the preposition *de* in L2 Spanish is not a case assigner but the spell-out of genitive features. The clitic and the DP share and agree in genitive features as in direct object clitic-doubling structures (Suñer 1988). In sentences such as (54) the genitive object incorporates into the theta grid of the verb and can be doubled by the clitic marked with genitive, a feature not associated with clitics in general Spanish. In this respect, transfer of an L1 feature is not necessarily an automatic process that is restricted to a single category. In fact the mapping of genitive features onto the preposition *de* 'of' as a spell-out and not as a case assigner allows a new set of mappings of features onto the clitic *le* as a morphological expression.

Cross-linguistic influence in the mapping of features onto morphology as a form of transfer from the L1 can also result in a widening of the feature specification of clitics in L2 Spanish. Kalt (2002) found evidence of a wider interpretation of dative clitics in the L2 Spanish of thirty-eight Southern Quechua–Spanish bilingual children in a comprehension study that used a picture selection task. This wider interpretation includes oblique readings such as benefactives and locatives. In other varieties of Spanish, clitics are coindexed with indirect objects rather than with oblique benefactives, as shown by the contrast between (60) and (61). In Quechua, on the other hand, a first-person object marker *-wa* in combination with the aspectual suffix *-pu* has a benefactive interpretation, as shown in (62):

(60)   *Mi   madre   l-e$_k$ =   dar-á   el   libro (a Ana$_k$)*
         My   mother CL-3 SG.DAT = give-FUT.3 SG the book   (to Ana)
         'My mother will give the book to Ana.'

(61)   **Mi   madre m-e$_k$ =   dar-á   el   libro*
         My   mother CL.1 SG-BEN =   give-FUT.3 SG the book
         a   Ana   (para mí$_k$)
         to   Ana   (for me$_k$)
         'My mother will give Ana the book for me.'

(62)   *Mama-y   Ana-man libru-ta   haywa-pu-wa-nqa.*
         Mom-1.POSS Ana-DAT book-ACC give-BEN-1.OBJ-3 SG.FUT
         'My mom gave Ana the book for me.'   (Kalt 2012: 175)

Kalt (2002) tested sentences without clitics and with reflexive and oblique objects expressed by clitics. The results of her study showed the lowest levels of accuracy by the Quechua–Spanish bilingual children in the strict dative interpretation of sentences with an indirect object clitic *le*, the interpretation in general Spanish of sentence (63).

(63)   *Ana$_i$ l-e$_j$ pone la   chompa.*
         Ana   CL-3 SG.DAT puts the sweater
         'Ana puts his sweater on.'

The results of the bilingual children were significantly different from those of a group of Spanish monolingual children who clearly favored the indirect object interpretation. They are consistent with the idea that transfer of the Quechua benefactive feature widens the possible interpretations of the clitic. In fact, Kalt's account (Kalt 2012) attributes the variability in interpretation to a pattern of reassociation in the L2 Spanish of the aspectual benefactive features of the suffix *-pu* and the case features of a direct object marker (*-wa* in the example) to the Spanish clitic *le*. This association is possible due to the fact that *le-* has a dative case feature and an interpretation of the dative that in some circumstances is compatible with that of the benefactive. These results are consistent with a reassignment of features associated with the clitic *le* that allows for a wider range of non-argumental cases and it is indicative of how some of the transfer processes found in bilingual speech if persistent and transmitted to younger generations might result in important morphosyntactic changes.

Kalt (2012) sought further confirmation that the wider range of options comes from the L1. She reports on a subsequent study conducted in Quechua with Quechua L1 children. In Southern Quechua first and second direct and indirect objects may be morphologically marked but third-person indirect objects are not, as shown in sentence (64). The results of Kalt's study show that several interpretations are possible for a third-person indirect object null morpheme. It can be an individual other than the subject, the subject itself, or a location.

(64)   *Ana   chumpa-ta   chura-Ø-n.*
         Ana   sweater-ACC   put-Ø-3 sg.obj-3 sg.sbj
         'Ana put the sweater (on somebody specified in discourse / on somebody unspecified / there/ somewhere).'   (Kalt 2012: 183)

These data point in the direction of a process of transfer that is highly complex, in which the activation of features from the L1 such as benefactive and their mapping onto L2 morphology, in this case the clitic *le*, may result in an overt morphological form in the L2 that has no correspondence in the L1 paradigm.

As mentioned in the introduction to this chapter, Sánchez (2004) presents evidence of functional convergence in a study of oral production of thirty Southern Quechua–Spanish bilingual children (10 to 16 years old). The Spanish of these bilingual children shows evidence of the mapping of reported evidentiality and past tense features onto the Spanish morphological forms that spell out aspect and tense features, as shown in examples (17)–(20). On the basis of these data Sánchez (2004) proposes a re-elaboration of the *Functional Convergence Hypothesis* (*FCH*), originally proposed in Sánchez (2003) as follows:

> Convergence, the common specification for equivalent functional features in the two languages spoken by the bilingual in a language contact situation, takes place when the languages have partially similar matrices of features associated with the same functional category. Frequent activation of the two matrices triggers convergence in features.   (Sánchez, 2004: 150)

The FHC predicts that among Quechua–Spanish bilinguals who activate Quechua and Spanish frequently, the activation of aspectual or discourse-oriented features in Spanish affects the bilingual Quechua representations, and activation of evidentiality features in Quechua affects bilingual Spanish representations. In addition to evidence for the first type of mapping strategy found in the Spanish data, the bilingual Quechua data also exhibited an incipient emergence of discourse-oriented background and foreground distinctions associated with the attested past morpheme, similar to those found in Spanish in association with imperfective morphology.

Sánchez (2006) also presents evidence of functional convergence in the mapping of some grammaticalized aspectual features associated in Quechua with syncretic derivational morphology onto independent verbs in Spanish in a study of picture-based narratives of thirty Lamas Quechua[7]–Spanish bilingual children (aged 9 to 13). In this case, convergence takes place in the mapping of volitive and imminent modal/aspectual features of the Quechua syncretic derivational morpheme -naya onto the Spanish modal verb querer 'to want,' as shown in (65) and (66):

(65)   *Miku-naya-yka-n.*
         Eat-DES-PROG-3 SG
         '(S/he) wants to/is about to eat.'

(66)   *Está quer-iendo   com-er.*
         Is   want-TV-PROG eat-TV-INF
         '(S/he) wants to/is about to eat.'

The latter form was not found in the narratives of a comparison group of twenty-five Spanish-dominant children. The results of the study showed that bilingual children used the desiderative form alone and in conjunction with progressive forms in Quechua:

(67)   *Sapitu urma-naya-n yaku-pi.*
         Toad   fall-DES-3 SG water-LOC
         'The toad wants to fall in the water.'

(68)   *Kay achku muku-chi-naya-yka-n   kay sapitu-ta.*
         This dog   bit -CAUS-DES-PROG-3 SG this toad-ACC
         'This dog is wanting to have this toad bit.'

In their Spanish narratives, the children used modal progressive forms with a desiderative/imminent interpretation:

(69)   *Un wamrillu (e)stá queriendo agarr-a-r   su   sapo.*
         A   boy   (i)s wanting   grab-TV-INF his toad
         'A boy wants/is about to grab his toad.'   (Sánchez 2006: 545)

While in Quechua the modal desiderative feature and the aspectual imminent feature are syncretically mapped onto the morpheme -naya, in Spanish there is

---

[7] In Sánchez (2006) I use the term Kechwa to refer to the Quechua language following the use of the Lamas community.

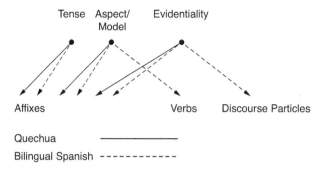

Figure 3.1 *Feature mapping in Quechua and Spanish*

no corresponding bound morpheme. Therefore, in this case convergence requires a different type of mapping to spell out the features and this is accomplished by mapping the volitive and imminent features onto a lexical item, the modal verb *querer* 'to want,' in such a way that its interpretation can be determined according to the context. The imminent interpretation is favored by the progressive periphrastic form.

These emergent verb forms provide support for a view in which some functional features that are relevant for interpretation in one language, such as evidentiality, tense, and aspect, can be associated in the bilingual lexicon with morphological forms in the phonetic inventory of the other language. This indicates that the organization of the lexicon includes multiple mapping strategies of features onto morphological forms in both languages, as shown in Figure 3.1, which is based on a similar diagram proposed by Muysken (2004: 163).

Figure 3.1 shows the mapping of tense, aspect, and evidentiality features in Quechua and Spanish onto affixes and at the same time the mapping of some aspectual/modal features onto verbal periphrastic forms and discourse particles (phonologically independent words such as *dice* 'says') in Bilingual Spanish. It is the need to morphologically express features such as evidentiality that is at the base of emerging morphosyntactic features in a language contact situation.

In addition to new patterns of feature–morphology mapping, Quechua–Spanish bilingualism also illustrates transfer of mapping strategies at the syntax–pragmatics interface that involves the spell-out of functional features. Camacho, Paredes, and Sánchez (1997) show that the Spanish of Southern Quechua speakers is characterized by null objects with definite antecedents. They found evidence of null objects with definite antecedents in the speech of three groups of Southern Quechua–L2 Spanish bilinguals with different proficiency levels. These are examples of null objects with definite referents:

(70) a.   *¿Y Uds. preparaban el desayuno_i para los pensionistas?*
            'And did you prepare breakfast for the guests?'
     b.   *Sí, mis hermanas e_i preparaban.*
            'Yes, my sisters prepared it.'

(71) a.   *¿Extrañas mucho a tu papá$_i$?*
                 'Do you miss your father?'
     b.   *Sí, sí e$_i$ extraño.*
                 'Yes, yes I miss him.'

(72) a.   *¿Qué pasó?– me dijo – Lo$_i$ había atropellado una moto*
                 'What happened? – he told me–. A motorcycle has run her over
                 le dije, entonces:
                 I told him, then:
     b.   *Hemos llevado e$_i$ ya al Hospital del Niño, ya e$_i$*
                 Then we took her to the hospital;
                 hemos llevado e$_i$ al Emergencia.
                 'we took her to the Emergency room.'

(73) a.   *¿Qué hace, la mata (el lobo) o no la mata a la oveja$_i$?*
                 What does the wolf do? Does it kill the sheep?
     b.   *Sí mata e$_i$, sí mata e$_i$*
                 Yes, it kills (it), yes it kills it.'
                 (Camacho *et al.* 1997: 59)

Camacho *et al.* (1997) analyze these null objects as licensed by a topic operator. Licensing of these objects is not due to a lack of morphological marking in Spanish, as shown by the fact that there is an overt clitic in example (72a). In that example, the topic of discourse is introduced as a clitic in the sentence that answers the question *¿Qué pasó?* 'What happened?' Because it is an answer to a question that requires new information, the whole sentence is new information and the clitic is not the topic of conversation. It is used possibly to refer back to a referent that is shared knowledge by speaker and hearer or that has been previously introduced but is not necessarily the topic of this fragment of discourse. However, once it has been introduced it becomes a topic and appears as a null object in (72b). This type of licensing is also found in Quechua, as shown in the use of a null object and subject to describe a picture in which a boy holds a frog that has been seen in a previous picture:

(74)   *Chari-ya-n.*
              Hold-DUR-3 SG
              '(He) is holding (him)'   (Sánchez 2003: 104)

In these cases, the relevant third-person and accusative case features are not mapped onto overt verbal morphology in Quechua. Unlike overt pronouns that are independent words marked for case in Quechua, the null object appears in contexts in which there is a third-person topic object, as in (56). It is the mapping strategy of Quechua, namely the lack of third-person object overt morphology, that is at the source of the definite null objects in L2 Spanish. Independent evidence for such a mapping has also been found in the L2 Spanish of Chinese speakers (Cuza, Pérez-Leroux, and Sánchez, 2013).

Sánchez (2003) also found evidence of null objects with definite antecedents in the Spanish of two groups of Central Quechua–Spanish and Southern

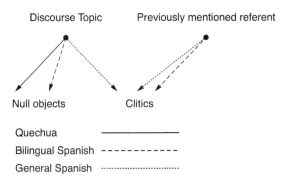

Figure 3.2 *Discourse properties morphological mapping in Quechua and Bilingual Spanish*

Quechua–Spanish bilingual children (ages 9 to 13). The data were narratives elicited in Quechua and Spanish using pictures. The Quechua narratives had null objects as the second most frequent type of direct object after overt DPs. The Spanish narratives had a higher frequency of clitics and structures with clitic doubling than of null objects. Null objects had as their antecedents overt definite DPs previously mentioned in the text and antecedents not present in the text but shown in the pictures, a pattern also found in the Quechua narratives. This supports the notion that the null objects correspond to a discourse topic. Figure 3.2 illustrates the mapping of discourse topics and previously mentioned referents onto clitics in general Spanish. It also shows how Bilingual Spanish shares with Quechua the mapping of discourse topics and with general Spanish the mapping of previously mentioned referents.

More evidence of how bilingual acquisition of morphology is revealing of the mapping of functional features onto the morphology in the input received by bilinguals comes from a study of DP case marking in Quechua–Spanish bilingual code-switching by Sánchez (2012). This study examines convergence in case-mapping strategies in the oral speech of Quechua–Spanish bilingual children aged 9 to 13. While Quechua is a nominative–accusative language in which case is overtly marked on internal and external arguments of the verb as well as on DPs marked with oblique cases, Spanish lacks overt case marking of DPs. In Spanish oblique DPs are typically headed by prepositions while in Quechua they are marked with case suffixes. Bilingual children's code-mixing speech shows some evidence of the coexistence of Spanish prepositions with case suffixes as in:

(75)   *Chay niñito pusanayaykan al chay kochapi*
         Chay niñito pusa-naya-yka-n   al   chay kocha-pi.
         That boy   go-DES-PROG-3 SG to- the that lake-LOC
         'That boy was about to go to the lake.'

These data show that in Quechua suffixes are not lexical heads but actual suffixes that are the spell-out of case features and are therefore compatible with prepositions in code-mixing utterances. In this particular case, bilingual code-mixing shows evidence of the coexistence of two types of morphological marking: prepositions as independent words that assign case and suffixes that are the spell-out of case.

Overall, the evidence presented in this subsection points in the direction of a nuanced view of the interface of the lexicon, feature specification, and morphology that shows that the organization of the lexicon in bilingual individuals includes multiple mapping strategies of features onto morphological forms in both languages.

Euskara and Spanish in contact

As Silva-Corvalán (1997) notes, the typological systems of Euskara and Spanish have remained quite different despite many centuries of contact, most notably the case-marking and head-direction patterns in each language. Euskara is an ergative language in which there is one grammatical case for the subjects of transitive verbs (ergative case), and another case for the subjects of intransitive verbs and direct objects (absolutive case), as shown in examples (76)–(78):

Transitive verb
(76)   *Nik liburua-Ø irakurri dut*
          Ni-k   liburu-a- Ø   irakurri dut
          I-ERG book-DET-ABS read   AUX-3 SG.ABS-1 SG.ERG
          'I have read the books.'

Unaccusative verb
(77)   *Ni eseri naiz*
          Ni-Ø   eseri naiz
          I-ABS   sit   AUX-1 SG.ABS
          'I have sat.'

Unergative verb
(78)   *Nik korritu dut*
          Ni-k   korritu dut
          I-ERG run   AUX-3 SG.ABS-1 SG.ERG
          'I have run.'

In (76), the subject of a transitive verb such as *irakurri* 'to read' is marked with the ergative morpheme -*k*, and the direct object receives absolutive case, which is zero-marked (Ø). In contrast, the subject of an unaccusative verb such as *eseri* 'to sit' in example (77) has the same absolutive case marker as the direct object of a transitive verb (Ø) and the subject of an unergative verb has the same ergative marker -*k* as the subject of a transitive verb, as shown in example (78).

In contrast, Spanish has a nominative–accusative case-marking pattern in which all subjects receive nominative case, which is not morphologically marked. This case assignment takes place, regardless of their argument structure, as shown in (79)–(81).

Unaccusative verb
(79)   *Ellos han llegado tarde*
         Ellos   h -an   lleg-a   -do   tarde
         They-NOM have-3 PL arrive-TV -PST.PRT late
         'They have arrived late.'

Unergative verb
(80)   *Ellos han dormido*
         Ellos   h-an   dorm-i-do
         They-NOM have-3 PL sleep-TV-PST.PRT
         'They have slept.'

Transitive verb
(81)   *Ellos han leído los libros.*
         Ellos   h-an   le -í-do   los libros.
         They-NOM have-3 PL read-TV-PST.PRT the books
         'They have read the books.'

As these examples show, Spanish does not discriminate morphologically between unaccusative and unergative verbs.

A second syntactic feature which distinguishes Euskara from Spanish is the order of constituents in a sentence. In Euskara, unlike in Spanish or English, phrases and sentences are right-headed. This means that verbs appear after their complements, relative pronouns appear after the sentence they head, and determiners and postpositions appear after nouns. For example, Euskara sentences have an unmarked subject-object-verb order such, as in (82):

(82)   *Guk liburu asko irakurri dugu.*
         Guk   liburu asko irakurri dugu.
         We-ERG book a lot read   AUX-ABS.3SG-ERG.1SG
         'We have read a lot of books.'

Notice that in addition to the object preceding the verb, the verb precedes the auxiliary. In Spanish, the order of these constituents is the opposite; the direct object follows the verb, and the verb follows the auxiliary, as in (83):

(83)   *Nosotros hemos leído muchos libros.*
         Nosotros h-emos   le -í-do   muchos libros.
         We-NOM have-1PL read-TV-PST.PRT many   books
         'We have read many books.'

This pattern of the head of a phrase on the right for Euskara and on the left for Spanish is repeated recursively to form all the elements of a sentence. Similarly, embedded clauses in Euskara are situated to the left of the embedding element, whereas in Spanish, they are on the right, as shown in (84):

Euskara
(84)   *Ikusi duen gizona*
         Ikusi duen   gizon-a
         seen AUX-ABS.3 SG.ERG.3SG-REL man-DET
         'The man that she saw.'

Table 3.1 *Euskara–Spanish typological contrasts*

Grammatical feature	Spanish	Euskara
Head direction	Head initial	Head final
Unmarked word order	SVO	SOV
Case of transitive subjects	Nominative	Ergative
Case of intransitive subjects	Nominative	Ergative (unergatives)
		Absolutive (unaccusatives)
Morphological typology	Fusional	Agglutinative

Spanish

(85)   *El hombre que he visto.*

El   hombre   que   he   visto.

DET man   REL   have.1SG.PRS   see.PST.PRT

'The man that I saw.'

Spanish and Euskara are both synthetic languages, meaning that grammatical morphemes are typically encoded in verbal and nominal affixes rather than separate words. Euskara, however, is morphologically agglutinative, whereas Spanish is fusional. In an agglutinative language such as Euskara, an auxiliary consists of a stack of affixes which each convey a distinct meaning. This difference is illustrated in (86) and (87); in the Euskara example, although the auxiliary *daramazkit* 'I carry them' is one word, there are distinguishable affixes which mark the verbal stem and other morphemes. In contrast, in the Spanish verb *llevo* 'I carry' in (87), there is one morpheme (*-o*) which conveys several meanings at once:

Euskara

(86)   *Bi liburu-Ø daramazkit*

Bi   liburu- Ø   da   rama   zki   t

Two book-ABS PRS. carry. PL   ERG.1SG

'I carry two books.'

Spanish

(87)   *Llevo dos libros.*

Llev-o   dos   libros.

Carry-1 SG.PRS two books

'I carry two books.'

The typological contrasts between Euskara and Spanish are summarized in Table 3.1.

Although the grammatical effects of contact between Euskara and Spanish have been studied very little, this influence has been reciprocal; contact with Spanish has affected Euskara and the Spanish spoken in the Basque Autonomous Community (Landa 1995; Urrutia Cárdenas 1996). Landa and Franco (1996) suggested that null objects with definite referents in Basque Spanish have the same properties as the null category *pro*, a null pronoun. Landa (1995) proposes that influence from Euskara may allow for fewer restrictions on the pragmatic contexts that allow null objects to appear in this dialect of Spanish as opposed to other varieties. The following example from Landa and Franco (1999) shows the availability of null objects with definite referents in Basque Spanish:

(88)   *T-e*   *he*   *traído*   *el*   *coche$_i$*
         CL.2 SG.DAT   have   brought   the   car
         porque   *hace*   *ruido,*   *pero*   *si*   *no*
         because   makes   noise,   but   if   not
         puedes   *mirar*   *e$_i$*   *hoy*   *miras*   *e$_i$*   *mañana.*
         can   look   e$_i$ today   look   e$_i$ tomorrow
         'I brought you the car because it makes a noise, but if you can't take a look at it today, look at it tomorrow.'

Notice that in this case, as in the case of Quechua–Spanish bilingualism, we find that the two null objects in the sentence have their referent clearly established in discourse. As in the case of Quechua–Spanish bilinguals, the null objects are consistent with the transfer of a particular mapping strategy that allows null pronominals to not be phonologically expressed.

Another important aspect of how Spanish has been influenced by contact with Euskara is revealed in the pronominal system. As is true in much of Spain, the Spanish dialect spoken in the Basque Country is *leísta*. *Leísmo* is the substitution of the dative clitic *le* for the accusative clitic *lo* and less frequently, for *la* when marking direct objects. The most extreme instance of this phenomenon is shown in (90), in a set of sentences in Basque Spanish that contrast with sentence (89) in other varieties of Spanish that use accusative clitics, as shown in (90b) and (90c). Use of *leísmo* in other varieties is related to the humanness and animacy of the direct object, and it tends to be used the most with human direct objects, as well as with benefactive or affected objects.

Leísta *Spanish*

(89)   <u>*Le*</u> *he visto (a tu padre/ madre /perro).*
         <u>*Le*</u>   *he*   *visto (a tu padre/ madre /perro).*
         CL.3SG-DAT   have- 1SG   seen   (your father/mother/dog)
         'I have seen him/her (your father/mother/dog).'

*Non-*leísta *Spanish*

(90) a.   <u>*Lo/le*</u> *he visto (a tu padre).*
            <u>*L-o*</u> /<u>*l-e*</u>   *h-e*   *visto (a tu padre).*
            CL.3SG-ACC.M /CL.3SG-DAT   have-1SG   seen   (to your father)
            'I have seen him/her (your father).'

     b.   <u>*La*</u> *he visto (a tu madre).*
            <u>*L-a*</u>   *h -e*   *visto (a tu madre).*
            CL.3 SG-ACC.F   have-1 SG   seen   (your mother)
            'I have seen him/her (your mother).'

     c.   <u>*Lo*</u> *he visto (tu perro).*
            <u>*L-o*</u>   *h -e*   *visto (tu perro).*
            CL.3 SG-ACC.M   have-1 SG   seen   (your dog)
            'I have seen him/her (your father/mother/dog).'

The Spanish spoken in the Basque Country has been greatly affected by bilingualism. In Basque Spanish, clitics which refer to all animate objects, regardless of case or gender, are marked with dative case (Fernández-Ordóñez 1999). However, studies by Klein-Andreu (1981, 1999) and Fernández-Ordóñez (1994, 1999) make it clear that *leísmo* in spoken Spanish cannot be described adequately by this simple generalization. Taking a sociolinguistic approach to the distribution of *leísmo*, these researchers have found that there is considerable variation in Peninsular Spanish as to the use of *leísmo* in different dialects. Speakers of Basque Spanish are *leísta* to varying degrees depending on sociolinguistic factors such as degree of bilingualism and socio-cultural level (Urrutia-Cárdenas 1996).

As we saw in the previous section on Quechua–Spanish bilingualism and above in this section, Basque Spanish is characterized by a pronominal system that diverges from that of other varieties of Spanish in that dative marking is overextended and at the same time, at the syntax–pragmatics interface, it allows for null objects that are the discourse topic. This type of cross-linguistic influence, as the previous sources of evidence, indicates the need to study the relationship between lexical categories such as verbs, their argument structure, and the morphosyntactic expression of case as well as the need to explore the relationship between overt and null expression of direct objects and their pragmatic function.

Spanish and English in contact

In the case of contact between English and Spanish there is an important difference with respect to the two contact situations previously presented. While Quechua and Basque are morphologically rich languages that exhibit a different social status from that of Spanish, English is a language with a morphological paradigm that is less complex than that of Spanish and with a higher social status in the Spanish–English communities. This is a contact situation in which Spanish is not a socially dominant language and there is considerable morphosyntactic variation across Spanish dialects in contact with English (Bayley and Bonnici 2009). The complexities of dialectal variation in Spanish–English contact situations in the US have been extensively documented and analyzed from a variety of perspectives including sociolinguistic and pragmatic analyses (Silva-Corvalán 1991, 1994, 1997; Bills and Vigil 1999; Roca and Lipski 1999; Cameron, and Flores-Ferrán 2004; Flores-Ferrán 2004; Travis 2007; Otheguy, Zentella, and Livert 2007; Otheguy and Zentella 2012, among others) and acquisitional perspectives (Cuza and Frank 2011; Cuza 2013; Montrul 2004a, 2004b, 2008, 2009, and 2011; Rothman 2009; Silva-Corvalán and Montanari 2008, among others).

From a sociolinguistic perspective there has been extensive exploration of the contrast between overt and null subjects and the potential effects of contact with English on a preference for overt subjects (Cameron and Flores-Ferrán 2004; Flores-Ferrán 2004; Otheguy *et al.* 2007; Otheguy and Zentella 2012).

From an acquisitional perspective, research on Spanish in the USA has focused on a variety of related issues that range from the expression of null and overt subjects (Montrul 2008) to the instability in the tense–aspect–mood system of US Spanish heritage bilingual speakers (Montrul 2009; Cuza 2010). Other studies have explored syntactic characteristics such as the lack of subject–verb inversion (Cuza 2013), the availability of postverbal subjects (Zapata, Sánchez, and Toribio 2005; Montrul 2009), and topicalization as clitic-left dislocation (Zapata *et al.* 2005). The following examples illustrate these characteristics:

Prevalence of overt subjects

(91)   *Había una chica que vivía con su mamá y *ella va a visitar a su abuela.*
          Y *ella trajo toda la comida para un regalo para la abuela . . . Cuando
          Caperucita llegó, *ella estaba arreglando todos los flores que *ella recogía
          durante su camino, y *ella no notaba que el lobo estaba en la cama.

          'There was a girl who lived with her mother and she goes to visit her
          grandmother. And she brought all the food for a present for her
          grandmother . . . When Little Riding Hood arrived, she was fixing all the
          flowers that she had gathered during her way, and she did not notice that
          the wolf was in the bed.'   (Montrul 2009: 134)

This example illustrates the oral production of a heritage speaker who obtained an intermediate proficiency score in an independent proficiency measure. It is characterized by an overproduction of overt pronouns.

Instability of tense–aspect morphology, use of progressive forms as generic

(92) a.   *Mi amiga Sara baila.*
          Mi   amiga   Sara   baila.
          My   friend   Sara   dances
     b.   *Mi amiga Sara está bailando*
          Mi   amiga   Sara   está   bailando
          My   friend   Sara   is   dancing   (Cuza 2010: 264)

Cuza (2010) notes the use of progressive verb forms, as in (92b), restricted in most varities of Spanish to an ongoing interpretation of the event, to one with a generic interpretation, such as the one that the present tense (92a) has in other varieties.

Lack of verb–subject inversion

(93)   *¿Qué compró Juan?*
          ¿Qué   compró   Juan?
          What   bought   Juan
          'What did Juan buy?'

(94)   **¿Qué Juan compró?*
          *¿Qué   Juan   compró?
          What   Juan   bought
          'What did Juan buy?'

(95)   *Me pregunto qué compró Juan.*
         Me   pregunto   qué   compró   Juan.
         CL.1SG.DAT wonder   what   bought   Juan
         'I wonder what Juan bought.'

(96)   **Me pregunto qué Juan compró.*
         *Me   pregunto   qué   Juan   compró.
         CL.1SG.DAT wonder   what   Juan   bought
         'I wonder what Juan bought.'   (Cuza 2010: 76)

Examples (94) and (96) are sentences in which the expected verb–subject inversion found in most varieties of Spanish is absent. These sentences are ungrammatical in those varieties. Cuza (2010) found evidence of high levels of acceptance (76 percent) for sentences such as (96) among adult heritage bilinguals but only 24 percent acceptance with main sentences. This is in line with Austin, Blume, and Sánchez's (2013) findings in a longitudinal study on young Spanish–English bilingual children who did not experience significant loss of verb–subject inversion in main sentences.

Topicalization instead of clitic left dislocation
(97) a.   *La piñata la compra Ignacio.*
           La   piñata   l -a =   compr-a   Ignacio.
           The piñata   CL.3SG-F-ACC =   buy-PRS.3SG Ignacio.
           'Ignacio buys the piñata.'
     b.   *La piñata compra Ignacio.*
           La   piñata   compr-a   Ignacio.
           The piñata   buy-PRS.3SG Ignacio.
           'Ignacio buys the piñata.'   (Zapata, Sánchez and Toribio 2005: 390)

Sentence (97b) is illustrative of the written production of adult heritage bilinguals in a sentence completion task with a definite noun phrase as a prompt. This type of sentence diverges from the clitic left-dislocated structure found in most varieties of Spanish that requires a clitic when the object is fronted.

In addition to these characteristics, there is also extensive research on Spanish–English code-switching among US Spanish–English bilinguals from pioneering work (Pfaff 1979; Poplack 1980) that has focused on the restrictions imposed by grammar on code-switching, and more recent work (Toribio 2002; 2004; van Gelderen and MacSwan 2008) that focuses on the high levels of proficiency required to code-switch.

In this subsection, we will focus on recent research from an acquisitional perspective that illustrates how the mapping of English functional values onto Spanish morphological forms might play a role in the outcome of Bilingual Spanish representations. Due to differences in the morphological paradigms of English and Spanish, reduced or simplified systems emerge in different varieties of US Bilingual Spanish (Silva-Corvalán 1997; Montrul 2006, 2008, 2009; Montrul and Bowles 2009; Montrul 2011; Cuza and Frank 2011; Montrul and Foote 2013; Austin *et al.* 2013, among others). The existence of this difference has given rise to the exploration of this phenomenon as the result of incomplete acquisition or attrition by authors such as Montrul (2008, 2009, 2011), Polinsky (2006, 2011a), and Rothman (2009) among others (see Chapter 1). From an acquisitional perspective the debate on whether bilingual heritage speakers in the USA have experienced loss or limited exposure to input has produced a vast and important body of research and experimental data from bilingual populations. As argued by Putnam and Sánchez (2013), this wealth of data can be studied from the perspective of the process that leads to heritage bilingual competence or as its result. We will present evidence of some of the morphosyntactic patterns studied in the literature on Bilingual Spanish in the USA from an acquisitional perspective and we will argue that, when taken as a process, they are indicative of convergence between morphological patterns in English and Spanish that is related to the way in which lexical items are associated with functional features.

The main morphosyntactic features of US Spanish we focus on in this section are tense, aspect, and mood in the verbal domain (Silva-Corvalán 1994, 2003; Montrul 2006, 2009) and *Differential Object Marking* (DOM) in the nominal domain (Montrul 2004a; Montrul and Bowles 2009). We will analyze them in light of our previous discussion linking activation of the bilingual lexicon to the emergence of morphosyntactic features.

As noted in Chapter 1, one of the main characteristics that have been identified in the growing literature on bilingual speakers of Spanish in the USA is the different configuration of the verbal paradigm with respect to the syncretic morphological marking of tense, mood, and aspect. Since the early work by Silva-Corvalán (1994) on the simplification of the verbal paradigm of Spanish–English bilinguals in Los Angeles, a growing body of work has enriched our knowledge of the mapping of syntactic features onto morphology. The main issue that has been debated regarding the development of heritage Spanish in the USA is the extent to which the apparent "simplification" of the tense–mood–aspect system of Spanish as spoken by heritage bilinguals in the USA can be attributed to contact with English, the socially dominant language. The following examples illustrate the notion of simplification proposed by Silva-Corvalán (1994) and also attested in other studies such as Montrul (2009). The following pair of sentences shows the contrast between bilingual speakers' use of the indicative mood form of the verb in the subordinate sentence while in other non-bilingual varieties of Spanish a subjunctive form is used:

US Spanish (Los Angeles)
(98)   *Ahí lo voy a dejar hasta que se cae.*
         Ahí   l -o   voy   a dej -a -r   hasta que
         There CL3SG-M.ACC = go.PRS.1SG to leave-TV-INF until COMP

         se   ca-e.
         REFL fall-PRS.IND.3 SG
         'I am going to leave it there until it falls.' (Silva-Corvalán 1994: 264)

Other varieties

(99)   *Ahí lo voy a dejar hasta que se caiga.*

    Ahí   l-o   voy   a dej -a-r   hasta que

    There CL.3SG-M.ACC go.PRS.1SG to leave-TV-INF until COMP

    se   caiga.

    REFL   fall.PRS.SBJ.3 SG

    'I am going to leave it there until it falls.'

The claim of simplification is based on the overextension of indicative forms to contexts in which the subjunctive is used in other varieties of Spanish. Another instance of the simplification proposed is the overextension of preterit forms to contexts in which in other Spanish varieties imperfective forms are expected or vice versa, as the following examples from Montrul (2009) illustrate:

Imperfect for preterit

(100)   **Yo fui el único hombre que tenían*

    *Yo fui   el   único hombre que ten -í -a -n

    I   was the only man   REL have-TV -PST.IPFV -3PL

    'I was the only son they had.'

Preterit for imperfective

(101)   **En la casa mi mamá era la única que habló español y las demás hablaron en inglés.*

    *En l-a   casa   mi mama era l-a   únic-a que habl-ó

    In   the-F house-F my mom was the-F only-F REL speak-PRT.PFV.3 SG

    español y l-a-s demás   habl-a-ron   en inglés.

    Spanish and the-F-PL other_ones speak-TV-PRT.PFV.3 PL in English.

    'At home my mom was the only one who spoke Spanish and the other ones only spoke English.'   (Montrul 2009: 245)

In order to test the extent of these phenomena in bilingual heritage speakers, Montrul (2009) conducted two studies with sixty-five adult heritage speakers of Spanish who were raised in the Midwestern region of the USA. The bilingual participants were divided in three groups: advanced, intermediate, and low according to their proficiency scores in an independent test. In the first study Montrul tested the speakers' ability to distinguish between preterit and imperfective forms using an oral production test based on elicitation of a narrative, a written morphology recognition task, and a sentence completion judgment task based on a similar task used in Slabokova and Montrul (2002) and Montrul and Slabokova (2003).

Of particular relevance for the understanding of the relationship between bilinguals' access to the lexicon associated with functional features is the relationship between types of events and states denoted by the meanings of verbs and Spanish aspectual morphology. According to the *Lexical Aspect Hypothesis* proposed for first language acquisition by Shirai and Li (2000), morphological aspectual distinctions between forms such as the preterit and the imperfect are acquired following a sequence that is related to the lexical aspect of verbs. Vendler's

(1967) classification of verbs according to lexical aspects distinguishes between states, activities, achievements, and accomplishments, as illustrated in the examples below from Montrul (2009). In Spanish these different verb types can be inflected for perfective and imperfective morphology, as shown in Montrul's examples. According to the *Lexical Aspect Hypothesis*, acquisition of preterit forms with accomplishment verbs precedes their acquisition with stative verbs. In a similar way, acquisition of imperfective forms with stative verbs precedes their acquisition with accomplishment verbs. In fact, as noted by Montrul, the latter association is not the preferred one for most Spanish speakers without a larger context:

State
(102) *Juan estuvo/estaba enfermo.*
     Juan estuvo   /est-a-ba   enfermo.
     Juan be. PST.PFV.3SG / be-TV-PST.PFV.3SG ill
     'Juan was ill.'   (Montrul 2009: 244)

Activity
(103) *Patricio trabajó / trabajaba en un banco.*
     Patricio trabaj-ó   / trabaj-a-ba   en un banco.
     Patricio work-PST.PFV.3SG / work-TV-PST.IPFV.3SG in a   bank
     'Patricio worked in a bank.'   (Montrul 2009: 244)

Accomplishment
(104) *Pedro pintaba / pintó la pared.*
     Pedro pint-a -ba   / pint-ó   la   pared.
     Pedro paint-TV-PST.IPFV.3SG paint-PST.PRET.3 SG the wall
     'Pedro painted the wall.'   (Montrul 2009: 244)

Achievement
(105) *María salió / ?salía de vacaciones.*
     María sal -I -ó   / ?sal -í -a   de vacaciones.
     María go_out-TV-PST.PFV.3SG / go_out-TV-PST.IPFV.3SG of vacations
     'María went on vacation.'   (Montrul 2009: 244)

The results of this first study showed a 3.8 percent divergence from the expected uses. There were cases of preterit for imperfective and of imperfective forms used in contexts that were expected to favor the preterit:

(106) *La niña roja no notó que estuvo un lobo atrás de ella.*
     La niña roja no not-ó   que *estuvo
     The girl red not note-PST.PFV.3SG that *be.PST.PFV.3 SG
     un lobo atrás   de ella
     a   wolf behind of her
     'The red girl did not notice that a wolf was behind her.'

Expected form
(107) *La niña roja no notó que estaba un lobo atrás de ella.*
     La niña roja no not-ó   que est-a-ba
     The girl red not note-PST.PFV.3SG that be-TV-PST.IPFV.3SG

un lobo atrás   de ella
a   wolf behind of her
'The red girl did not notice that a wolf was behind her.'

The results of the written recognition task showed higher levels of accuracy with the perfective than with the imperfective forms, especially among speakers with the lowest levels of proficiency. Results of the sentence conjunction judgment task also showed higher levels of accuracy with perfective than with imperfective forms. In particular, these results lead Montrul to conclude that, while heritage speakers know the preterit/imperfect contrast as shown by the other tasks, they have more difficulty with verbs that denote states in the preterit and with imperfect forms with achievement verbs. Montrul (2009) notes that these results are compatible with the *Regression Hypothesis* originally proposed by Jakobson (1968) and with Sorace's (2000, 2006) *Interface Hypothesis*.

These results can also be accounted for by assuming a stronger association between the activation of some lexical classes of verbs and that of perfective and imperfective values of aspect as a functional feature and their mapping onto morphology. Higher activation of preterit forms and the lexical aspect in accomplishment verbs reinforces this relationship, but lower activation of perfective forms with stative verbs weakens it. It should not be surprising then that lower levels of activation of lexical items and feature values become even weaker when there are imbalances in the dominance of bilingual speakers that favor a language that does not express the distinction morphologically. Convergence in the specification seems to be in its earlier stages.

In the second study also reported in Montrul (2009), a similar set of tests was used to probe the heritage speakers' knowledge of the indicative/subjunctive contrast. In this case, results showed even greater difficulties in producing and judging the contrast in different contexts. Production tasks showed uses of indicative for subjunctive and vice versa:

Indicative for subjunctive
(108)   Es necesario que él sepa que él o ella *tenga un problema y que *sea
          necesario.
          'It is necessary that he knows that he or she has a problem and that it is
          necessary.'   (Montrul 2009: 279)

Subjunctive for indicative
(109)   No creo que *es bueno para tu salud tomar tanto alcohol. Es importante
          que t. *pones escuela antes de salir de fiestas con tus amigos. Es necesario
          que tu buscas ayuda de otras personas para que t. *puedes tomar menos.
          (subject 111, low proficiency)

          'I don't think it is good for your health to drink so much alcohol. It is
          important that you put school before going to parties with your friends. It is
          necessary that you find help from other people so that you can drink less.'
          (Montrul 2009: 279)

While both types of overextension were found, the percentage of indicative forms used in contexts that required subjunctive forms was higher (41.3 percent) than the opposite type of overtexension (6.7 percent). The sentence conjunction judgment task also showed differences between heritage speakers across proficiency levels, with heritage speakers with the lower proficiency showing difficulties discriminating between indicative and subjunctive forms in all contexts used in the task. Montrul (2009) treats these results as related to multiple factors involving the lexical–syntactic interface and the pragmatics interface. These findings can also be interpreted as forcing us to revisit the notion of "simplification" in favor of an alternative view in which a stronger activation of lexical verbs with indicative features and their corresponding verbal morphemes in the two languages progressively leads to a weaker association of lexical verbs with subjunctive features and their corresponding verbal morphemes.

In the realm of nominal morphology evidence of cross-linguistic influence has been presented in studies on differential object marking (Montrul 2009; Montrul and Bowles 2009). Unlike speakers of other varieties of Spanish, bilingual heritage speakers in the USA lack the obligatory preposition *a* that precedes animate direct objects in most varieties of Spanish. The lack of the preposition is shown in the following excerpt from a narrative collected by Montrul (2009):

(110)   Y lo que hizo el lobo era también comió la Caperucita. Lo que hizo el cazador para dar un lección al lobo fue cortar el estómago del lobo y quitar la abuela y la Caperucita.

          'And what the wolf did was also eat the Little Riding Hood. What the hunter did to teach a lesson to the wolf was to cut the wolf's stomach and take out the grandmother and the Little Riding Hood.'

Montrul and Bowles (2009) measured heritage bilinguals' knowledge of differential object marking in two experiments. In the first experiment, they tested heritage bilingual speakers and non-heritage Spanish speakers raised as monolinguals using a production and a written acceptability task. They found significant differences between the heritage bilinguals' performance in both tasks and that of non-heritage Spanish speakers. Heritage bilinguals in the three groups of proficiency (advanced, intermediate, and low) showed higher averages of acceptance of animate direct objects without *a* (10.5 percent, 26.9 percent, and 50 percent, respectively) than non-heritage bilinguals (<1.5 percent).

In the second experiment, they explored the extension of the lack of production of *a* and the acceptability of sentences without it to cases of structural dative case with ditransitive verbs including animate and inanimate objects, double object constructions (grammatical in English but not in Spanish), dative clitic doubling as well as clitic left dislocation structures and objects with inherent dative case such as those that occur with psychological verbs. The following examples illustrate the structures analyzed:

Ditransitive verbs with animate indirect object

(111)   *Angela envió regalos a su novio.*

       Angela envió regalos a   su   novio.

       Angela sent   gifts   ACC her boyfriend

       'Angela sent gifts to her boyfriend.'

Double object construction (no a*)*

(112)   **Estela dio María el libro.*

       *Estela dio   Ø María el   libro.

       Estela   gave   Ø María the   book

       'Estela gave Maria the book.'

Dative clitic doubling (with a*)*

(113)   *Teresa le devolvió el dinero a Pepe.*

       Teresa le =   devolvió el dinero a Pepe.

       Teresa CL.3SG.DAT = returned the money to Pepe.

       'Teresa returned the money to Pepe.'

Clitic left dislocation (with a*)*

(114)   *A su jefe le envió chocolates Paula.*

       A   su   jefe   le =   envió chocolates Paula.

       To her boss CL.3 SG.DAT = sent   chocolates Paula

       'To her boss Paula sent chocolates.'

Psychological verbs

(115)   *A Juan le gusta Patricia.*

       A   Juan le =   gusta Patricia.

       DOM Juan CL.3 SG.DAT = likes   Patricia

       'Juan likes Patricia.'

The results of the second experiment showed varying degrees of variability in the acceptability rates of these constructions across the three groups of heritage bilinguals (low, intermediate, and advanced) that were less consistent than the results of the group of monolingually raised Spanish speakers. Montrul and Bowles (2009) propose that these results are evidence of a simplification of the Spanish grammar of heritage bilinguals. In line with the general perspective we have adopted in this chapter, we would like to argue that these results can also be analyzed along the lines of convergence in features and their mapping onto morphology such that the animate feature that surfaces in the morphology of Spanish as the differential object marker *a* receives lower levels of activation in heritage bilinguals. This lessens its role as a trigger of morphological differential object marking across the different structures tested by Montrul and Bowles (2009), especially in speakers with lower levels of proficiency, and case assignment converges towards the English pattern of null morphology for accusative marking in a similar fashion to the convergence towards the overextension of absolute marking in bilingual Euskara and the overextension of accusative case in Quechua.

    To summarize, in this last section of the chapter we have presented evidence from several studies on Euskara–Spanish, Quechua–Spanish, and

Spanish–English bilingualism that supports a view of cross-linguistic influence as a process that involves activation of functional features and convergence in the mapping of features onto morphology from both languages.

3.5   Conclusions

In this chapter, we have presented an overview of some of the main theoretical proposals put forth in the literature on the development of the bilingual lexicon and of bilingual syntax in children and in adults. We have presented studies that have allowed the field of bilingualism to move from initial debates on unitary versus binary systems of representation to a more complex view of lexical and syntactic bilingual development that involves the interplay of different language subcomponents. The association of functional features and lexical items has been discussed as one of the factors that accounts for cross-linguistic influence. The different proposals have been illustrated with data from studies on bilingualism in Spanish and languages such as Euskara, Quechua, and English.

Conclusions

In this book, we have examined how the outcomes of bilingualism are shaped by factors at the individual level such as age of acquisition and the amount and type of input, as well as societal support for the minority language in the form of bilingual education and other initiatives. We have also discussed how societal maintenance of bilingualism differs within the three multilingual contexts which are the focus of this book: Peru, Spain, and the United States. By analyzing previous research on the effects of these variables on bilingual speakers' linguistic representations, as well as their minds and brains, we have attempted to provide a better understanding of some emerging conceptual views of the bilingual speaker.

In the first chapter of the book, we examined how the concept of bilingualism has evolved from early definitions, which included the expectation that bilinguals should behave like monolinguals, as in Bloomfield's definition of bilingualism as the "native-like control of two languages" (Bloomfield 1933: 55–56). Increasingly, contemporary theories of bilingualism view differences between bilinguals and monolinguals as expected and normal, rather than deficiencies on the part of the bilingual. In addition, we discussed how heritage speakers challenge some of our previous assumptions, namely that the first language acquired is always the dominant one, as well as the assumption of the critical period hypothesis that critical period effects are chiefly the result of the age of onset of acquisition of the second language, given that in the case of heritage learners it is the first language which undergoes these effects.

In the second chapter, we discussed recent research showing that the two languages of a bilingual are highly interconnected at the lexical, syntactic, and phonological levels. Furthermore, research has found that the continual interaction between the languages of a bilingual has important repercussions for cognitive development in bilingual children beginning early in infancy. These include enhanced executive function skills stemming from bilinguals' need to monitor and inhibit one of their languages, as well as enhanced literacy abilities for bilingual children acquiring same-script languages. Bilingualism also produces neuroanatomical changes in multilingual speakers, including enhanced subcortical auditory processing and increased gray-matter density in the inferior parietal cortex, an effect that is modulated by language proficiency and age of acquisition. Finally, in the second chapter we presented evidence regarding the factors that affect L1 and L2 attrition in bilinguals, including age of second language immersion, availability and type of input, and proficiency levels in each language.

The third chapter examined several theories which have been proposed to account for lexical and syntactic development in bilingual children and adults. While early theoretical accounts assumed that lexical and syntactic development occurred separately, more recent approaches have proposed that their acquisition is interconnected, a theoretical linguistic advance which finds empirical support in the studies of the bilingual lexicon by cognitive psychologists. In this chapter we also presented research findings that have allowed the field of bilingualism to move from initial debates on unitary versus binary systems of representation to a more nuanced view of the development of the bilingual lexicon and syntax that involves the interplay of different language subcomponents.

The overall picture that emerges from the three chapters in this book is one in which the cognitive and linguistic development in bilinguals illustrates the complexities of how language is represented, accessed, and processed in the human mind that go beyond accounts based on the study of monolingual development.

References

Abutalebi, J., Cappa, S., and Perani, D. (2001). The bilingual brain as revealed by functional neuroimaging. *Bilingualism: Language and Cognition*, 4, 2: 179–190.

Abutalebi, J., and Green, D. (2007). Bilingual language production: The neurocognition of language representation and control. *Journal of Neurolinguistics*, 20, 3: 242–275.

Adams, M. J. (1990). *Beginning to read: Thinking and learning about print*. Cambridge, MA: MIT Press.

Adger, D. and Smith, J. (2010). Variation in agreement: A lexical feature-based approach. *Lingua*, 120, 5: 1109–1134.

Albareda-Castellot, B., Pons, F., and Sebastián-Gallés, N. (2011). The acquisition of phonetic categories in bilingual infants: New data from an anticipatory eye movement paradigm. *Developmental Science*, 14, 2: 395–401.

Aldekoa, J. and Garder, N. (2002). Turning knowledge of Basque into use: Normalisation plans for schools. *International Journal of Bilingual Education and Bilingualism*, 5, 6: 339–354.

Altarriba, J. (1992). The representation of translation equivalents in bilingual memory. *Advances in Psychology*, 83: 157–174.

Amaral, L. and T. Roeper (2014a). Multiple grammars and second language representation. *Second Language Research*, 30: 3–36.

(2014b). Why minimal multiple rules provide a unique window into UG and L2. *Second Language Research*, 30: 97–107.

American Council on the Teaching of Foreign Languages. (2012). ACTFL Proficiency Guidelines. http://actflproficiencyguidelines2012.org

Amorrortu, E. (2003). *Basque sociolinguistics: Language, society, and culture*. Reno, NV: University of Nevada Press.

Anderson, R. (1999a). Impact of language loss on grammar in a bilingual child. *Communication Disorders Quarterly*, 21: 4–16.

(1999b). Loss of gender agreement in L1 attrition: Preliminary results. *Bilingual Research Journal*, 23: 319–338.

(2004). First language loss in Spanish-speaking children: Patterns of loss and implications for clinical practice. In *Bilingual language developments and disorders in Spanish–English speakers*, ed. B. Goldstein. Baltimore: Brookes, pp. 187–212.

Anton-Mendez, I. and Gollan, T. (2010). Not just semantics: Strong frequency and weak cognate effects on semantic association in bilinguals. *Memory and Cognition*, 38, 6: 723–739.

Aparicio, F. (1998). Whose Spanish, whose language, whose power? An ethnographic inquiry into differential bilingualism. *Indiana Journal of Hispanic Literatures*, 12, 1: 5–26.

Appel, R. and Muysken, P. (1987). *Language contact and bilingualism*. London: Edward Arnold.

Archila-Suerte, P., Zevin, J., Bunta, F., and Hernández, A. E. (2012). Age of acquisition and proficiency in a second language independently influence the perception of non-native speech. *Bilingualism: Language and Cognition*, 15, 1: 190–201.

Archila-Suerte, P., Zevin, J., Ramos, A. I., and Hernández, A. E. (2013). The neural basis of non-native speech perception in bilingual children. *NeuroImage*, 67: 51–63.

Arzamendi, J. and Genesee, F. (1997). Reflections on immersion education in the Basque Country. In *Immersion education: International perspectives*, ed. R. Johnson and R. Swain. Cambridge University Press, pp. 151–166.

Au, T. K. F., Knightly, L. M., Jun, S. A., and Oh, J. S. (2002). Overhearing a language during childhood. *Psychological Science*, 13, 3: 238–243.

Aucamp, A. J. (1926). *Bilingual education and nationalism: With special reference to South Africa*. Pretoria: J. L. Van Schaik.

Austin, J. (2001). Language differentiation and the development of morphosyntax in bilingual children acquiring Basque and Spanish. Unpublished Ph.D. dissertation, Cornell University.

(2007). Grammatical interference and the acquisition of ergative case in bilingual children learning Basque and Spanish. *Bilingualism: Language and Cognition*, 10, 3: 315–331.

(2009). Delay, interference and bilingual development: The acquisition of verbal morphology in children learning Basque and Spanish. *International Journal of Bilingualism*, 13, 4: 447–479.

(2010). Rich inflection and the production of finite verbs in child language. *Morphology*, 20, 1: 41–69.

(2013). Markedness, input frequency, and the acquisition of inflection: Evidence from Basque–Spanish bilingual children. *International Journal of Bilingualism*, 17, 3: 259–283.

Austin, J., Blume, M., and Sánchez, L. (2013). Syntactic development in the L1 of Spanish–English bilingual children. *Hispania*, 96, 3: 542–561.

Aydin, K., Ucar, A., Oguz, K. K., Okur, O. O., Agayev, A., Unal, Z., and Ozturk, C. (2007). Increased gray matter density in the parietal cortex of mathematicians: A voxel-based morphometry study. *American Journal of Neuroradiology*, 28, 10: 1859–1864.

Bachman, L. F. (1990). *Fundamental considerations in language testing*. Oxford University Press.

Bahrick, H. (1984). Semantic memory content in permastore: Fifty years of memory for Spanish learned in school. *Journal of Experimental Psychology: General*, 113, 1: 1–29.

Bailey, N., Madden, C., and Krashen, S. (1974). Is there a "natural sequence" in adult second language learning? *Language Learning* 21: 235–243.

Baker, C. (2011). *Foundations of bilingual education and bilingualism.* 5th edition. Bristol: Multilingual Matters.

Baker, C., and Hinde, J. P. (1984). Language background classification. *Journal of Multilingual and Multicultural Development*, 5: 43–56.

Baker, M. and Vinokurova, N. (2010). Two modalities of case assignment: Case in Sakha. *Natural Language and Linguistic Theory*, 28: 593–642.

Bardovi-Harlig, K. (2004). Pragmatic competence of the advanced learner. Paper prepared for the High-level language ability research hub. Department of Education.

Bardovi-Harlig, K., and Stringer, D. (2010). Variables in second language attrition. *Studies in Second Language Acquisition*, 32, 1: 1–45.

    (2013). The lexicon in second language attrition: What happens when the cat's got your tongue? In *Memory, Language, and Bilingualism: Theoretical and Applied Approaches*, ed. J. Altarriba and L. Isurin. Cambridge University Press, pp. 291–318.

Bates, E., Devescovi, A., and D'Amico, S. (1999). Processing complex sentences: A crosslinguistic study. *Language and Cognitive Processes*, 14: 68–123.

Bassetti, B. (2007). Bilingualism and thought: Grammatical gender and concepts of objects in Italian–German bilingual children. *International Journal of Bilingualism*, 11, 3: 251–273.

Bayley, R., and Bonnici, L. M. (2009). Recent research on Latinos in the USA and Canada, Part 1: Language maintenance and shift and English varieties. *Language and Linguistics Compass*, 3, 5: 1300–1313.

Becker, M. (2000). The development of copula in child English: The lightness of be. Unpublished Ph.D. dissertation, University of California, Los Angeles.

    (2004). Copula omission is a grammatical reflex. *Language Acquisition*, 12: 157–167.

Bedore, L. M., Peña, E. D., García, M., and Cortez, C. (2005). Conceptual versus monolingual scoring: When does it make a difference? *Language, Speech, and Hearing Services in Schools*, 36: 188–200.

Bel, A. (1998). Teoria lingüística i adquisició del llenguatge. Anàlisi comparada dels trets morfològics en català i en castellà. Unpublished Ph.D. dissertation. Universitat Autònoma de Barcelona.

Bel, Aurora. (2001). The projection of aspect: A key in the acquisition of finiteness? In *Research on Child language acquisition: Proceedings of the 8th Conference of the International Association for the Study of Child Language*, ed. M. Almgren, A. Barreña, M.-J. Ezeizabarrena, I. Idiazabal, and B. MacWhinney. Somerville: Cascadilla Press, pp. 297–313.

Belazi, H., Rubin, E. and J. Toribio (1994). Code switching and X-bar theory: The functional head constraint. *Linguistic Inquiry* 25, 2: 221–237.

Belletti, A. (2001). Inversion as focalization. In *Subject inversion in Romance and the theory of Universal Grammar*, ed. Aafke Hulk and Jean-Yves Pollock. Oxford University Press, pp. 60–90.

    (2004). Aspects of the low IP area. In *The structure of IP and CP: The cartography of syntactic structures*, ed. Luigi Rizzi, vol. 2. New York: Oxford University Press.

Bellugi, U. (1967). The acquisition of negation. Unpublished Ph.D. dissertation, Harvard University.

Benasich, A. A., and Tallal, P. (2002). Infant discrimination of rapid auditory cues predicts later language impairment. *Behavioural Brain Research*, 136, 1: 31–49.

Ben-Zeev, S. (1977). The influence of bilingualism on cognitive strategy and cognitive development. *Child Development*, 48, 3: 1009–1018.

Berman, R. and Olshtain, E. (1983). Features of first language transfer in second language attrition. *Applied Linguistics*, 4, 3: 222–234.

Bernardini, P. and Schlyter, S. (2004). Growing syntactic structure and code-mixing in the weaker language: The Ivy hypothesis. *Bilingualism: Language and Cognition*, 7, 1: 49–69.

Bernolet, S., Hartsuiker, R. J., and Pickering, M. J. (2007). Shared syntactic representations in bilinguals: Evidence for the role of word-order repetition. *Journal of Experimental Psychology: Learning, Memory, and Cognition*, 33: 931–949.

Beziers, M. and Van Overbeke. M. (1968). *Le bilinguisme*. Louvain: Librarie Universitaire.

Bhatia, T. K. and Ritchie, W. C. (1999). The bilingual child: Some issues and perspectives. In *The handbook of child language acquisition*, ed. W. C. Ritchie and T. J. Bhatia. San Diego, CA: Academic Press, pp. 569–365.

(eds.) (2006). *The handbook of bilingualism*. Malden, MA: Wiley-Blackwell.

Bhatt, R. M., and Bolonyai, A. (2011). Code-switching and the optimal grammar of bilingual language use. *Bilingualism: Language and Cognition*, 14, 4: 522–546.

Bialystok, E. (2001). *Bilingualism in development: Language, literacy, and cognition.* Cambridge University Press.

(2007). Acquisition of literacy in bilingual children: A framework for research. *Language learning*, 57, s1: 45–77.

(2009). Bilingualism: The good, the bad, and the indifferent. *Bilingualism: Language and Cognition*, 12,1: 3–11.

Bialystok, E., and Barac, R. (2012). Emerging bilingualism: Dissociating advantages for metalinguistic awareness and executive control. *Cognition*, 122: 67–73.

Bialystok, E., Craik, F. I. M., Green, D. W., and Gollan, T. H. (2009). Bilingual minds. *Psychological Science in the Public Interest*, 10: 89–129.

Bialystok, E., Craik, F. I., Klein, R., and Viswanathan, M. (2004). Bilingualism, aging, and cognitive control: evidence from the Simon task. *Psychology and Aging*, 19, 2: 290–303.

Bialystok, E., Craik, F. and Luk, G. (2008). Cognitive control and lexical access in younger and older bilinguals. *Journal of Experimental Psychology: Learning, Memory, and Cognition*, 34: 859–873.

Bialystok, E., Majumder, S., and Martin, M. M. (2003). Developing phonological awareness: Is there a bilingual advantage? *Applied Psycholinguistics*, 24, 1: 27–44.

Bills, G. D. (2005). Las comunidades lingüísticas y el mantenimiento del español en Estados Unidos. In *Contactos y contextos lingüísticos: El español en los Estados Unidos y en contacto con otras lenguas*, ed. L. A. Ortiz-López and M. Lacorte Frankfurt: Vervuet; Madrid: Iberoamericana, pp. 55–83.

Bills, G. D., and Vigil, N. A. (1999). Ashes to ashes: The historical basis for dialect variation in New Mexican Spanish. *Romance Philology*, 53, 1: 43–68.

Birdsong, D. (1999). Introduction: Whys and why nots of the critical period hypothesis for second language acquisition. In *Second language acquisition and the critical period hypothesis*, ed. D. Birdsong. Mahwah, NJ and London: Lawrence Erlbaum, pp. 1–22.

(2005). Nativelikeness and non-nativelikeness in L2A research. *International Review of Applied Linguistics in Language Teaching*, 43: 319–328.

Bishop, D. V. M. (2002). The role of genes in the etiology of specific language impairment. *Journal of Communication Disorders*, 35, 4: 311–328.

(2006). What causes specific language impairment in children? *Current Directions in Psychological Science*, 15, 5: 217–221.

Block, N. (1995). The mind as the software of the brain. In *An invitation to cognitive science: Thinking*, ed. D. Osherson. Cambridge, MA: MIT Press, vol. 3, pp. 377–426.

Bloom, L. (1970). *Language development: Form and function in emerging grammars.* Cambridge, MA: MIT Press.

Bloomfield, L. (1933). *Language.* George Allen and Unwin: London.

Bongaerts, T., Planken, B., and Schils, E. (1995). Can late learners attain a native accent in a foreign language? A test of the critical period hypothesis. In *The age factor in second language acquisition*, ed. D. Singleton and Z. Lengyel. Clevedon: Multilingual Matters, pp. 30–50.

Bosque, I, and Gutiérrez-Rexach, J. (2009). *Fundamentos de sintaxis formal.* Madrid: Akal.

Boudreault, P. and Mayberry, R. I. (2006). Grammatical processing in American Sign Language: Age of first language acquisition effects in relation to syntactic structure. *Language and Cognitive Processes*, 21: 608–635.

Boukrina, O. (2012). Neural networks underlying language processing in same script bilinguals: an investigation of functional specificity in the visual word form area. Unpublished Ph.D. dissertation, Rutgers University – Graduate School Newark.

Bowers, J. S., Mattys, S. L., and Gage, S. H. (2009). Preserved implicit knowledge of a forgotten childhood language. *Psychological Science*, 20, 9: 1064–1069.

Branum-Martin, L., Mehta, P. D., Fletcher, J. M., Carlson, C. D., Ortiz, A., Carlo, M., and Francis, D. J. (2006). Bilingual phonological awareness: Multilevel construct validation among Spanish-speaking kindergarteners in transitional bilingual education classrooms. *Journal of Educational Psychology*, 98, 1: 170–181.

Brown, R. (1973). *A first language: The early stages.* Cambridge, MA: Harvard University Press.

Brysbaert, B., and Duyck, W. (2010). Is it time to leave behind the Revised Hierarchical Model of bilingual language processing after fifteen years of service? *Bilingualism: Language and Cognition*, 13, 3: 359–371.

Bullock, B. (2009). Prosody in contact in French: A case study from a heritage variety in the USA. *International Journal of Bilingualism*, 13, 2: 165–194.

Bullock, B. E., Hinrichs, L., and Toribio, A. J. (2014). World Englishes, code-switching, and convergence. In *The Oxford handbook of World Englishes*, ed. M. Filppula, J. Klemola, and D. Sharma. Oxford University Press.

Bullock, B. E. and Toribio, A. J. (2004). Convergence as an emergent property in bilingual speech. *Bilingualism: Language and Cognition*, 7: 91–93.

(eds.). (2009). *The Cambridge handbook of linguistic code-switching.* Cambridge University Press.

Butler, Y. G. and Hakuta, K. (2006). Bilingualism and second language acquisition. In *The handbook of bilingualism*, ed. T. K. Bhatia and W. C. Ritchie. Malden, MA: Blackwell, pp. 114–144.

Camacho, J. (2012). Ser and estar: The individual/stage-level distinction and aspectual predication. In *The handbook of Hispanic linguistics*, ed. J. I. Hualde, A. Olarrea, and E. O'Rourke. Chichester: John Wiley, pp. 453–476.

Camacho, J., Paredes, L., and Sánchez, L. (1995). The genitive clitic and the genitive construction in Andean Spanish. *Probus*, 7(2), 133–146.

   (1997). Null objects in bilingual Andean Spanish. In *Proceedings of the 21st annual Boston University Conference on Language Development*, ed. E. Hughes, M. Hughes, and A. Greenhill. Sommerville, MA: Cascadilla Press, pp. 55–66.

Cameron, R., and Flores-Ferrán, N. (2004). Perseveration of subject expression across regional dialects of Spanish. *Spanish in Context*, 1, 1: 41–65.

Canale, M. (1983). From communicative competence to communicative language pedagogy. In *Language and communication*, ed. J. C. Richards and R. W. Schmidt. London: Longman, pp. 2–27.

Canale, M. and Swain, M. (1980). Theoretical bases of communicative approaches to second language teaching and testing. *Applied Linguistics*, 1: 1–47.

Caramazza, A. and Brones, I. (1979). Lexical access in bilinguals. *Bulletin of the Psychonomic Society*, 13, 4: 212–214.

   (1980). Semantic classification by bilinguals. *Canadian Journal of Psychology/Revue Canadienne de Psychologie*, 34, 1: 77–81.

Carlson, G. N. (1977). Reference to kinds in English. Unpublished Ph.D, dissertation, University of Massachusetts, Amherst.

Carreira, M. (2012). Spanish as a heritage language. In *The Handbook of Hispanic Linguistics*, ed. J. Hualde, A. Olarrea, and E. O'Rourke. Malden, MA: Wiley-Blackwell, pp. 765–782.

Cashman, H. R. (2006). Who wins in research on bilingualism in an anti-bilingual state? *Journal of Multilingual and Multicultural Development*, 27, 1: 42–60.

Castro-Caldas, A., Petersson, K. M., Reis, A., Stone-Elander, S., and Ingvar, M. (1998). The illiterate brain: Learning to read and write during childhood influences the functional organization of the adult brain. *Brain*, 121, 6: 1053–1063.

Cenoz, J. (2008). Achievements and challenges in bilingual and multilingual education in the Basque Country. *AILA Review* 21: 13–30.

Cerrón-Palomino, R. (1987). *Lingüística quechua*. Cusco: Centro de Estudios Rurales Andinos "Bartolomé de las Casas."

   (2003). *Castellano andino: Aspectos sociolingüísticos, pedagógicos y gramaticales*. Lima: Pontificia Universidad Católica del Perú.

Chee, M. W., Tan, E. W., and Thiel, T. (1999). Mandarin and English single word processing studied with functional magnetic resonance imaging. *Journal of Neuroscience*, 19, 8: 3050–3056.

Chomsky, N. (1981). *Lectures on government and binding*. Dordrecht: Kluwer.

   (1995). *The Minimalist Program*. Cambridge, MA: MIT Press.

   (1998). Minimalist inquiries: The framework. *MIT Occasional Papers Papers in Linguistics*, 15 Cambridge, MA: MIT.

   (2000). Linguistics and brain science. In *Image, language, brain*, ed. A. Marantz, Y. Miyashita, and W. O'Neil. Cambridge, MA: MIT Press, pp. 13–23.

(2001). Beyond explanatory adequacy. *MIT Occasional Papers In Linguistics*, 20. Cambridge, MA: MIT.

Chun M., M. (2000). Contextual cueing of visual attention. *Trends in Cognitive Sciences*, 4: 170–178.

Clahsen, H., and Muysken, P. (1989). The UG paradox in L2 acquisition. *Second Language Research*, 5, 1: 1–29.

Cohen, A. (1975). *A sociolinguistic approach to bilingual education: Experiments in the American Southwest*. Rowley, MA: Newbury House.

(1976). The acquisition of Spanish grammar through immersion: Some findings after four years. *Canadian Modern Language Review*, 32, 5: 562–574.

(1986). Forgetting foreign language vocabulary. In *Language attrition in progress*, ed. B. Weltens, K. de Bot, and T. J. Van Els. Dordrecht: Foris, vol. 2, pp. 143–158.

(1989). Attrition in the productive lexicon of two Portuguese third language speakers. *Studies in Second Language Acquisition*, 11, 2: 135–149.

Collier, V. P. and Thomas, W. P. (2004). The astounding effectiveness of dual language education for all. *NABE Journal of Research and Practice*, 2, 1: 1–20.

Cook, V. (1991). *Second language learning and language teaching*. London: Edward Arnold.

(1995). Multicompetence and effects of age. In *The age factor in second language acquisition*, ed. D. Singleton and Z. Lengyel. Clevedon: Multilingual Matters, pp. 51–66.

Cooper, R. (1971). Degree of bilingualism. In *Bilingualism in the barrio*, ed. J. Fishman, R. Cooper, and R. Ma, R. Bloomington: Indiana University Press, pp. 273–294.

Costa, A., Caramazza, A., and Sebastian-Galles, N. (2000). The cognate facilitation effect: implications for models of lexical access. *Journal of Experimental Psychology: Learning, Memory, and Cognition*, 26, 5: 1283–1296.

Costa, A., Colomé, A., Gómez, O., and Sebastián-Gallés, N. (2003). Another look at cross-language competition in bilingual speech production: Lexical and phonological factors. *Bilingualism: Language and Cognition*, 6, 3: 167–179.

Costa, A., Hernández, M., and Sebastián-Gallés, N. (2008). Bilingualism aids conflict resolution: Evidence from the ANT task. *Cognition*, 106, 1: 59–86.

Costa, A., Miozzo, M., and Caramazza, A. (1999). Lexical selection in bilinguals: Do words in the bilingual's two lexicons compete for selection? *Journal of Memory and Language*, 41, 3: 365–397.

Costa, M., Santesteban, M., and Ivanova, I. (2006). How do highly proficient bilinguals control their lexicalization process? Inhibitory and language-specific selection mechanisms are both functional. *Journal of Experimental Psychology: Learning, Memory, and Cognition*, 32, 5: 1057–1074.

Crawford, J. (1992). *Hold your tongue: Bilingualism and the politics of English only*. Reading, MA: Addison Wesley.

Crystal, D. (1997). *English as a global language*. Cambridge University Press.

(2000). *Language death*. Cambridge University Press.

Cuetos, F., and Mitchell, D. C. (1988). Cross-linguistic differences in parsing: Restrictions on the use of the Late Closure strategy in Spanish. *Cognition*, 30, 1: 73–105.

Cummins, J. (1987). Bilingualism, language profiency, and metalinguistic development. In *Childhood bilingualism: Aspects of linguistic, cognitive, and social development*, ed. P. Homel, M. Palif, and D. Aaronson. Hillsdale, NJ: Lawrence Erlbaum, pp. 57–74.

(1999). Alternative paradigms in bilingual education research: Does theory have a place? *Educational Researcher*, 28, 7: 26–32.

(2000). Putting language proficiency in its place: Responding to critiques of the conversational/academic language distinction. In *English in Europe: The acquisition of a third language*, ed. J. Cenoz and U. Jessner. Clevedon: Multilingual Matters, pp. 54–83.

Curtiss, S. (1977). *Genie: A psycholinguistic study of a modern-day "wild child."* New York: Academic Press.

(1988). The special talent of grammar acquisition. In *The exceptional brain: Neuropsychology of talent and special abilities*, ed. L. K. Obler and D. Fein. New York: Guildford Press, pp. 364–386.

(1989). The independence and task-specificity of language. In *Interaction in human development*, eds. M. H. Bornstein and J. S. Bruner. Hillsdale, NJ: Lawrence Erlbaum, pp. 105–137.

(1994). Language as a cognitive system: Its independence and selective vulnerability. In *Noam Chomsky: Critical assessments*, ed. C. Otero. New York: Routledge, vol. 4, pp. 210–256.

(1996). The case of Chelsea: A new case of the critical period. Unpublished MS, University of California, Los Angeles.

Curtiss, S., Fromkin, V., and Krashen, S. (1978). Language development in the mature (minor) right hemisphere. *ITL Review of Applied Linguistics*, 39–40: 23–37.

Cuza, A. (2010). On the L1 attrition of the Spanish present. *Hispania*, 93, 2: 256–272.

(2013). Crosslinguistic influence at the syntax proper: Interrogative subject-verb inversion in heritage Spanish. *International Journal of Bilingualism*, 17, 1: 71–96.

Cuza, A. and Frank, J. (2011). Transfer effects at the syntax-semantics interface: The case of double-*que* questions in Heritage Spanish. *Heritage Language Journal*, 8, 2: 66–88.

Cuza, A., Pérez-Leroux, A. T., and Sánchez, L. (2013). The role of semantic transfer in clitic drop among simultaneous and sequential Chinese–Spanish bilinguals. *Studies in Second Language Acquisition*, 35, 1: 93–125.

De Bot, K. (1992). A bilingual production model: Levelt's "Speaking" model adapted. *Applied Linguistics*, 13: 1–24.

(2002). Language attrition: Where are we and where are we going? Paper presented at the International Conference on First Language Attrition, Amsterdam. Available at www.let.vu.nl/events/2002/langatt.nsf/extern/home.

De Bot, K., Gommans, P., and Rossing, C. (1991). L1 loss in an L2 environment: Dutch immigrants in France. In *First language attrition*, ed. H. W. Seliger and R. M. Vago. Cambridge University Press, pp. 87–98.

DeGraff, M. (1999). *Language creation and language change: Creolization, diachrony, and development*. Cambridge, MA: MIT Press.

De Groot, A. M. (1993). Word-type effects in bilingual processing tasks. In *The bilingual lexicon*, ed. R. Schreuder and B. Weltens. Amsterdam: John Benjamins, pp. 27–51.

De Groot, A. (2011). *Language and cognition in bilinguals and multilinguals*. New York and Hove: Psychology Press.

De Groot, A., Dannenburg, L., and van Hell, J. (1994). Forward and backward word translation by bilinguals. *Journal of Memory and Language*, 33, 5: 600–629.

De Groot, A. and Nas, G. (1991). Lexical representation of cognates and noncognates in compound bilinguals. *Journal of Memory and Language*, 30, 1: 90–123.

De Houwer, A. (1990). *The acquisition of two languages from birth: A case study*. Cambridge University Press.

(2005). Early bilingual acquisition: focus on morphosyntax and the Separate Development Hypothesis. In *The handbook of bilingualism: Psycholinguistic Approaches*, ed. J. Kroll and A. De Groot. Oxford University Press, pp. 30–48.

(2007). Parental language input patterns and children's bilingual use. *Applied Psycholinguistics*, 28, 3: 411–424.

(2009). *Bilingual first language acquisition*. Bristol: Multilingual Matters.

Dehaene, S., Pegado, F., Braga, L. W., Ventura, P., Nunes Filho, G., Jobert, A., Dehaene-Lambertz, G., Kolinsky, R., Morais, J., and Cohen, L. (2010). How learning to read changes the cortical networks for vision and language. *Science*, 330, 6009: 1359–1364.

Dehaene-Lambertz, G. and Gliga, T. (2004). Common neural basis for phoneme processing in infants and adults. *Journal of Cognitive Neuroscience*, 16, 8: 1375–1387.

Del Percio, C., Rossini, P. M., Marzano, N., Iacoboni, M., Infarinato, F., Aschieri, P., and Eusebi, F. (2008). Is there a "neural efficiency" in athletes? A high-resolution EEG study. *NeuroImage*, 42, 4: 1544–1553.

Desmet, T., and Declercq, M. (2006). Cross-linguistic priming of syntactic hierarchical configuration information. *Journal of Memory and Language*, 54, 4: 610–632.

Desmet, T., and Duyck, W. (2007). Bilingual language processing. *Language and Linguistics Compass*, 1, 3: 168–194.

Deuchar, M. and S. Quay. (2000). *Bilingual acquisition: Theoretical implications of a case study*. Oxford University Press.

Dijkstra, T., Timmermans, M. and Schriefers, H. (2000). On being blinded by your other language: Effects of task demands on interlingual homograph recognition. *Journal of Memory and Language*, 42: 445–464.

Dijkstra, T and W. Van Heuven. (2002). The architecture of the bilingual word recognition system: From identification to decision. *Bilingualism: Language and Cognition*. 5, 3: 175–197.

Dijkstra, T., Van Heuven, W. J., and Grainger, J. (1998). Simulating cross-language competition with the bilingual interactive activation model. *Psychologica Belgica*, 38, 177–196.

Döpke, S. (1998). Competing language structures: The acquisition of verb placement by Bilingual German–English children. *Journal of Child Language*, 25: 555–584.

(2000). *Cross-linguistic structures in simultaneous bilingualism.* Amsterdam: John Benjamins.

Douglas, D. (1988). Testing listening comprehension in the context of the ACTFL proficiency guidelines. *Studies in Second Language Acquisition*, 10: 245–261.

Douglas, J. E. and Button, A. (1978). The development of speech and mental processes in a pair of twins: A case study. *Journal of Child Psychology and Psychiatry*, 19, 1: 49–56.

Dronkers, N. (1987). Chelsea's cognitive and neuropsychological status. Paper presented at the Orton Dyslexia Society Annual Meeting, San Francisco.

Dulay, H. and Burt, M. (1974). Natural sequences in child second language acquisition. *Language Learning*, 24: 37–53.

Durgunoğlu, A. Y., Nagy, W. E., and Hancin-Bhatt, B. J. (1993). Cross-language transfer of phonological awareness. *Journal of Educational Psychology*, 85, 3: 453–465.

Dussias, P. E. (2001). Sentence parsing in fluent Spanish–English bilinguals. In *One mind, two languages: Bilingual language processing*, ed. J. Nicol. Cambridge: Blackwell, pp. 159–176.

(2003). Syntactic ambiguity resolution in L2 learners. *Studies in Second Language Acquisition*, 25, 4: 529–557.

(2004). Parsing a first language like a second: The erosion of L1 parsing strategies in Spanish–English Bilinguals. *International Journal of Bilingualism*, 8, 3: 355–371.

Dussias, P. E. and Sagarra, N. (2007). The effect of exposure on syntactic parsing in Spanish–English bilinguals. *Bilingualism: Language and Cognition*, 10, 1: 101–116.

Duyck, W. (2005). Translation and associative priming with cross-lingual pseudo-homophones: Evidence for nonselective phonological activation in bilinguals. *Journal of Experimental Psychology: Learning, Memory, and Cognition*, 31: 1340–1359.

Edwards, J. (2006). Foundations of bilingualism. In *The handbook of bilingualism*, eds. T. K. Bhatia and W. C. Ritchie. Malden, MA: Blackwell, pp. 7–31.

Ellis, R. (1985). *Understanding Second Language Acquisition.* Oxford University Press.

(1994). *The Study of Second Language Acquisition.* Oxford University Press.

Emmorey, K., Bellugi, U., Friederici, A., and Horn, P. (1995). Effects of age of acquisition on grammatical sensitivity: Evidence from on-line and off-line tasks. *Applied Psycholinguistics*, 16: 1–23.

Escobar, A. (1978). *Variaciones sociolingüísticas del castellano en el Perú.* Lima: Instituto de Estudios Peruanos.

(1994). Andean Spanish and Bilingual Spanish: Linguistic characteristics. In *Language in the Andes*, eds. P. Cole, G. Hermon, and M. D. Martin. Newark, DE: University of Delaware, pp. 51–73.

(2010). El español en los Estados Unidos. In *Introducción a la lingüística española*, J. I. Hualde, A. Olarrea, A. M. Escobar, and C. Travis. Cambridge University Press, pp. 445–502.

(2011). Spanish in contact with Quechua. In *The handbook of Hispanic sociolinguistics*, ed. M. Díaz-Campos. Malden, MA: Blackwell, pp. 323–352.

(2012). Revisiting the "present perfect": Semantic analysis of Andean colonial documents. *Lingua*, 122, 5: 470–480.

Etxeberria, F. (1997). Bilingualism and biculturalism in the Basque Country. *Educational Review*, 49, 2: 141–149.

Eubank, L. (1993). On the transfer of parametric values in L2 development. *Language Acquisition*, 3, 3: 183–208.

Ezeizabarrena, M. J. (1996). *Adquisición de la morfología verbal en esukera y castellano por niños bilingües*. Bilbao: Servicio Editorial de la Universidad del País Vasco.

(1997). Imperativos en el lenguaje de niños bilingües. *Actas do I Simposio Internacional do Bilingüismo*. University of Vigo, pp. 328–341. http://webs.uvigo .es/ssl/actas1997/03/Ezeizabarrena.pdf. Accessed on 14 May, 2012.

(2012). The (in)consistent ergative marking in early Basque: L1 vs. child L2. *Lingua*, 122, 3: 303–317.

Ezeizabarrena, M. J. and Aeby, S. (2010). Les phénomènes de code-switching dans les conversations adulte-enfant(s) en basque-espagnol: Une approche syntaxique. *Corpus*, 9: 53–80.

Fabbro, F. (1999). *The neurolinguistics of bilingualism*. Hove: Psychology Press.

(2001a). The bilingual brain: Cerebral representation of languages. *Brain and Language*, 79, 2: 211–222.

(2001b). The bilingual brain: Bilingual aphasia. *Brain and Language*, 79, 2: 201–210.

Fabbro, F., and Paradis, M. (1995). Differential impairments in four multilingual patients with subcortical lesions. In *Aspects of bilingual aphasia*, ed. M. Paradis. Oxford: Pergamon Press, pp. 139–176.

Fabbro, F., Skrap, M., and Aglioti, S. (2000). Pathological switching between languages following frontal lesion in a bilingual patient. *Journal of Neurology, Neurosurgery, and Psychiatry*, 68: 650–652.

Ferguson, C. A. (1959). *Diglossia. Word*, 15: 325–340.

Fernández, E. M. (2003). *Bilingual sentence processing: Relative clause attachment in English and Spanish*. Amsterdam: John Benjamins.

Fernández Fuertes, R., Liceras, J., Pérez-Tattam, R., Carter, D., Martínez-Sanz, C., and Alba de la Fuente, A. (2008). The nature of the pronominal system and verbal morphology in Bilingual Spanish/English child data: Linguistic theory and learnability issues. In *Selected Proceedings of the 10th Hispanic Linguistics Symposium*, ed. J. Bruhn and E. Valenzuela. Somerville, MA: Cascadilla Proceedings Project. www.lingref.com, document #1785, pp. 51–63.

Fernández, R. and Liceras, J. (2010). Copula omission in the English developing grammar of English/Spanish bilingual children. *International Journal of Bilingual Education and Bilingualism* 13, 5: 525–551.

Fernández Leborans, M. (1999). El nombre propio. In *Gramática descriptiva de la lengua española*, ed. I. Bosque and V. Demonte. Madrid: Espasa Calpe, vol. 1, pp. 77–128.

Fernández-Ordóñez, I. (1994). Isoglosas internas del castellano. El sistema referencial del pronombre átono de tercera persona. *Revista de Filología Española*, 74, 1: 71–125.

(1999). Leísmo, laísmo y loísmo. In *Gramática descriptiva de la lengua española*. ed. I. Bosque and V. Demonte Madrid: Espasa Calpe, vol. 1, pp. 1317–1393.

Firth, Uta. (2003). *Autism: Explaining the enigma*. Malden, MA: Wiley-Blackwell.

Fisher, S. (2005). Dissection of molecular mechanisms underlying speech and language disorders. *Applied Psycholinguistics*, 26(01), 111–128.

Fishman, J. (1967). Bilingualism with and without diglossia; diglossia with and without bilingualism. *Journal of Social Issues*, 23, 2: 29–38.

(1991). *Reversing language shift: theoretical and empirical foundations of assistance to threatened languages*. Clevedon: Multilingual Matters.

Flege, J. E. (1988). Factors affecting degree of perceived foreign accent in English sentences. *Journal of the Acoustical Society of America*, 84: 70–79.

(1987). A critical period for learning to pronounce foreign languages? *Applied Linguistics*, 8: 162–177.

Flege, J. and Davidian, R. (1984). Transfer and developmental processes in adult foreign language speech production. *Applied Psycholinguistics*, 5: 323–347.

Flege, J. E. and Liu, S. (2001). The effect of experience on adults' acquisition of a second language. *Studies in Second Language Acquisition*, 23: 527–552.

Flege, J. E., Yeni-Komshian, G. H., and Liu, S. (1999). Age constraints on second-language acquisition. *Journal of Memory and Language*, 41: 78–104.

Flores-Ferrán, N. (2004). Spanish subject personal pronoun use in New York City Puerto Ricans: Can we rest the case of English contact? *Language Variation and Change*, 16, 1: 49–73.

Flynn, S. (1983). Differences between first and second language acquisition. In *Acquisition of symbolic skills*, ed. D. Rogers and J. Sloboda. London and New York: Plenum Press, pp. 485–500.

(1987). L2 Acquisition of pronoun anaphora: Resetting the parameter. In *Studies in the acquisition of anaphora: Defining the constraints*, ed. B. Lust. Dordrecht: D. Reidel, vol. 2., pp. 227–243.

Flynn, S. and Manuel, S. (1991). Age dependent effects in language acquisition: An evaluation of "Critical Period" hypotheses. In *Point/counterpoint: Universal Grammar in the second language*, ed. L. Eubank. Amsterdam: John Benjamins, pp. 118–145.

Forbes, J. N., Poulin-Dubois, D., Rivero, M. R., and Sera, M. D. (2008). Grammatical gender affects bilinguals' conceptual gender: Implications for linguistic relativity and decision making. *Open Applied Linguistics Journal*, 1: 68–76.

Foster-Cohen, S. (2001). First language acquisition... second language acquisition: What's Hecuba to him or he to Hecuba? *Second Language Research*, 17: 329–344.

Frenck-Mestre, C. and Pynte, J. (1997). Syntactic ambiguity resolution while reading in second and native languages. *Quarterly Journal of Experimental Psychology A*, 50, 1: 119–148.

Friederici, A. D. (2009). Pathways to language: Fiber tracts in the human brain. *Trends in Cognitive Sciences*, 13, 4: 175–181.

Friederici, A. D., Friedrich, M., and Weber, C. (2002). Neural manifestation of cognitive and precognitive mismatch detection in early infancy. *NeuroReport*, 13, 10: 1251–1254.

Fromkin, V., Curtiss, S., Krashen, S., Rigler, D., and Riqler, M. (1974). The linguistic development of Genie. *Language*, 50: 528–554.

Galambos, S. J., and Goldin-Meadow, S. (1990). The effects of learning two languages on levels of metalinguistic awareness. *Cognition*, 34, 1: 1–56.

Galambos, S. J., and Hakuta, K. (1988). Subject-specific and task-specific characteristics of metalinguistic awareness in bilingual children. *Applied Psycholinguistics*, 9, 2: 141–162.

García, E. (2008). Bilingual education in the United States. In *An introduction to bilingualism: Principles and processes*, ed. J. Altarriba, and R. R. Heredia. Mahwah, NJ: Lawrence Erlbaum, pp. 321–343.

García, O. (2008). *Bilingual education in the 21st century: A global perspective*. Malden, MA: Wiley-Blackwell.

Gaser C, and Schlaug G. (2003). Brain structures differ between musicians and non-musicians. *Journal of Neuroscience*, 23: 21–24.

Gass, S. (1979). Language transfer and universal grammatical relations. *Language Learning*, 29, 2: 327–344.

Gass, S. and Glew, M. (2008). Second language acquisition and bilingualism. In *An introduction to bilingualism: Principles and processes*, ed. J. Altarriba and R. R. Heredia. Mahwah, NJ: Lawrence Erlbaum, pp. 265–294.

Gass, S. M., and Selinker, L. (eds.). (1992). *Language transfer in language learning*, revised edition. Amsterdam: John Benjamins.

Gawlitzek-Maiwald, I. and Rosemary, T. (1996). Bilingual bootstrapping. *Linguistics* 34, 5: 901–926.

Genesee, F. (1988). Neuropsychology and second language acquisition. In *Issues in Second Language Acquisition*, ed. L. M. Beebe. Boston: Heinle and Heinle, pp. 81–112.

(1989). Early bilingual development: One language or two? *Journal of Child Language*, 13: 537–60.

Genesse, F., Boivin, I., and Nicoladis, E. (1996). Talking with strangers: A study of bilingual children's communicative competence. *Applied Psycholinguistics*, 17: 427–442.

Genesee, F., Nicoladis, E., and Paradis, J. (1995). Language differentiation in early bilingual development. *Journal of Child Language*, 22: 611–631.

Geranmayeh, F., Brownett, S., Leech, R., Beckmann, C., Woodhead, Z. and Wise, R. (2012). The contribution of the inferior parietal cortex to spoken language production. *Brain and Language*, 121, 1: 47–57.

Gerard, L. and Scarborough, D. (1989). Language-specific lexical access of homographs by bilinguals. *Journal of Experimental Psychology: Learning, Memory and Cognition*, 15: 305–313.

Glusker, P. (1987). *Chelsea*. Paper presented at the Orton Dyslexia Society Annual Meeting, San Francisco.

Goldin-Meadow, S. (2003). *The resilience of language: What gesture creation in deaf children can tell us about how all children learn language*. New York: Psychology Press

Goldin-Meadow, S. and Feldman, H. (1977). The development of language-like communication without a language model. *Science*, 197: 401–403.

Goldin-Meadow, S. and Mylander, C. (1984). Gestural communication in deaf children: The effects and noneffects of parental input on early language development. *Monographs of the Society for Research in Child Development*, 49, 3/4: 1–151.

Gollan, T. H. and Acenas, L. A. R. (2004). What is a TOT? Cognate and translation effects on tip-of-the-tongue states in Spanish–English and Tagalog–English bilinguals. *Journal of Experimental Psychology Learning Memory and Cognition*, 30, 1: 246–269.

Gollan, T. H., Fennema-Notestine, C., Montoya, R. I., and Jernigan, T. L. (2007) The bilingual effect on Boston Naming Test performance. *Journal of the International Neuropsychological Society*, 13: 197–208.

Gollan, T. H., Montoya, R. I., Cera, C., and Sandoval, T. C. (2008). More use almost always means a smaller frequency effect: Aging, bilingualism, and the weaker links hypothesis. *Journal of Memory and Language*, 58, 3: 787–814.

Gollan, T. H., Montoya, R. I., Fennema-Notestine, C. and Morris, S. K. (2005). Bilingualism affects picture naming but not picture classification. *Memory and Cognition*, 33: 1220–1234.

Gollan, T. H., and Silverberg, N. B. (2001). Tip-of-the-tongue states in Hebrew–English bilinguals. *Bilingualism: Language and Cognition*, 4: 63–84.

González, J. E. J. and Garcia, C. R. H. (1995). Effects of word linguistic properties on phonological awareness in Spanish children. *Journal of Educational Psychology*, 87, 2: 193–201.

Goodale, M., and Milner, D. (1992). Separate visual pathways for perception and action. *Trends in Neurosciences*, 15, 1: 20–25.

Gottardo, A., and Mueller, J. (2009). Are first-and second-language factors related in predicting second-language reading comprehension? A study of Spanish-speaking children acquiring English as a second language from first to second grade. *Journal of Educational Psychology*, 101, 2: 330–344.

Grabner, R. H., Stern, E., and Neubauer, A. C. (2000). When intelligence loses its impact: Neural efficiency during reasoning in a familiar area. *International Journal of Psychophysiology*, 49, 2: 89–98.

Green, D. (1985). Control, activation and resource: A framework and a model for the control of speech in bilinguals. *Brain and Language*, 27: 210–223.

(1998). Mental control of the bilingual lexico-semantic system. *Bilingualism: Language and Cognition*, 1: 67–81.

Green, D. W., Crinion, J., and Price, C. J. (2007). Exploring cross-linguistic vocabulary effects on brain structures using voxel-based morphometry. *Bilingualism, Language and Cognition*, 10, 2: 189–199.

Griffin, P., Burns, M. S., and Snow, C. E. (eds.). (1998). *Preventing reading difficulties in young children*. Washington, DC: National Academies Press.

Grimshaw, G. M., Adelstein, A., Bryden, M. P., and MacKinnon, G. E. (1998). First language acquisition in adolescence: Evidence for a critical period for verbal language development. *Brain and Language*, 63: 237–255.

Grinstead, J., Cantú-Sánchez, M., and Flores-Ávalos, B. (2008). Canonical and epenthetic plural marking in Spanish-speaking children with specific language impairment. *Language Acquisition*, 15, 4: 329–349.

Grinstead, J., MacSwan, J., Curtiss, S., and Gelman, R. (1998). The autonomy of number and grammar in development. In *Proceedings of the 22nd Boston University Conference on Language Development*, ed. A. Greenhill, M. Hughes, H. Littlefield, and H. Walsh. Somerville: Cascadilla Press, pp. 303–313.

Grosjean, F. (1982). *Life with two languages: An introduction to bilingualism.* Cambridge, MA: Harvard University Press.

(1985). The bilingual as a competent but specific speaker-hearer. *Journal of Multilingual and Multicultural Development*, 6: 467–77.

(1989). Neurolinguists, beware! The bilingual is not two monolinguals in one person. *Brain and Language*, 36, 1: 3–15.

(1998). Studying bilinguals: Methodological and conceptual issues. *Bilingualism: Language and Cognition*, 1: 131–149.

(1999). The bilingual's language modes. In *One mind, two languages: Bilingual language processing*, ed. J. L. Nicol. Oxford: Blackwell, pp. 1–25.

(2006). Studying bilinguals: Methodological and conceptual issues. In *The handbook of bilingualism*, ed. T. K. Bhatia and W. C. Ritchie. Malden, MA: Blackwell, pp. 32–63.

(2008). *Studying bilinguals.* Oxford University Press.

Guiberson, M., Barrett, K., Jancoset, E., and Yoshinaga Itano, C. (2006). Language maintenance and loss in preschool-age children of Mexican immigrants: A longitudinal study. *Communications Disorders Quarterly*, 28, 1: 4–17.

Guion, S. (2003). The vowel systems of Quichua–Spanish bilinguals: Age of acquisition effects on the mutual influence of the first and second languages. *Phonetics*, 60, 2: 98–128.

Gürel, A. (2004). Selectivity in L2-induced L1 attrition: A psycholinguistic account. *Journal of Neurolinguistics*, 17, 1: 53–78.

Haboud, M. (2004). Quichua language vitality: An Ecuadorian perspective. *International Journal of the Sociology of Language*, 167: 69–81.

Haddican, W. (2005). Standardization, functional shift and language change in Basque. *Estudios de Sociolingüística*, 6, 1: 87–112.

Haier, R. J., Siegel Jr., B. V., Nuechterlein, K. H., Hazlett, E., Wu, J. C., Paek, J., and Buchsbaum, M. S. (1988). Cortical glucose metabolic rate correlates of abstract reasoning and attention studied with positron emission tomography. *Intelligence*, 12, 2: 199–217.

Haier, R. J., Siegel, B., Tang, C., Abel, L., and Buchsbaum, M. S. (1992). Intelligence and changes in regional cerebral glucose metabolic rate following learning. *Intelligence*, 16, 3: 415–426.

Hakuta, K. (1986). *Mirror of language: The debate on bilingualism.* New York: Basic Books.

Halliday, M. A. K., McKintosh, A. and Strevens, P. (1970). The users and uses of language. In *Readings in the sociology of language*. ed. J. A. Fishman. The Hague: Mouton, pp. 139–169.

Hamers, J. and Blanc, M. (2000). *Bilinguality and bilingualism.* Cambridge University Press.

Hansen, L. (2001). Language attrition: The fate of the start. *Annual Review of Applied Linguistics*, 21: 60–73.

Hansen, L., and Chen, Y. L. (2001). What counts in the acquisition and attrition of numeral classifiers. *JALT Journal*, 23, 1: 83–100.

Harley, B. (1986). *Age in second language acquisition*. San Diego: College-Hill Press.

Hartsuiker, R. J. and Pickering, M. J. (2008). Language integration in bilingual sentence production. *Acta Psychologica*, 128, 3: 479–489.

Hartsuiker, R. J., Pickering, M. J., and Veltkamp, E. (2004). Is syntax separate or shared between languages? Cross-linguistic syntactic priming in Spanish–English bilinguals. *Psychological Science*, 15, 6: 409–414.

Haugen, E. (1953). *The Norwegian language in America*. Philadelphia: University of Pennsylvania Press.

Hauser-Grüdli, N., Arencibia-Guerra, L., Witzmann, F., Leray, E., and Muller, N. (2010). Cross-linguistic influence in bilingual children: Can input frequency account for it? *Lingua*, 120, 11: 2638–2650.

Hawkins, R. and Chan, C. Y.-H. (1997). The partial availability of Universal Grammar in second language acquisition: The "failed functional features hypothesis." *Second Language Research*, 13, 3: 187–226.

Hayashi, B. (1999). Testing the regression hypothesis: The remains of the Japanese negation system in Micronesia. In *Second language attrition in Japanese contexts*, ed. L. Hansen. Oxford University Press, pp. 154–168.

Heredia, R. (1996). Bilingual memory: A re-revised version of the Hierarchical Model of Bilingual Memory. *Newsletter of the Center for Research in Language*, 10, 3–6.

(1997). Bilingual memory and hierarchical models: A case for language dominance. *Current Directions in Psychological Science*, 6, 2: 34–39.

Hermans, D., Bonagerts, T., De Bot, K., and Schreuder, R. (1998). Producing words in a foreign language: Can speakers prevent interference from their first language? *Bilingualism: Language and Cognition* 1, 3: 213–229.

Hernandez, A. E., Dapretto, M., Mazziotta, J., and Bookheimer, S. (2001). Language switching and language representation in Spanish–English bilinguals: An fMRI study. *NeuroImage*, 14, 2: 510–520.

Hernandez, A. E. and Li, P. (2007). Age of acquisition: Its neural and computational mechanisms. *Psychological Bulletin*, 133, 4: 638–650.

Hernández-Chávez, E., Burt, M., and Dulay, H. (1978). Language dominance and proficiency testing: some general considerations. *NABE Journal*, III, 1: 41–54.

Hernández Pina, F. (1984). *Teorías psicosociolingüísticas y su aplicación a la adquisición del español como lengua materna*. Madrid: Siglo XXI.

Hickok, G. (2009). The functional neuroanatomy of language. *Physics of Life Reviews*, 6: 121–143.

Hickok, G. and Poeppel, D. (2007). The cortical organization of speech processing. *Nature Reviews Neuroscience*, 8: 393–402.

Hidalgo, M. (1996). A profile of language issues in contemporary Mexico. In *Spanish in contact: Issues in bilingualism*, ed. A. Roca and J. B. Jensen. Somerville, MA: Cascadilla Press, pp. 45–72.

Hoekstra, T. and Hyams, N. (1998). Aspects of root infinitives. *Lingua*, 106,1): 81–112.

Hohenstein, J., Eisenberg, A. R., and Naigles, L. (2006). Is he floating across or crossing afloat? Cross-influence of L1 and L2 in Spanish–English bilingual adults. *Bilingualism: Language and Cognition* 9: 249–261.

Hoffmann, Charlotte. (1991). *Introduction to bilingualism*. Harlow: Longman.

Holm, J. (2000). *An introduction to pidgins and creoles*. Cambridge University Press.

Hölzel, B. K., Carmody, J., Vangel, M., Congleton, C., Yerramsetti, S. M., Gard, T., and Lazar, S. W. (2011). Mindfulness practice leads to increases in regional brain gray matter density. *Psychiatry Research: Neuroimaging*, 191, 1: 36–43.

Hopp, H. (2013). Grammatical gender in adult L2 acquisition: Relations between lexical and syntactic variability. *Second Language Research*, 29, 1: 33–56.

Hopp, H. and Schmid, M. (2013). Perceived foreign accent in first language attrition and second language acquisition: The impact of age of acquisition and bilingualism. *Applied Psycholinguistics*, 34, 2: 361–394.

Hualde, J. I., Olarrea, A., Escobar, A. M., and Travis, C. (2010). *Introducción a la lingüística hispánica*. Cambridge University Press.

Huerta-Macías, Ana. (1981). Code-switching: All in the family. In *Latino language and communicative behavior*, ed. R. P. Durán. Norwood. NJ: Ablex, pp. 153–160.

Hulk, A. (1997). The acquisition of French object pronouns by a Dutch/French bilingual child. In *Language acquisition: Knowledge, representation and processing. Proceedings of the GALA 1997 conference on language acquisition*, ed. A. Sorace, C. Heycock, and R. Shillcock. Edinburgh University Press, pp. 521–526

Hulk, A. and Müller, N. (2000). Bilingual first language acquisition at the interface between syntax and pragmatics. *Bilingualism: Language and Cognition* 3, 3: 227–244.

Hymes, D. H. (1967). Models of the interaction of language and social setting. *Journal of Social Issues*, 23, 2: 8–38.

    (1972). On communicative competence. In *Sociolinguistics: Selected readings*, ed. J. B. Pride and J. Holmes. Harmondsworth: Penguin, pp. 269–293.

Indefrey, P. (2006). A Meta-analysis of hemodynamic studies on first and second language processing: Which suggested differences can we trust and what do they mean? *Language Learning*, 56, 1: 279–304.

Instituto Nacional de Estadística de Bolivia. www.ine.gob.bo

Ionin, T. and Montrul, S. (2010). The role of L1 transfer in the interpretation of articles with definite plurals. *Language Learning* 60, 4: 877–925.

Ioup, G. (1995). Evaluating the need for input enhancement in post-critical period language acquisition. In *The age factor in second language acquisition: A research update*, ed. D. Singleton and Z. Lengyel. Clevedon: Multilingual Matters, pp. 95–123.

Isurin, L. (2000). Deserted islands or a child's first language forgetting. *Bilingualism: Language and Cognition*, 3: 151–166.

Isurin, L., Winford, D., and de Bot, K. (eds.). (2009). *Multidisciplinary approaches to code switching* (Studies in Bilingualism, 41). Amsterdam: John Benjamins.

Itard, J. M. G. (1962). *The wild boy of Aveyron (L'enfant sauvage)*, trans. G. and M. Humphrey. New York: Applenton-Century-Crofts.

Jackendoff, R. (2002). *Foundations of language: Brain, meaning, grammar and evolution*. Oxford University Press.

Jacobson, P. F. (2012). The effects of language impairment on the use of direct object pronouns and verb inflections in heritage Spanish speakers: A look at attrition, incomplete acquisition and maintenance. *Bilingualism: Language and Cognition*, 15, 1: 22–38.

Jakobson, R. (1938). Sur la théorie des affinités phonologiques entre les langues. *Actes du Congrès International des Linguistes* 4, 45–58.

(1968). *Child language, aphasia, and phonological universals*. The Hague and Paris: Mouton.

Jiménez González, J. and García, C. (1995). Effects of word linguistic properties on phonological awareness in Spanish children. *Journal of Educational Psychology*, 87, 2: 193–201.

Johnson, J. S. and Newport, E. L. (1989). Critical period effects in second language learning: the influence of maturational state of acquisition of English as a second language. *Cognitive Psychology*, 21: 60–99.

(1991). Critical period effects on universal properties of language: The status of subjacency in the acquisition of a second language. *Cognition*, 39, 3: 215–258.

Jones, P. E. (1995). Contradictions and unanswered questions in the Genie case: A fresh look at the linguistic evidence. *Language and Communication*, 15: 261–280.

Jones, Ō. P., Green, D. W., Grogan, A., Pliatsikas, C., Filippopolitis, K., Ali, N., Lee, H., Ramsden, S., Gazarian, K., Prejawa, S., Seghier, M., and Price, C. J. (2012). Where, when and why brain activation differs for bilinguals and monolinguals during picture naming and reading aloud. *Cerebral Cortex*, 22, 4: 892–902.

Jordaan, H., and Yelland, A. (2003). Intervention with multilingual language impaired children by South African speech-language therapists. *Journal of Multilingual Communication Disorders*, 1,1: 13–33.

Kakazu, Y. and Lakshmanan, U. (2000). The status of IP and CP in child L2 acquisition. In *Social and cognitive factors in second language acquisition: Selected proceedings of the 1999 second language research forum*, ed. B. Swierzbin, F. Morris, M. Anderson, C. Klee, and E. Tarone. Somerville, MA: Cascadilla Press, pp. 201–221.

Kalt, S. (2002). Second language acquisition of Spanish morpho-syntax by Quechua-speaking children. Ph.D. dissertation, University of Southern California.

(2009). Bilingual children's object and case marking in Cusco Quechua. In *University of British Columbia's Working Papers in Linguistics, Proceedings of the Workshop on the Constituent Structure of the 13th and 14th Workshop on the Structure and Constituency of the Languages of the Americas* (vol. 26). Retrieved from: http://kellogg.nd.edu/STLILLA/proceedings/Kalt_Susan.pdf

(2012). Cambios morfosintácticos en castellano impulsados por el quechua hablante. In P. Dankel, V. F. Mallat, J. C. Godenzzi, and S. Pfänder (eds.), El español andino. *Espacios comunicativos y cambios gramaticales*, 41, (pp. 165–192). Neue Romania.

Kaufman, D. and Aronoff, M. (1991). Morphological disintegration and reconstruction in first language attrition. In *First language attrition*, ed. H. Seliger and R. Vago. Cambridge University Press, pp. 175–189.

Keijzer, M. (2010). The regression hypothesis as a framework for first language attrition. *Bilingualism: Language and Cognition*, 13, 1: 9–18.

Kim, K. H., Relkin, N. R., Lee, K. M., and Hirsch, J. (1997). Distinct cortical areas associated with native and second languages. *Nature*, 388, 6638: 171–174.

Kinsbourne, M. (1975). The ontogeny of cerebral dominance. *Annals of the New York Academy of Science*, 263: 244–250.

Kinsbourne, M. and Hiscock, M. (1977). Does cerebral dominance develop? In *Language development and neurological theory*, ed. S. Segalowitz and F. Gruber. New York: Academic Press, pp. 171–191.

Kirsner, K., Smith, M., Lockhart, R., King, R., and Jain, M. (1984). The bilingual lexicon: Language-specific units in an integrated network. *Journal of Verbal Learning and Verbal Behavior*, 23, 4: 519–539.

Klee, C. (1996). The Spanish of the Peruvian Andes: The influence of Quechua on Spanish language structure. In *Spanish in Contact: Issues in Bilingualism*, ed. A. Roca and J. B. Jensen. Somerville, MA: Cascadilla Press, pp. 73–91.

Klee, C. and Lynch, A. (2009). *El español en contacto con otras lenguas*. Washington, DC: Georgetown University Press.

Klein, D., Milner, B., Zatorre, R. J., Meyer, E., and Evans, A. C. (1995). The neural substrates underlying word generation: a bilingual functional-imaging study. *Proceedings of the National Academy of Sciences*, 92, 7: 2899–2903.

Klein, D., Zatorre, R. J., Milner, B., Meyer, E., and Evans, A. C. (1994). Left putaminal activation when speaking a second language: Evidence from PET. *Neuroreport*, 5, 17: 2295–2297.

Klein-Andreu, F. (1981). Distintos sistemas de empleo de *le, la, lo*: Perspectivas sincrónica, diacrónica y sociolingüística. *Thesaurus* 36, 35–46.

    (1999). Grammatical and lexical behavior in the development of the Spanish third person clitics. In *Between grammar and lexicon*, ed. E. Contini-Morava and Y. Tobin. Amsterdam and Philadelphia: John Benjamins, pp. 159–183.

Kohnert, K. (2010). Bilingual children with primary language impairment: Issues, evidence and implications for clinical actions. *Journal of Communication Disorders*, 43, 6: 456–473.

Kolers, P. (1966). Interlingual facilitation of short-term memory. *Journal of Verbal Learning and Verbal Behavior*, 5: 311–319.

Köpke, B. (2004). Neurolinguistic aspects of attrition. *Journal of Neurolinguistics*, 17: 3–30.

Köpke, B., and Schmid, M. S. (2003). Language attrition: the next phase. In *First language attrition: The next phase. Proceedings of the International Conference on First Language Attrition: Interdisciplinary perspectives on methodological issues*, ed. M. S. Schmid, B. Köpke, M. Keijser, and L. Weilemar. Amsterdam: John Benjamins, pp. 1–44.

Kovács, Á. and Mehler, J. (2009). Flexible learning of multiple speech structures in bilingual infants. *Science*, 325 (5940), 611–612.

Kovelman, I., Baker, S., and Pettito, L. (2008). Bilingual and monolingual brains compared: A functional Magnetic Resonance Imaging investigation of syntactic processing and a possible "neural signature" of bilingualism. *Journal of Cognitive Neuroscience*, 20, 1: 153–169.

Krashen, S. D. (1973) Latralization, language learning, and the critical period. Some new evidence. *Language Learning*, 23, 63–74.

(1996a). The case against bilingual education. In *Georgetown University Round Table on Languages and Linguistics (GURT) 1996: Linguistics, Language Acquisition, and Language Variation Current Trends and Future Prospects*, ed. J. E. Alatis. Washington, DC: Georgetown University Press, pp. 55–69.

(1996b). *Under Attack: The Case Against Bilingual Education*. Culver City: Language Education Associates.

Krashen, S. D., Long, M. A., and Scarcella, R. C. (1979). Age, rate and eventual attainment in second language acquisition. *Tesol Quarterly*, 13: 573–582.

Kratzer, A. (1995). Stage level and individual level predicates. In *The generic book*, ed. G. Carlson and J. Pelletier. Chicago University Press, pp. 125–175.

Krizman, J., Marian, V., Shook, A., Skoe, E., and Kraus, N. (2012). Subcortical encoding of sound is enhanced in bilinguals and relates to executive function advantages. *Proceedings of the National Academy of Sciences*, 109, 20: 7877–7881.

Kroll, J., Bobb, S., Misra, M., and Guo, T. (2008). Language selection in bilingual speech: Evidence for inhibitory processes. *Acta Psychologica*, 128: 416–430.

Kroll, J. F., Bobb, S. C., and Wodniecka, Z. (2006). Language selectivity is the exception not the rule: Arguments against a fixed locus of language selection in bilingual speech. *Bilingualism: Language and Cognition*, 9: 119–135.

Kroll, J. F. and Stewart, E. (1994). Category interference in translation and picture naming: Evidence for asymmetric connections between bilingual memory representations. *Journal of Memory and Language*, 33: 149–174.

Kroll, J. F. and Tokowicz, N. (2005). Models of bilingual representation and processing: Looking back and to the future. In *Handbook of bilingualism: Psycholinguistic approaches*, ed. J. F. Kroll and A. M. B. De Groot. New York: Oxford University Press, pp. 531–553.

Kuhberg, H. (1992). Longitudinal L2-attrition versus L2-acquisition, in three Turkish children-empirical findings. *Second Language Research*, 8, 2: 138–154.

Kuhl, P. K., Williams, K. A., Lacerda, F., Stevens, K. N., and Lindblom, B. (1992). Linguistic experience alters phonetic perception in infants by 6 months of age. *Science*, 255, 5044: 606–608.

Kulick, D. (1992). *Language shift and cultural reproduction: Socialization, self, and syncretism in a Papua New Guinean village*. Cambridge University Press.

Kuo, L. J., and Anderson, R. C. (2010). Beyond cross-language transfer: Reconceptualizing the impact of early bilingualism on phonological awareness. *Scientific Studies of Reading*, 14, 4: 365–385.

Kuperberg, G. (2007). Neural mechanisms of language comprehension: Challenges to syntax. *Brain Research*, 1146: 23–49.

Kupisch, T. (2003). Cross-linguistic influence in the acquisition of determiners in German–Italian Bilinguals. In *Proceedings of the Annual Boston University Conference on Language Development 27 (2)*, ed. B. Beachley, A. Brown, and F. Conlin. Somerville, MA: Cascadilla Press, 461–472.

(2007). Determiners in bilingual German–Italian children: What they tell us about the relation between language influence and language dominance. *Bilingualism: Language and Cognition* 10, 1: 57–78.

Kutas, M. and Hillyard, S. A. (1980). Reading senseless sentences: Brain potentials reflect semantic incongruity. *Science*, 207, 4427: 203–205.

Lado, R. (1957). *Linguistics across cultures*. Ann Arbor: University of Michigan Press.

Lagrou, E., Hartsuiker, R. J., and Duyck, W. (2011). Knowledge of a second language influences auditory word recognition in the native language. *Journal of Experimental Psychology: Learning, Memory, and Cognition*, 37, 4: 952–965.

Lakshmanan, U. (1994). *Universal grammar in child second language acquisition*. Amsterdam: John Benjamins.

(2009). Child second language acquisition. In *The New handbook of second language acquisition*, ed. W. Ritchie and T. Bhatia. Sheffield: Emerald Publishers, pp. 377–399.

Landa, A. (1995). Conditions on null objects in Basque Spanish and their relation to leísmo and clitic doubling. Ph.D. dissertation, University of Southern California.

Landa, A. and Franco, J. (1996). Two issues in null objects in Basque Spanish: Morphological decoding and grammatical permeability. In *Grammatical Theory and Romance Languages*, ed. K. Zagona. Amsterdam: John Benjamins, pp. 159–168.

(1999). Converging and diverging grammars. *Anuario del Seminario de Filología Vasca "Julio de Urquijo"*, 33, 2: 569–581.

Lanza, E. (1992). Can bilingual two-year-olds code-switch? *Journal of Child Language*, 19: 633–658.

(2004). *Language mixing in infant bilingualism: A sociolinguistic perspective*. Oxford University Press.

Lardiere, D. (1998). Dissociating syntax from morphology in a divergent L2 end-state grammar. *Second Language Research*, 14, 4: 359–375.

(2003). Second language knowledge of [±past] vs. [±finite]. In *Proceedings of the 6th Generative Approaches to Second Language Acquisition Conference (GASLA 2002)*, ed. J. M. Liceras, H. Zobl, and H. Goodluck. Somerville, MA: Cascadilla Press, pp. 176–189.

(2005). On morphological competence. In *Proceedings of the 7th Generative Approaches to Second Language Acquisition Conference* (GASLA 2004), ed. L. Dekydtspotter, R. Sprouse, and A. Liljestrand. Somerville, MA: Cascadilla Press, pp. 178–192.

Lee. H. L., Devlin, J. T., Shakeshaft, C., Stewart, L. H., Brennan, A., Glensman, J., Pitcher, K., Crinion, J., Mechelli, A., Frackowiak, R. S. J., Green, D. W., and Price, C. J. (2007). Anatomical traces of vocabulary acquisition in the adolescent brain. *Journal of Neuroscience*, 27: 1184–1189.

Lefebvre, C. (1988). *Creole genesis and the acquisition of grammar: The case of Haitian Creole*. Cambridge University Press.

Legate, J. A., and Yang, C. (2007). Morphosyntactic learning and the development of tense. *Language Acquisition*, 14, 3: 315–344.

Lehtonen, M., Hultén, A., Rodríguez-Fornells, A., Cunillera, T., Tuomainen, J., and Laine, M. (2012). Differences in word recognition between early bilinguals and monolinguals: Behavioral and ERP evidence. *Neuropsychologia*, 50, 7: 1362–1371.

Lenneberg, E. H. (1967). *Biological foundations of language*. New York: Riley.

Leonard, M., Torres, C., Travis, K., Brown, T, Hagler Jr., D, Dale, A., Elman, J., and Halgren, E. (2011). Language proficiency modulates the recruitment of non-classical language areas in bilinguals. *PloS One*, 6, 3. Retrieved from: www.plosone.org/article/info%3Adoi%2F10.1371%2Fjournal.pone .0018240.

Leopold, W. F. (1949/1970). *Speech development of a bilingual child: A linguist's record*. New York: Ams Press.

Levelt, W. J. (1989). *Speaking: From intention to articulation*. Cambridge, MA: MIT Press.

(1992). Accessing words in speech production: Stages, processes and representations. *Cognition*, 42, 1–3: 1–22.

Lewis, M. P., Simons, G. F., and Fenning, C. D. (eds.) (2013). *Ethnologue: Languages of the world*, 17th edition. Dallas, Texas: SIL International. Online version: www.ethnologue.com.

Liceras, J. (2011). Beyond (or besides) interfaces? On narrow syntax, directionality and input. *Linguistic Approaches to Bilingualism*, 1, 1: 54–57.

Liceras, J., Fernández Fuertes, R., Perales, S., Pérez-Tattam, R. and Spradlin, K. T. (2008). Gender and gender agreement in bilingual native and non-native grammars: A view from child and adult functional-lexical mixing. *Lingua* 118: 827–851.

Liceras, J. M., Fernández Fuertes, R., and de la Fuente, A. A. (2012). Overt subjects and copula omission in the Spanish and the English grammar of English–Spanish bilinguals: On the locus and directionality of interlinguistic influence. *First Language*, 32, 1–2: 88–115.

Liceras, J. M., Spradlin, K. T., and Fernández Fuertes, R. (2005). Bilingual early functional-lexical mixing and the activation of formal features. *International Journal of Bilingualism*, 9, 2: 227–252.

Liceras, J. M., Spradlin, K.T., Senn, C., Sikorska, M., Fernández Fuertes, R., de la Fuente, E. A. (2003). Second language acquisition and bilingual competence: The Grammatical Features Spell-out Hypothesis. Paper presented at the European Association of Second Language Acquisition (EuroSLA-13), Edinburgh, September 19–21, 2003.

Lindholm, K. and Padilla, A. (1978). Language mixing in bilingual children. *Journal of Child Language* 5: 327–335.

Lindsey, K. A., Manis, F. R., and Bailey, C. E. (2003). Prediction of first-grade reading in Spanish-speaking English-language learners. *Journal of Educational Psychology*, 95, 3: 482–494.

Lipski, J. M. (2008). *Varieties of Spanish in the United States*. Washington, DC: Georgetown University Press.

Liu, H., Bates, E., and Li, P. (1992). Sentence interpretation in bilingual speakers of English and Chinese. *Applied Psycholinguistics*, 13: 451–484.

Liu, H., Hu, Z., Guo, T., and Peng, D. (2010). Speaking words in two languages with one brain: Neural overlap and dissociation. *Brain Research*, 1316: 75–82.

Loebell, H. and Bock, K. (2003). Structural priming across languages. *Linguistics*, 41, 5: 791–824.

Long, M. H. (1990). Maturational constraints on language development. *Studies in Second Language Acquisition* 12, 3: 251–285.

López, L. E. (1997). La eficacia y validez de lo obvio: Lecciones aprendidas desde la evaluación de procesos educativos bilingües. In *Multilingüismo y educación bilingüe en América y España*, ed. J. Calvo Pérez and J. C. Godenzzi. Cuzco: Centro de Estudios Regionales Andinos "Bartolomé de las Casas," pp. 53–97.

López Ornat, S. L., Mariscal, S., Fernández, A., and Gallo, P. (1994). *La adquisición de la lengua española*. Madrid: Siglo XXI.

Luján, M. (1981). The Spanish copulas as aspectual indicators. *Lingua* 54: 165–210.

Luk, G., Green, D. W., Abutalebi, J., and Grady, C. (2012). Cognitive control for language switching in bilinguals: A quantitative meta-analysis of functional neuroimaging studies. *Language and Cognitive Processes*, 27, 10: 1479–1488.

Lust, B. (ed.). (1987). *Studies in the acquisition of anaphora,* vol. 2: *Applying the constraints*. Dordrecht: Reidel.

Lust, B., Flynn, S., Blume, M., Park, S., Cang, C., and Yang, S. (2014). Assessing child bilingualism: Direct assessment of bilingual syntax amends caretaker report. *International Journal of Bilingualism*. doi: 10.1177/1367006914547661.

MacKay, I., Flege, J. and Imai, S. (2006). Evaluating the effects of chronological age and sentence duration on degree of perceived foreign accent. *Applied Psycholinguistics*, 27: 157–183.

Mackey, W. (1968). The description of bilingualism. In *Readings in the sociology of language*, ed. J. Fishman. The Hague: Mouton, pp. 554–584.

    (1970). A typology of bilingual education. *Foreign Language Annals* 3, 4: 596–608.

    (2006) Bilingualism in North America. In *The handbook of bilingualism*, ed. T. K. Bhatia, and W. C. Ritchie. Malden, MA: Blackwell, pp. 607–641.

Macnamara, J. (1967). The bilingual's linguistic performance: A psychological overview. *Journal of Social Issues*, 23: 59–77.

MacSwan, J. (2000). The architecture of the bilingual language faculty: Evidence from intrasentential code switching. *Bilingualism: Language and Cognition*, 3: 37–54.

    (2012). Code-switching and grammatical Theory. In *The handbook of bilingualism and multilingualism*, ed. T. K. Bhatia and W. Ritchie. Oxford: Blackwell, pp. 323–350.

MacSwan, J., and Rolstad, K. (2005). Modularity and the facilitation effect: Psychological mechanisms of transfer in bilingual students. *Hispanic Journal of Behavioral Sciences*, 27, 2: 224–243.

Maguire E. A., Gadian, D. G., Johnrude, I. S., Good, C. S., Ashburner, J., Frackowiak, R. S. J., Frith, C. D. (2000). Navigation-related structural changes in the hippocampi of taxi drivers. *Proceedings of the National Academy of Sciences, USA*, 97: 4398–4403.

Marantz, A. (2000). Case licensing. In *Arguments and case: Explaining Burzio's Generalization*, ed. E. Reuland. Amsterdam: John Benjamins, pp. 11–30.

Marian, V. and Kaushanskaya, M. (2007). Cross-linguistic transfer and borrowing in bilinguals. *Applied Psycholinguistics*, 28: 369–390.

Martohardjono, G. (1993): Wh-movement in the acquisition of a second language: A cross-linguistic study of three languages with and without movement. Unpublished Ph.D. dissertation, Cornell University.

Martohardjono, G, and Flynn, S. (1995). Language transfer: What do we really mean? In *The Current State of Interlanguage*, ed. L. Eubank, L. Selinker, and M. Sharwood Smith. Philadelphia: John Benjamins, pp. 205–217.

Masullo, P. (1992). Incorporation and case theory in Spanish: A crosslinguistic perspective. Ph.D. dissertation, University of Washington.

Mayberry, R. I. and Eichen, E. B. (1991). The long-lasting advantage of learning sign language in childhood: Another look at the critical period for language acquisition. *Journal of Memory and Language*, 30: 486–512.

McClelland, J. L. and Rumelhart, D. E. (1981). An interactive activation model of context effects in letter perception, Part I: An account of basic findings. *Psychological Review*, 88, 5: 375–407.

McCormack, P. D. (1977). Bilingual linguistic memory: The independence-interdependence issue revisited. In *Bilingualism*, ed. P. A. Horney. New York: Academic Press, pp. 57–66.

McLaughlin, B. (1978). *Second-language acquisition in childhood*. Hillside, NJ.: Lawrence Erlbaum.

McWhorter, J. (2001). *The power of Babel: The natural history of language*. New York: Times Books.

Mechelli A., Crinion, J. T., Noppeney, U., O'Doherty, J., Ashburner, J., Frackowiak, R. S., and Price, C. J. (2004). Neurolinguistics: structural plasticity in the bilingual brain. *Nature*, 431: 757.

Mechelli, A., Price, C. J., Friston, K. J., and Ashburner, J. (2005). Voxel-based morphometry of the human brain: Methods and applications. *Current Medical Imaging Reviews*, 1, 2: 105–113.

Mehotcheva, T. H. (2010). After the fiesta is over: Foreign language attrition of Spanish in Dutch and German Erasmus students. Ph.D. dissertation, GRODIL series (86), University of Groningen / RECERCAT, Pompeu Fabra University. Retrieved from http://vinson2.upf.edu/handle/10230/12648

Meijer, P. J., and Fox Tree, J. E. (2003). Building syntactic structures in speaking: A bilingual exploration. *Experimental Psychology*, 50, 3: 184–195.

Meisel, J. M. (1986). Word order and case marking in early child language. Evidence from simultaneous acquisition of two first languages: French and German. *Linguistics*, 24, 1: 123–183.

  (1989). Early differentiation of languages in bilingual children. In *Bilingualism across the life span. Aspects of acquisition, maturity, and loss*, ed. K. Hyltenstam and L. Obler. Cambridge University Press, pp. 13–40.

  (1992). Functional categories and verb placement. In *Functional categories and V2 phenomena in language acquisition* (Studies in Theoretical Psycholinguistics, 16), ed. J. M. Meisel. Dordrecht: Kluwer Academic Publishers, pp. 1–21.

  (2001). The simultaneous acquisition of two first languages: Early differentiation and subsequent development of grammars. In *Trends in bilingual acquisition*, ed. J. Cenoz and F. Genesse. Amsterdam: John Benjamins, pp. 11–41.

  (2004). The bilingual child. In *The handbook of bilingualism*, ed. T. K. Bhatia and W. C. Ritchie. Malden, MA: Blackwell, pp. 91–113.

Merino, B. J. (1983). Language loss in bilingual Chicano children. *Journal of Applied Developmental Psychology*, 4, 277–294.

Montrul, S. (2002). Incomplete acquisition and attrition of Spanish tense/aspect distinctions in adult bilinguals. *Bilingualism: Language and Cognition*, 5, 1: 39–68.

(2004a). Subject and object expression in Spanish heritage speakers: A case of morpho-syntactic convergence. *Bilingualism, Language and Cognition*, 7: 125–142.

(2004b). *The acquisition of Spanish: Morphosyntactic development in monolingual and bilingual L1 acquisition and adult L2 acquisition.* Amsterdam and Philadelphia: John Benjamins.

(2006). On the bilingual competence of Spanish Heritage Speakers: Syntax, lexical-semantics and processing. *International Journal of Bilingualism*, 10, 1: 37–69.

(2008). *Incomplete acquisition in bilingualism: Re-examining the age factor.* Amsterdam and Philadelphia: John Benjamins.

(2009). Knowledge of tense-aspect and mood in Spanish heritage speakers. *International Journal of Bilingualism*, 13, 2: 239–269.

(2011). Multiple interfaces and incomplete acquisition. *Lingua*, 121, 4: 591–604.

Montrul, S., Bhatt, R., and Bhatia, A. (2012). Erosion of case and agreement in Hindi heritage speakers. *Linguistic Approaches to Bilingualism*, 2, 2: 141–176.

Montrul, S. and Bowles, M. (2009). Back to basics: Incomplete knowledge of Differential Object Marking in Spanish heritage speakers. *Bilingualism: Language and Cognition* 12: 363–383.

Montrul, S. and Foote, R. (2013). Age of acquisition interactions in bilingual lexical access: A study of the weaker language of L2 learners and heritage speakers. *International Journal of Bilingualism*. Published online before print May 8, 2012, doi: 10.1177/1367006912443431.

Montrul, S. and Ionin, T. (2010). Transfer effects in the interpretation of definite articles by Spanish heritage speakers. *Bilingualism: Language and Cognition*. 13, 4: 449–473.

Montrul, S. and Perpiñán, S. (2011). Assessing differences and similarities between instructed heritage language learners and L2 learners in their knowledge of Spanish tense-aspect and mood (TAM) morphology. *Heritage Language Journal*, 8, 1: 90–133.

Montrul, S. and Potowski, K. (2007). Command of gender agreement in school-age Spanish–English bilingual children. *International Journal of Bilingualism*, 11, 3: 301–328.

Montrul, S. and Slabakova, R. (2003). Competence similarities between native and near-native speakers. *Studies in Second Language Acquisition*, 25, 3: 351–398.

Moorcroft, R. and Gardner, R. C. (1987). Linguistic factors in second language loss. *Language Learning*, 37, 3: 327–340.

Morais, J., Cary, L., Alegria, J., and Bertelson, P. (1979). Does awareness of speech as a sequence of phonemes arise spontaneously? *Cognition*, 7: 323–331.

Morales, J., Calvo, A., and Bialystok, E. (2012). Working memory development in monolingual and bilingual children. *Journal of Experimental Child Psychology*, 114: 187–202.

Morford, J. P., Wilkinson, E., Villwock, A., Piñar, P., and Kroll, J. F. (2011). When deaf signers read English: Do written words activate their sign translations? *Cognition*, 118, 2: 286–292.

Müller, N. (1998). Transfer in bilingual first language acquisition. *Bilingualism: Language and Cognition*, 1, 3: 151–171.

Müller, N. and Hulk, A. (2001). Crosslinguistic influence in bilingual language acquisition: Italian and French as recipient languages. *Bilingualism: Language and Cognition*, 4, 1: 1–53.

Muysken, P. (1981). Halfway between Spanish and Quechua: The case for relexification. In *Historicity and Variation in Creole Studies*, ed. A. Highfield and A. Valdman, Ann Arbor: Karoma Press, pp. 52–78.

(2001). *Bilingual speech*. Cambridge University Press.

(2004). Quechua and Spanish, evidentiality and aspect: Commentary on Liliana Sánchez. *Bilingualism: Language and Cognition*, 7, 2: 163–164.

(2008). *Functional categories*. Cambridge University Press.

Myers-Scotton, C. M. (2002). *Contact linguistics: Bilingual encounters and grammatical outcomes*. Oxford University Press.

(2006). *Multiple voices: An introduction to bilingualism*. Malden, MA: Blackwell.

Näätänen, R. (2001). The perception of speech sounds by the human brain as reflected by the mismatch negativity (MMN) and its magnetic equivalent (MMNm). *Psychophysiology*, 38, 1: 1–21.

Nagasawa, S. (1999). Learning and losing Japanese as a second language: A multiple case study of American university students. In *Second language attrition in Japanese contexts*, ed. L. Hansen. Oxford University Press, pp. 169–200.

Nair, R. B. (1984). Monosyllabic English or disyllabic Hindi? Language acquisition in a bilingual child. *Indian Linguistics*, 54: 51–90.

Neufeld, G. G. (1977). Toward a theory of language learning ability. *Language Learning* 29: 227–240.

Newport, E. (1990). Maturational constraints in language learning. *Cognitive Science*, 14: 11–28.

Newport, E. L. and Supalla, T. (1999). Sign languages. In *The MIT encyclopedia of the cognitive sciences*, ed. R. Wilson and F. Keil. Cambridge, MA: MIT Press, pp. 758–760.

(2000). Sign language research at the millennium. In *The signs of language revisited: An anthology in honor of Ursula Bellugi and Edward Klima*, ed. K. Emmorey and H. Lane. Mahwah, NJ: Lawrence Erlbaum Associates, pp. 94–103.

Nicoladis, E., and Grabois, H. (2002). Learning English and losing Chinese: A case study of a child adopted from China. *International Journal of Bilingualism*, 6, 4: 441–454.

Nicolay, A., and Poncelet, M. (2012). Cognitive advantage in children enrolled in a second-language immersion elementary school program for three years. *Bilingualism: Language and Cognition*, 1, 1: 1–11.

Niemiec, E. (2010). Between us bilinguals: A fairly unbiased dissertation on monolingual and bilingual views of code-switching. Unpublished Ph.D. dissertation, Warsaw University.

Odlin, T. (1989). *Language transfer: Cross-linguistic influence in language learning*. Cambridge University Press.

Oh, J. S., Au, T. K. F., and Jun, S. (2010). Early childhood language memory in the speech perception of international adoptees. *Journal of Child Language*, 37, 5: 1123–1132.

Oh, J. S., Jun, S. A., Knightly, L. M., and Au, T. K. F. (2003). Holding on to childhood language memory. *Cognition*, 86, 3: 53–64.

Olshtain, E. (1989). Is second language attrition the reversal of second language acquisition? *Studies in Second Language Acquisition*, 11, 2: 151–165.

Ormazabal, J. and Romero, J. (2013). Object clitics, agreement and dialectal variation, *Probus*. doi: 10.1515/probus-2013–0012.

Oroz Bretón, N. and Sotés Ruiz, P. (2006) Bilingual education in Navarre: Achievements and challenges. *Language, Culture, and Curriculum*, 21, 1: 21–38.

Ortiz, A. A., Robertson, P. M., Wilkinson, C. Y., Liu, Y. J., McGhee, B. D., and Kushner, M. I. (2011). The role of bilingual education teachers in preventing inappropriate referrals of ELLs to special education: Implications for response to intervention. *Bilingual Research Journal*, 34, 3: 316–333.

Osterhout, L. and Holcomb, P. (1992). Event-related brain potentials elicited by syntactic anomaly. *Journal of Memory and Language*, 31: 785–806.

Otheguy, R., and Zentella, A. C. (2012). *Spanish in New York: Language contact, dialectal leveling, and structural continuity*. Oxford University Press.

Otheguy, R., Zentella, A. C., and Livert, D. (2007). Language and dialect contact in Spanish in New York: Toward the formation of a speech community. *Language*, 8, 4: 770–802.

Ouhalla, J. (1991). *Functional categories and parametric variation*. London: Routledge.

Pallier, C., Dehaene, S., Poline, J. B., LeBihan, D., Argenti, A. M., Dupoux, E., and Mehler, J. (2003). Brain imaging of language plasticity in adopted adults: Can a second language replace the first? *Cerebral Cortex*, 13, 2: 155–161.

Paradis, J., Crago, M., and Genesee, F. (2005/2006). Domain-general versus domain-specific accounts of Specific Language Impairment: Evidence from bilingual children's acquisition of object pronouns. *Language Acquisition* 13, 1: 33–62.

Paradis, J. and Genesee, F. (1996). Syntactic acquisition in bilingual children: Autonomous or interdependent? *Studies in Second Language Acquisition*, 18, 1: 1–25.

(1997). On continuity and the emergence of functional categories in bilingual first-language acquisition. *Language Acquisition* 6, 2: 91–124.

Paradis, J. and Navarro, S. (2003). Subject realization and crosslinguistic interference in the bilingual acquisition of Spanish and English: What is the role of the input? *Journal of Child Language* 30: 371–393.

Paradis, M. (1985). On the representation of two languages in one brain. *Language Sciences*, 7, 1: 1–39.

(1990). Language lateralization in bilinguals: Enough already! *Brain and Language*, 39, 4: 576–586.

(1993). Linguistic, psycholinguistic, and neurolinguistic aspects of "interference" in bilingual speakers: The activation threshold hypothesis. *International Journal of Psycholinguistics*, 9, 2: 133–145.

(1995). Introduction: The need for distinctions. In *Aspects of bilingual aphasia*, ed. M. Paradis. Oxford: Pergamon Press, pp. 1–9.

(2004). *A neurolinguistic theory of bilingualism*. Amsterdam: John Benjamins.

(2007). L1 attrition features predicted by a neurolinguistic theory of bilingualism. In *Language attrition: Theoretical perspectives*, ed. B. Köpke. Amsterdam: John Benjamins, pp. 121–133.

(2009). *Declarative and procedural determinants of second languages*. Amsterdam: John Benjamins.

Patkowski, M. S. (1980). The sensitive period for the acquisition for the acquisition of syntax in a second language. *Language Learning*, 30, 2: 449–472.

Pavlenko, A. (2000). L2 influence on L1 in late bilingualism. *Issues in Applied Linguistics*, 11, 2: 175–205.

Pearson, B. Z., Fernández, S., and Oller, D. K. (1995). Cross-language synonyms in the lexicons of bilingual infants: One language or two? *Journal of Child Language* 22: 345–368.

Pease-Álvarez, L., Hakuta, K., and Bayley, R. (1996). Spanish proficiency and language use in a California Mexicano community. *Southwest Journal of Linguistics* 15, 1–2: 137–151.

Penfield, W. (1963). *The second career*. Boston: Little Brown and Company.

Penfield, W. and Roberts, L. (1959). *Speech and brain mechanisms*. Princeton University Press.

Perani, D., and Abutalebi, J. (2005). The neural basis of first and second language processing. *Current Opinion in Neurobiology*, 15, 2: 202–206.

Perani, D., Abutalebi, J., Paulesu, E., Brambati, S., Scifo, P., Cappa, S. F., and Fazio, F. (2003). The role of age of acquisition and language usage in early, high-proficient bilinguals: An fMRI study during verbal fluency. *Human Brain Mapping*, 19, 3: 170–182.

Perani, D., Paulesu, E., Sebastián Galles, N., Dupoux, E., Dehaene, S., Bettinardi, V, and Mehler, J. (1998). The bilingual brain. Proficiency and age of acquisition of the second language. *Brain*, 121, 10: 1841–1852.

Pérez-Leroux, A. T. (1998). The acquisition of mood selection in Spanish relative clauses. *Journal of Child Language* 25: 585–604.

Petersson, K. M., Reis, A., Askelöf, S., Castro-Caldas, A., and Ingvar, M. (2000). Language processing modulated by literacy: A network analysis of verbal repetition in literate and illiterate subjects. *Journal of Cognitive Neuroscience*, 12, 3: 364–382.

Pfaff, C. W. (1979). Constraints on language mixing: Intrasentential code-switching and borrowing in Spanish/English. *Language*, 55, 2, 291–318.

Pinker, S. (1994). *The language instinct*. New York: William Morris and Company.

Pladevall Ballester, E. (2010). Child L2 development of syntactic and discourse properties of Spanish subjects. *Bilingualism: Language and Cognition*, 13, 2: 185–216.

Platzack, C. (2001). The vulnerable C-domain. *Brain and Language*, 77, 3: 364–377.

Polinsky, M. (2006). Incomplete acquisition: American Russian. *Journal of Slavic Linguistics*, 14: 191–262.

(2007). Reaching the end point and stopping midway: Different scenarios in the acquisition of Russian. *Russian Linguistics* 31: 157–199.

(2011a). Reanalysis in adult heritage language. *Studies in Second Language Acquisition*, 33, 2: 305–328.

(2011b). Annotated bibliography of research in heritage languages. *Oxford Bibliographies, Linguistics*. Oxford University Press. doi: 10.1093/OBO/9780199772810–0067

Poplack, S. (1980). Sometimes I'll start a sentence in Spanish y termino en español: Toward a typology of code-switching. *Linguistics*, 18, 7–8: 581–618.

Potowski, K. (2013). Language maintenance and shift. In *The Oxford handbook of sociolinguistics*, ed. R. Bayley, R. Cameron, and C. Lucas. Oxford University Press, pp. 321–339.

Pozzi-Escot, I. (1988). La educación bilingüe en el Perú: Una mirada retrospectiva y prospectiva. In *Pesquisas en lingüística andina*, ed. L. E. López. Lima: Consejo Nacional de Ciencia y Tecnología, pp. 37–77.

Prat, C. S., and Just, M. A. (2011). Exploring the neural dynamics underpinning individual differences in sentence comprehension. *Cerebral Cortex*, 21, 8: 1747–1760.

Prat, C. S., Keller, T. A., and Just, M. A. (2007). Individual differences in sentence comprehension: A functional magnetic resonance imaging investigation of syntactic and lexical processing demands. *Journal of Cognitive Neuroscience*, 19, 12: 1950–1963.

Putnam, M. and Sánchez, L. (2013). What's so incomplete about incomplete acquisition? A prolegomenon to modeling heritage language grammars. *Linguistic Approaches to Bilingualism* 3, 4: 378–504.

Quay, S. (2008). Dinner conversations with a trilingual two-year-old: Language socialization in a multilingual context. *First Language* 28, 1: 5–33.

Quiroga, T., Lemos-Britton, Z., Mostafapour, E., Abbott, R. D., and Berninger, V. W. (2002). Phonological awareness and beginning reading in Spanish-speaking ESL first graders: Research into practice. *Journal of School Psychology*, 40, 1: 85–111.

Radford, A. (2004). *English syntax: An introduction*. Cambridge University Press.

Ramírez, M., Pérez, M. Valdez, G., and Hall, B. (2009). Assessing the long-term effects of an experimental bilingual-multicultural programme: implications for dropout prevention, multicultural development and immigration policy. *International Journal of Bilingual Education and Bilingualism* 12, 1: 47–59.

Ramus, F., Nespor, M., and Mehler, J. (1999). Correlates of linguistic rhythm in the speech signal. *Cognition*, 73: 265–292.

Rastle, K., Davis, M., and New, B. (2004). The broth in my brother's brothel: Morpho-orthographic segmentation in visual word recognition. *Psychonomic Bulletin and Review*, 11, 6: 1090–1098.

Restrepo, M. (1998). Identifiers of predominantly Spanish-speaking children with language impairment. *Journal of Speech, Language, and Hearing Research*, 41, 6: 1398–1411.

Restrepo, M. and Kruth, K. (2000). Grammatical characteristics of a Spanish–English bilingual child with specific language impairment. *Communication Disorders Quarterly*, 21, 2: 66–76.

Rivarola, J. A. (1989). Bilingüismo histórico y español andino. In *Actas del IX Congreso de la Asociación Internacional de Historia. AIH, Berlín, 1986*, ed. S. Neumeister. Frankfurt: Vervuert, pp. 153–164.

Rivera-Gaxiola, M., Klarman, L., Garcia-Sierra, A., and Kuhl, P. K. (2005). Neural patterns to speech and vocabulary growth in American infants. *NeuroReport*, 16, 5: 495–498.

Rivera-Gaxiola, M., Silva-Pereyra, J., and Kuhl, P. K. (2005). Brain potentials to native and non-native speech contrasts in 7- and 11-month-old American infants. *Developmental Science*, 8, 2: 162–172.

Roca, A. and Lipski, J. M. (eds.). (1999). *Spanish in the United States: Linguistic contact and diversity*. Berlin: Walter de Gruyter.

Rodríguez-Mondoñedo, M. (2008). The acquisition of differential object marking in Spanish. *Probus*, 20(1), 111–145.

Roeper, T. (1999). Universal bilingualism. *Bilingualism: Language and Cognition*, 2, 3: 169–186.

Roeper, T. and Green, L. (2007). Node labels and features: Stable and unstable dialects and variation in acquisition. *Linguistic Variation Yearbook* 7, 1: 1–27.

Romaine, S. (1992). The evolution of linguistic complexity in pidgin and creole languages. In *The evolution of human languages*, eds. J. Hawkins and M. Gell-Mann. Reading, MA: Addison Wesley, pp. 213–238.

    (1995). *Bilingualism*. Oxford and Cambridge, MA: Blackwell.

Rossell, C. H. and Baker, K. (1996). The educational effectiveness of bilingual education. *Research in the Teaching of English*, 30, 1: 7–68.

Rothman, J. (2009). Understanding the nature and outcomes of early bilingualism: Romance languages as heritage languages. *International Journal of Bilingualism*, 13, 2: 155–163.

Rozencvejg, V. J. (1976). *Linguistic interference and convergent change*. The Hague: Mouton.

Ruiz, R. (1984). Orientations in language planning. *NABE Journal*, 8: 15–34.

Rymer, R. (1993). *Genie: Escape from a Silent Childhood*. London: Michael Joseph.

Salaberry, R. (2000). *The development of past tense morphology in L2 Spanish*. Amsterdam: John Benjamins.

Salamoura, A., and Williams, J. N. (2006). Lexical activation of cross-language syntactic priming. *Bilingualism: Language and Cognition*, 9: 299–307.

    (2007). Processing verb argument structure across languages: Evidence for shared representations in the bilingual lexicon. *Applied Psycholinguistics*, 28: 627–660.

Sánchez, L. (1996). Syntactic structures in nominals: A comparative study of Spanish and Southern Quechua. Ph.D. dissertation, University of Southern California.

    (2003). *Quechua–Spanish bilingualism: Interference and convergence in functional categories*. Amsterdam: John Benjamins.

    (2004). Functional convergence in the tense, evidentiality and aspectual systems of Quechua–Spanish bilinguals. *Bilingualism: Language and Cognition*, 7, 2: 147–162.

    (2006). Kechwa and Spanish bilingual grammars: Testing hypotheses on functional interference and convergence. *International Journal of Bilingual Education and Bilingualism*, 9, 5: 535–556.

    (2012). Convergence in syntax/morphology mapping strategies: Evidence from Quechua–Spanish code mixing. *Lingua*. 122, 5: 511–528.

(2015). Crosslinguistic influences, functional interference, feature reassembly and functional convergence in Quechua–Spanish bilingualism. In *The acquisition of Spanish as a second language: Data from understudied language pairings*, ed. S. Perpiñan and T. Judy. Amsterdam: John Benjamins, pp. 19–48.

Sanchez-Casas, R., Davis, C. and García-Albea, J. (1992). Bilingual lexical processing: Exploring the cognate/-non-cognate distinction. *The European Journal of Cognitive Psychology* 4, 4: 293–310.

Saville-Troike, M. (1987). Dilingual discourse: The negotiation of meaning without a common code. *Linguistics* 25: 81–106.

Saville-Troike, Muriel. (2006). *Introducing second language acquisition*. Cambridge University Press.

Scarborough, D., Gerard, L, and Cortese, C. (1984). Independence of lexical access in bilingual word recognition. *Journal of Verbal Learning and Verbal Behavior*, 23, 1: 84–99.

Schlyter, S. (1994). Early morphology in Swedish as the weaker language in French–Swedish bilingual children. *Scandinavian Working Papers on Bilingualism*, 9: 67–86.

Schmid, M. (2002). *First Language Attrition, Use and Maintenance: The case of German Jews in Anglophone Countries*. Amsterdam and Philadelphia: John Benjamins.

(2007). The role of L1 use for L1 attrition. *Language Attrition: Theoretical Perspectives*, 33: 135–154.

Schmid, M. S. and Mehotcheva, T. (2012). Foreign language attrition. *Dutch Journal of Applied Linguistics*, 1, 1: 102–124.

Schmitt, C. (1996). Aspect and the syntax of noun phrases. Unpublished Ph.D. dissertation, University of Maryland.

Schmitt, C. and Miller, K. (2007). Making discourse-dependent decisions: The case of the copulas *ser* and *estar* in Spanish. *Lingua*, 117: 1907–1929.

Schrauf, R. W. (2008). Bilingualism and aging. In *An introduction to bilingualism: Principles and processes*, ed. J. Altarriba and R. R. Heredia. Mahwah, NJ: Lawrence Erlbaum, pp. 105–127.

Schwartz, A. I. and Kroll, J. F. (2006). Bilingual lexical activation in sentence context. *Journal of Memory and Language*, 55: 197–212.

Schwartz, B. D. (2003). Why child L2 acquisition? In *Proceedings of GALA 2003*, ed. J. van Kampen and S. Baauw. Utrecht: Netherlands Graduate School of Linguistics, vol. 1, pp. 47–66.

Schwartz, B. D. and Sprouse, R. A. (1996). L2 cognitive states and the Full Transfer/Full Access model. *Second Language Research*, 12, 1: 40–72.

Schwieter, J. and Sunderman, G. (2008). Language switching in bilingual speech production. *The Mental Lexicon* 3, 2: 214–238.

Seliger, H. W. and Vago, R. M. (1991). *First language attrition*. Cambridge University Press.

Sera, M. D., Berge, C., and del Castillo Pintado, J. (1994). Grammatical and conceptual forces in the attribution of gender by English and Spanish speakers. *Cognitive Development*, 9: 261–292.

Serratrice, L. (2007). Cross-linguistic influence in the interpretation of anaphoric and cataphoric pronouns in English–Italian bilingual children. *Bilingualism: Language and Cognition*, 10: 225–238.

Serratrice, L., Sorace, A. and Paoli, S. (2004). Crosslinguistic influence at the syntax-pragmatics interface: Subjects and objects in English–Italian bilingual and monolingual acquisition. *Bilingualism: Language and Cognition*, 7, 3: 183–205.

Shafer, V. L., Yu, Y. H., and Datta, H. (2011). The development of English vowel perception in monolingual and bilingual infants: Neurophysiological correlates. *Journal of Phonetics*, 39, 4: 527–545.

Shapiro, K., and Caramazza, A. (2003). Looming a loom: Evidence for independent access to grammatical and phonological properties in verb retrieval. *Journal of Neurolinguistics* 16: 85–111.

Sharwood Smith, M. A. (1983). On explaining language loss. In *Language development at the crossroads*, ed. R. Felix, and H. Wode. Tübingen: Gunter Narr, pp. 49–59.

Sherkina-Lieber, M. Pérez-Leroux, A.T., and Johns, A. (2011). Grammar without speech production. The case of Labrador Inuttitut heritage receptive bilinguals. *Bilingualism: Language and Cognition*, 14, 3: 301–317.

Shin, J. A., and Christianson, K. (2009). Syntactic processing in Korean–English bilingual production: Evidence from cross-linguistic structural priming. *Cognition*, 112, 1: 175–180.

Shirai, Y., and Li, P. (2000). *The acquisition of lexical and grammatical aspect*. Berlin: Mouton de Gruyter.

Siegel, J. (2004). Morphological elaboration. *Journal of Pidgin and Creole Languages* 19, 2: 333–362.

Signorini, A. (1998). La conciencia fonológica y la lectura. Teoría e investigación acerca de una relación compleja. *Lectura y Vida*, 19, 3: 15–22. Retrieved from: www.lecturayvida.fahce.unlp.edu.ar/numeros/a19n3/19_03_Signorini.pdf

Silva-Corvalán, C. (1991). Spanish language attrition in a contact situation with English. *First Language Attrition*. In *First language attrition*, ed. H. W. Seliger and R. M. Vago. Cambridge University Press, pp. 151–171.

  (1994). *Language contact and change: Spanish in Los Angeles*. Oxford University Press.

  ed. (1997). *Spanish in four continents: Studies in language contact and bilingualism*. Washington, DC: Georgetown University Press.

  (2003). Linguistic consequences of reduced input in bilingual first language acquisition. In *Linguistic theory and language development in Hispanic languages*, ed. S. Montrul and F. Ordóñez. Somerville, MA: Cascadilla Press, pp. 375–397.

  (2008). The limits of convergence in language contact. *Journal of Language Contact*, 2: 213–224.

Silva-Corvalán, C. and Montanari, S. (2008). The acquisition of *ser, estar* (and *be*) by a Spanish–English bilingual child: The early stages. *Bilingualism: Language and Cognition*, 11, 3: 341–360.

Silva-Corvalán, C. and Sánchez-Walker, N. (2007). Subjects in early dual language development: A case study of a Spanish–English bilingual child. In *Spanish in contact: Policy, social and linguistic inquiries*, ed. K. Potowski and R. Cameron. Amsterdam: John Benjamins, pp. 3–22.

Singh, J. A. L. and Zingg, R. M. (1942). *Wolf-children and feral man.* Hamden, CT: Shoe String Press. [Reprinted 1966, New York: Harper and Row.]

Singleton, D. (1989). *Language acquisition: The age factor.* Clevedon, Multilingual Matters.

(2005). The critical period hypothesis: A coat of many colors. *International Review of Applied Linguistics in Language Teaching*, 43: 269–285.

Sinka, I. and Schelleter, C. (1998). Morphosyntactic development in bilingual children. *International Journal of Bilingualism* 2, 3: 301–326.

Skuse, D. H. (1993). Extreme deprivation in early childhood. In *Language development in exceptional circumstances*, ed. D. Bishop and K. Mogford. Hove and Hillsdale, NJ: Lawrence Erlbaum, pp. 29–46.

Skutnabb-Kangas, T. and Toukomaa, P. (1976). Teaching migrant children's mother tongue and learning the language of the host country in the context of the sociocultural situation of the migrant family. Report written for UNESCO. Tampere: University of Tampere, Dept of Sociology and Social Psychology, Research Reports 15, 99.

Snodgrass, J. G. (1984). Concepts and their surface representations. *Journal of Verbal Learning and Verbal Behavior*, 23: 3–22.

Snow, C. E. (1983). Age differences in second language acquisition: Research findings and folk psychology. In *Second language acquisition studies*, ed. K. Bailey, M. Long, and S. Peck. Rowley, MA: Newbury House, pp. 141–150.

(1987). Relevance of the notion of a critical period to language acquisition. In *Sensitive periods in development*, ed. M. Bornstein. Hillsdale, NJ: Lawrence Erlbaum, pp. 183–209.

Snow, C. and Hoefnagel-Höhle, M. (1978a). Age differences in second language acquisition. In *Applied linguistics: Psycholinguistics*, ed. G. Nickel. Stuttgart: Hochschulverlag, pp. 293–309.

(1978b). The critical period for language acquisition: Evidence from second language learning. *Child Development* 49: 1114–28.

Soares, C. and Grosjean, F. (1984). Bilinguals in a monolingual and a bilingual speech mode: The effect on lexical access. *Memory and Cognition*, 12, 4: 380–386.

Sorace, A. (2000). Differential effects of attrition in the L1 syntax of near-native L2 speakers. In *Proceedings of the 24th Annual Boston University Conference on Language Development*, ed. S. C., Howell, S. A. Fish, and T. Keith-Lucas. Somerville, MA: Cascadilla Press, pp. 719–725.

(2003). Near-nativeness. In *Handbook of second language acquisition*, eds. C. Doughty and M. Long. Oxford: Blackwell, pp. 130–151.

(2006). Gradience and optionality in mature and developing grammars. In *Gradience in grammars: Generative perspectives*, ed. G. Fanselow, C. Fery, M. Schlesewsky, and R. Vogel. Oxford University Press, 106–123.

Sorace, A. and Serratrice, L. (2009). Internal and external interfaces in bilingual language development: Beyond structural overlap. *International Journal of Bilingualism.* 13, 2: 195–210.

Spivey, M. J., and Marian, V. (1999). Cross talk between native and second languages: Partial activation of an irrelevant lexicon. *Psychological Science*, 10, 3: 281–284.

Sundara, M., and Scutellaro, A. (2011). Rhythmic distance between languages affects the development of speech perception in bilingual infants. *Journal of Phonetics*, 39, 4: 505–513.

Suñer, M. (1988). The role of agreement in clitic-doubled constructions. *Natural Language & Linguistic Theory*, 6, 3: 391–434.

Szwed, M., Dehaene, S., Kleinschmidt, A., Eger, E., Valabrègue, R., Amadon, A., and Cohen, L. (2011). Specialization for written words over objects in the visual cortex. *NeuroImage*, 56, 1: 330–344.

Taki, Y., Kinomura, S., Sato, K., Goto, R., Wu, K., Kawashima, R., and Fukuda, H. (2011). Correlation between gray/white matter volume and cognition in healthy elderly people. *Brain and Cognition*, 75, 2: 170–176.

Thiery, C. (1978). True bilingualism and second language learning. In *Language interpretation and communication*, ed. D. Gerver and H. Sinaiko. New York: Plenum Press, pp. 147–151.

Thomas, W. and Collier, V. (2002). A national study of school effectiveness for language minority students' long-term academic achievement. UC Berkeley: Center for Research on Education, Diversity and Excellence. Retrieved from: http://escholarship.org/uc/item/65j213pt

Thomason, S. and Kauffman, T. (1988). *Language contact, creolization, and genetic linguistics*. Berkeley: University of California Press.

Thomason, S. G. (2003). Contact as a source of language change. In *The handbook of historical linguistics*, ed. B. D. Joseph and R. D. Janda. Oxford: Blackwell, pp. 687–712.

Tomiyama, M. (2000). Child second language attrition: A longitudinal case study. *Applied Linguistics*, 21, 3: 304–332.

(2008). Age and proficiency in L2 attrition: Data from two siblings. *Applied Linguistics*, 30, 2: 253–275.

Toribio, A. J. (2000). Language variation and the linguistic enactment of identity among Dominicans. *Linguistics* 38, 5: 1133–1159.

(2001). On the emergence of bilingual code-switching competence. *Bilingualism: Language and Cognition*, 4, 3: 203–231.

(2002). Spanish–English code-switching among US Latinos. *International Journal of the Sociology of Language*, 158: 89–120.

(2004). Convergence as an optimization strategy in bilingual speech: Evidence from code-switching. *Bilingualism: Language and Cognition*, 7, 2: 165–173.

Trask, R. L. (1997). *The history of Basque*. New York and London: Routledge.

Travis, C. (2007). Genre effects on subject expression in Spanish: Priming in narrative and conversation. *Language Variation and Change*, 19: 101–135.

Treffers-Daller, J., and Sakel, J. (2012). Why transfer is a key aspect of language use and processing in bilinguals and L2-users. *International Journal of Bilingualism*, 16, 1: 3–10.

Tsimpli, I., Sorace, A., Heycock, C., and Filiaci, F. (2004). First language attrition and syntactic subjects: A study of Greek and Italian near-native speakers of English. *International Journal of Bilingualism*, 8, 3: 257–277.

Ullman, M. T. (2001). A neurocognitive perspective on language: The declarative/procedural model. *Nature Reviews Neuroscience*, 2, 10: 717–726.

(2004). Contributions of memory circuits to language: The declarative/procedural model. *Cognition*, 92, 1: 231–270.

(2005). A cognitive neuroscience perspective on second language acquisition: The declarative/procedural model. In *Mind and context in adult second language acquisition: Methods, theory, and practice*, ed. C. Sanz. Washington, DC: Georgetown University Press, pp. 141–178.

Unsworth, S. (2003). Testing Hulk & Mueller (2000) on crosslinguistic influence: Root infinitives in a bilingual German/English child. *Bilingualism Language and Cognition*, 6, 2: 143–158.

(2013). Assessing the role of current and cumulative exposure in simultaneous bilingual acquisition: The case of Dutch gender. *Bilingualism: Language and Cognition*, 16, 1: 86–110.

Urrutia-Cárdenas, H. (1995). Morphosyntactic Features in the Spanish of the Basque Country. In C. Silva-Corvalán (ed.), *Spanish in four continents: Studies in language contact and bilingualism*. Washington, DC: Georgetown University Press, 243–259.

Valdés, G. and Figueroa, R. (1994). *Bilingualism and testing: A special case of bias*. Norwood, NJ. Ablex.

Valdés, G., and Gioffrion-Vinci, M. (2011). Heritage language students: The case of Spanish. In *The handbook of Hispanic sociolinguistics*, ed. M. Díaz-Campos. Malden, MA: Wiley-Blackwell, pp. 598–622.

van Gelderen, E., and MacSwan, J. (2008). Interface conditions and code-switching: Pronouns, lexical DPs, and checking theory. *Lingua*, 118, 6: 765–776.

Van Heuven, W. J., Dijkstra, T., and Grainger, J. (1998). Orthographic neighborhood effects in bilingual word recognition. *Journal of Memory and Language*, 39, 3: 458–483.

Vendler, Z. (1967). *Linguistics in philosophy*. Ithaca, NY: Cornell University Press.

Ventureyra, V., Pallier, C., and Yoo, H.Y. (2004). The loss of first language phonetic perception in adopted Koreans. *Journal of Neurolinguistics*, 17: 79–84.

Vigil, N. (2003). Enseñanza de castellano como lengua maternal en un modelo de educación intercultural. In *Actas del V Congreso Latinoamericano de Educación Intercultural Bilingüe: Realidad multilingüe y desafío intercultural: Ciudadanía, política y educación*, ed. R. Zariquiey. Lima: Fondo Editorial de la Pontificia Universidad Católica del Perú, pp. 247–261.

Vigneau, M., Beaucousin, V., Hervé, P., Duffau, H., Crivello, F., Houdé, O., Mazoyer, B., Tzourio-Mazoyer, N. (2006). Meta-analyzing left hemisphere language areas: Phonology, semantics, and sentence processing. *NeuroImage*, 30: 1414–1432.

Vihman, M. and McLaughlin, B. (1982). Bilingualism and second language acquisition in preschool children. In *Progress in cognitive development research: Verbal processes in children*, ed. C. J. Brainerd and M. Pressley. Berlin: Springer, pp. 35–58.

Volterra, V. and Taeschner, T. (1978). The acquisition and development of language by bilingual children. *Journal of Child Language*, 5, 2: 311–326.

Wartenburger, I., Heekeren, H. R., Abutalebi, J., Cappa, S. F., Villringer, A., and Perani, D. (2003). Early setting of grammatical processing in the bilingual brain. *Neuron*, 37, 1: 159–170.

Weber-Fox, C. M., and Neville, H. J. (1996). Maturational constraints on functional specializations for language processing: ERP and behavioral evidence in bilingual speakers. *Journal of Cognitive Neuroscience*, 8, 3: 231–256.

Wei, L. (2007). Dimensions of bilingualism. In *The bilingualism reader*, ed. L. Wei. London and New York: Routledge, pp. 3–23.

Weinreich, U. (1953). *Languages in contact. Findings and problems*. The Hague: Mouton.

Weltens, B. (1987). The attrition of foreign-language skills: A literature review. *Applied Linguistics*, 8, 1: 22–38.

Werker, J. F., and Tees, R. C. (1984). Cross-language speech perception: Evidence for perceptual reorganization during the first year of life. *Infant Behavior and Development*, 7, 1: 49–63.

Wexler, K., Schaeffer, J., and Bol, G. (2004). Verbal syntax and morphology in typically developing Dutch children and children with SLI: How developmental data can play an important role in morphological theory. *Syntax*, 7, 2: 148–198.

Wexler, K., Schütze, C. T., and Rice, M. (1998). Subject case in children with SLI and unaffected controls: Evidence for the Agr/Tns omission model. *Language Acquisition*, 7, 2–4: 317–344.

Whitehurst, G. J., and Lonigan, C. J. (1998). Child development and emergent literacy. *Child Development*, 69, 3: 848–872.

Wiley, T., and Valdés, G. (2000). Heritage language instruction in the United States: A time for renewal. *Bilingual Research Journal*, 24, 4, i–v. Available at http://brj.asu.edu/archive.html

Wode, H. (1977). On the systematicity of L1 transfer in L2 acquisition. *Proceedings from the 1977 Second Language Research Forum (SLRF)*. Los Angeles: University of California, Department of Applied Linguistics, pp. 160–169.

Yamamoto, M. (2001). *Language use in interlingual families: A Japanese–English sociolinguistic study*. Clevedon: Multilingual Matters.

Yang, S., Yang, H., and Lust, B. (2011). Early childhood bilingualism leads to advances in executive attention: Dissociating culture and language. *Bilingualism: Language and Cognition*, 14: 412–422.

Yip, V. and Matthews, S. (2000). Syntactic transfer in a Cantonese–English bilingual child. *Bilingualism: Language and Cognition*, 3: 193–208.

Zagona, Karen. (2002). *Spanish syntax*. Cambridge University Press.

Zalbide, M. and Cenoz, J. (2008). Bilingual education in the Basque Autonomous Community: Achievements and challenges. *Language, Culture and Curriculum* 21, 1: 5–20.

Zapata, G. C., Sánchez, L., and Toribio, A. J. (2005). Contact and contracting Spanish. *International Journal of Bilingualism*, 9, 3–4: 377–395.

Zavala, V. (2002). *Desencuentros con la escritura: Escuela y comunidad en los Andes peruanos*. Lima: Red para el desarrollo de las ciencias sociales en el Perú.

Zawiszewski, A., Gutiérrez, E., Fernández, B., and Laka, I. (2011). Language distance and nonnative language processing. Evidence from event-related potentials. *Bilingualism: Language and Cognition*, 14, 3: 400–411.

Zelazo, P. D. (2006). The dimensional change card sort (DCCS): A method of assessing executive function in children. *Nature Protocols*, 1, 1: 297–301.

Zentella, A. C. (1997). *Growing up bilingual: Puerto Rican children in New York*. Malden, MA: Blackwell.

Zimmermann, Klaus. (1997). Planificación de la identidad étnico-cultural y educación bilingüe para los amerindios. In *Multilingüismo y educación bilingüe en América y España*, ed. J. Calvo Pérez and J. C. Godenzzi. Cuzco: Centro de Estudios Regionales Andinos "Bartolomé de las Casas," pp. 31–52.

Zobl, H. (1980). The formal and developmental selectivity of LI influence on L2 acquisition. *Language Learning*, 30, 1: 43–57.

Zúñiga, M., Sánchez, L., and Zacharías, D. (2000). *Demanda y necesidad de educación bilingüe: Lenguas indígenas y castellano en el sur andino*. Lima, Peru: Ministerio de Educación (Peru's Ministry of Education), GTZ (German Technical Cooperation Agency), and KfW (German Financial Cooperation Agency).

Zwanziger, E., Allen, S., and Genesee, F. (2005). Crosslinguistic influence in bilingual acquisition: Subject omission in learners of Inuktitut and English. *Journal of Child Language*, 32, 4: 893–909.

Index